ALL COLOUR COLLECTION

365
MAIN
COURSE
DISHES

ALL COLOUR COLLECTION

365
MAIN
COURSE
DISHES

EBURY PRESS
LONDON

First published by Ebury Press
an imprint of The Random Century Group
Random Century House
20 Vauxhall Bridge Road
London SW1V 2SA

British Library Cataloguing-in-Publication Data
Ebury 365 all colour main course dishes.
I. Ebury Press
641.5

ISBN 0–09–175052–0

Editor Helen Southall
Designed by Bridgewater Design Limited
Photography by Sue Atkinson, Jan Baldwin, Martin Brigdale,
Laurie Evans, Melvin Grey, John Heseltine, Tim Imrie,
David Johnson, Paul Kemp, Don Last, James Murphy,
Peter Myers, Grant Symon, Paul Williams

Typeset in Garamond by Textype Typesetters, Cambridge
Printed and bound in Italy by New Interlitho S.p.a., Milan

COOK'S NOTES

★ Both metric and imperial measures are given in the recipes
in this book. Follow one set of measures only as they are not
interchangeable.

★ All spoon measures are level unless otherwise stated.

★ Microwave cooking instructions are given for many of the
recipes in this book. When using these, please note that HIGH
refers to 100% full power output of a 600–700 watt cooker;
MEDIUM refers to 60% of full power; LOW refers to 35% of
full power.

   If your microwave power output is lower than 600 watts,
it may be necessary to allow a longer cooking time than that
recommended in a recipe.

   No matter what the wattage of your oven, you should always
check food before the end of cooking time, to ensure that it
does not get overcooked.

CONTENTS

MEAT

This mouth-watering selection of meat-based dishes includes all types of meat and offal cooked in every way imaginable. From warming country casseroles to an elegant crown roast of lamb or a simply cooked, tender, juicy steak – you will be sure to find a recipe to please.

SIRLOIN STEAKS WITH MUSTARD

SERVES 4

50 g (2 oz) wholegrain mustard	30 ml (2 tbsp) chopped parsley
15 g (½ oz) plain flour	30 ml (2 tbsp) chopped thyme
four 175 g (6 oz) sirloin steaks	

1 Mix together the mustard and flour, then spread on top of each steak.
2 Line a grill pan with foil, sprinkle with the herbs and put the steaks on top. Cook under a preheated grill for 5–15 minutes, turning frequently, until the steaks are cooked to your liking. Serve at once.

——————— TO MICROWAVE ———————

Complete step 1. Preheat a large browning dish on HIGH for 5 minutes or according to manufacturer's instructions. Quickly put the herbs and steaks in the browning dish and cook on HIGH for 5–7 minutes.

STILTON STEAKS

SERVES 4

100 g (4 oz) Stilton cheese, crumbled	pepper
25 g (1 oz) butter, softened	four 100–175 g (4–6 oz) sirloin or fillet steaks
50–75 g (2–3 oz) walnut pieces, finely chopped	

1 Put the cheese in a bowl and mash with a fork. Add the butter and walnuts and mix in. Season to taste.
2 Put the steaks on the grill rack and season with plenty of pepper. Cook under a preheated grill for 5–15 minutes, turning frequently, until the steaks are cooked to your liking.
3 Remove the steaks from under the grill, sprinkle the cheese and nut mixture evenly over them and press down with a palette knife. Grill for a further minute or until the topping is melted and bubbling. Serve hot.

STEAK WITH CREAM SAUCE

SERVES 4

four 175 g (6 oz) fillet steaks	15 ml (1 tbsp) lemon juice
2 garlic cloves, crushed (optional)	30 ml (2 tbsp) Worcestershire sauce
salt and pepper	15–30 ml (1–2 tbsp) brandy
50 g (2 oz) butter	150 ml (5 fl oz) single cream
100 g (4 oz) button mushrooms, very thinly sliced	15 ml (1tbsp) finely chopped parsley
25 g (1 oz) onion, very finely chopped	parsley sprigs, to garnish

1 Rub the steaks with the garlic and season well.

2 Melt half the butter in a frying pan and fry the steaks over a high heat for about 2 minutes on each side to brown. If you like your steaks well done, cook for longer. Transfer to a warm serving dish and keep hot.

3 Heat the remaining butter in the frying pan and quickly fry the mushrooms and onion for about 5 minutes or until tender. Add the lemon juice, Worcestershire sauce and brandy and bring to the boil.

4 Stir in the cream and chopped parsley, bring almost to the boil, check the seasoning, then quickly pour over the steaks. Serve garnished with parsley sprigs.

JUGGED STEAK

SERVES 4

700 g (1½ lb) stewing steak, cut into 2.5 cm (1 inch) cubes	about 450 ml (¾ pint) beef stock
25 g (1 oz) plain wholemeal flour	225 g (8 oz) sausagemeat
1 medium onion, sliced	50 g (2 oz) fresh wholemeal breadcrumbs
4 cloves	30 ml (2 tbsp) chopped parsley
salt and pepper	15 ml (1 tbsp) redcurrant jelly
150 ml (¼ pint) port	

1 Toss the meat in the flour, shaking off excess, and put in an ovenprof casserole.

2 Add the onion and cloves and season to taste. Pour in the port and just enough stock to cover the meat.

3 Cover the casserole and cook in a preheated oven at 170°C (325°F) mark 3 for about 3 hours or until the meat is tender.

4 Meanwhile, mix together the sausagemeat, breadcrumbs and parsley and season to taste. With floured hands, form the mixture into eight balls.

5 Forty minutes before the end of the cooking time, stir the redcurrant jelly into the casserole. Add the forcemeat balls and cook, uncovered, until the forcemeat balls are cooked and brown. Skim off any excess fat and serve hot.

STRIPS OF BEEF IN WHISKY SAUCE

SERVES 4

15 g (½ oz) butter	75 ml (3 tbsp) whisky liqueur, such as Drambuie
700 g (1½ lb) sirloin steak, cut into strips	75 ml (3 fl oz) double cream
1 large onion, chopped	salt and pepper

1 Melt the butter in a frying pan. Add the beef strips and onion and cook for 5–10 minutes or until the beef is brown and cooked to taste.

2 Stir in the liqueur and cream. Heat gently to reduce slightly. Season to taste, then serve at once.

──────────── **TO MICROWAVE** ────────────

Preheat a large browning dish on HIGH for 5 minutes or according to manufacturer's instructions. Quickly put the butter, beef and onion in the browning dish. Cook on HIGH for 5–7 minutes or until the meat is cooked to taste, stirring frequently. Stir in the liqueur and season to taste. Cook on HIGH for 1 minute, then stir in the cream and serve at once.

BEEF OLIVES

SERVES 4

75 g (3 oz) streaky bacon rashers, finely chopped	salt and pepper
1 small onion, chopped	8 thin slices of topside beef, weighing about 700 g (1½ lb)
10 ml (2 tsp) chopped parsley	15 ml (1 tbsp) prepared English mustard
100 g (4 oz) fresh breadcrumbs	45 ml (3 tbsp) seasoned flour
50 g (2 oz) shredded beef suet	25 g (1 oz) butter
1.25 ml (¼ tsp) dried mixed herbs	30 ml (2 tbsp) vegetable oil
1 egg, size 6	450 ml (¾ pint) beef stock
1 lemon	2 medium onions, sliced

1 Mix the bacon with the chopped onion, parsley, breadcrumbs, suet, herbs and egg. Add the grated rind of ½ of the lemon and 5 ml (1 tsp) juice and season to taste.

2 Put the meat between two sheets of greaseproof paper and beat out with a meat mallet or rolling pin.

3 Spread mustard thinly over the meat, then divide the stuffing equally between the pieces. Roll up and secure with strong cotton or fine string. Toss in seasoned flour, reserving excess flour.

4 Heat the butter and oil in a shallow flameproof casserole into which all the beef olives will just fit. Add the olives and cook until well browned. Remove from the pan.

5 Stir the remaining seasoned flour into the pan residue and cook for 1–2 minutes or until lightly browned. Remove from the heat, gradually stir in the stock and bring to the boil. Season to taste, then return the meat to the pan.

6 Scatter the sliced onions over the meat. Cover and cook in a preheated oven at 170°C (325°F) mark 3 for 1½ hours.

MINCED BEEF KEBABS WITH HORSERADISH RELISH

SERVES 6

700 g (1½ lb) lean minced beef	salt and pepper
250 g (9 oz) grated onion	1 egg, beaten
135 ml (9 tbsp) horseradish sauce	plain flour, for coating
45 ml (3 tbsp) chopped thyme	150 ml (¼ pint) natural yogurt
250 g (9 oz) fresh white breadcrumbs	120 ml (8 tbsp) finely chopped parsley

1 Put the minced beef in a large bowl and mix in the onion, 90 ml (6 tbsp) of the horseradish, the thyme and breadcrumbs. Season to taste.
2 Add enough egg to bind the mixture together and, with floured hands, shape into 18 even-sized sausages. Cover and chill in the refrigerator until required.
3 Thread the kebabs lengthways on to six oiled skewers. Cook under a preheated grill for about 20 minutes, turning frequently.
4 Meanwhile, mix the yogurt with the remaining horseradish and the parsley. Serve the kebabs hot, with the sauce in a separate sauceboat.

--- **VARIATION** ---

For a more luxurious horseradish sauce, stir 30 ml (2 tbsp) grated fresh horseradish into a whipped mixture of 75 ml (3 fl oz) whipping cream and 150 ml (¼ pint) soured cream. Add 5 ml (1 tsp) vinegar, 2.5 ml (½ tsp) sugar and salt and pepper to taste.

BITKIS

SERVES 6

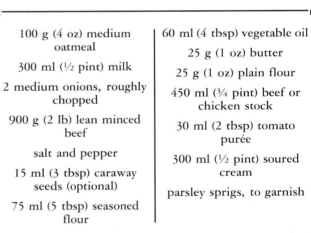

100 g (4 oz) medium oatmeal	60 ml (4 tbsp) vegetable oil
300 ml (½ pint) milk	25 g (1 oz) butter
2 medium onions, roughly chopped	25 g (1 oz) plain flour
900 g (2 lb) lean minced beef	450 ml (¾ pint) beef or chicken stock
salt and pepper	30 ml (2 tbsp) tomato purée
15 ml (3 tbsp) caraway seeds (optional)	300 ml (½ pint) soured cream
75 ml (5 tbsp) seasoned flour	parsley sprigs, to garnish

1 Soak the oatmeal in the milk overnight. Squeeze out excess milk and mix the oatmeal with the onions, minced beef and seasoning to taste.
2 Put this mixture twice through a mincer or mix in a food processor until smooth. Beat in 10 ml (2 tsp) of the caraway seeds, if using.
3 Shape in 18 round flat cakes, or bitkis. Coat with seasoned flour.
4 Heat the oil in a large frying pan, add the bitkis and cook until well browned. Place in a single layer in a large shallow ovenproof dish.
5 Melt the butter in a saucepan, add the plain flour and cook over low heat, stirring with a wooden spoon, for 2 minutes. Remove from the heat and gradually blend in the stock. Bring to the boil slowly, then simmer for 2–3 minutes, stirring. Stir in the tomato purée, soured cream and remaining caraway seeds, if using.
6 Pour the sauce over the bitkis and cook in a preheated oven at 180°C (350°F) mark 4 for about 1¼ hours or until the juices run clear. Garnish with parsley.

ITALIAN-STYLE MEATBALLS

SERVES 4

30 ml (2 tbsp) olive oil	50 g (2 oz) fresh white breadcrumbs
1 large onion, finely chopped	50 g (2 oz) Parmesan cheese, freshly grated
2 garlic cloves, crushed	1 egg, beaten
397 g (14 oz) can chopped tomatoes	20 small black olives, stoned
10 ml (2 tsp) dried mixed herbs	vegetable oil, for deep frying
10 ml (2 tsp) dried oregano	100 ml (4 fl oz) red or white dry Italian wine
salt and pepper	
450 g (1 lb) lean minced beef	

1 Heat the oil in a heavy-based saucepan, add the onion and half of the crushed garlic and fry gently for about 5 minutes or until soft and lightly coloured.

2 Add the tomatoes, half of the herbs and seasoning to taste. Bring to the boil, stirring, then lower the heat, cover and simmer for about 20 minutes

3 Meanwhile, make the meatballs. Put the minced beef in a bowl with the breadcrumbs, Parmesan, remaining garlic and herbs. Mix well, then season and bind with egg.

4 Pick up a small amount of the mixture, about the size of a walnut. Press one olive in the centre, then shape the mixture around it. Repeat to make 20 meatballs.

5 Heat the oil in a deep-fat fryer to 190°C (375°F). Deep-fry the meatballs in batches for 2–3 minutes or until lightly browned, then drain thoroughly on kitchen paper.

6 Stir the wine into the tomato sauce, than add 300 ml (½ pint) water and the meatballs. Shake the pan to coat the balls in the sauce, adding more water if necessary. Cover and simmer for 15 minutes, then season and serve.

CHINESE BEEF AND VEGETABLE STIR-FRY

SERVES 4

350 g (12 oz) fillet or rump steak, sliced into very thin strips	1 onion, thinly sliced
30 ml (2 tbsp) cornflour	1 garlic clove, crushed
60 ml (4 tbsp) soy sauce	2.5 cm (1 inch) piece of fresh root ginger, crushed
90 ml (6 tbsp) dry sherry	2 celery sticks, thinly sliced
30 ml (2 tbsp) dark soft brown sugar	1 red pepper, sliced into thin strips
30 ml (2 tbsp) wine vinegar	225 g (8 oz) mange-touts, halved
salt and pepper	
75 ml (5 tbsp) sesame or vegetable oil	

1 Put the steak in a bowl. Mix together the next five ingredients and season to taste. Pour over the steak, stir well to mix, then cover and leave to marinate for 1 hour.

2 Heat 30 ml (2 tbsp) of the oil in a wok or large frying pan. Add the onion, garlic and ginger and fry gently, stirring, for 5 minutes or until soft.

3 Heat another 15 ml (1 tbsp) of the oil in the pan. Add the celery and red pepper and fry, stirring, for a further 5 minutes or until tender but still crisp. Remove the vegetables from the pan with a slotted spoon.

4 Drain the steak from the marinade. Heat the remaining oil in the pan, add the steak and stir-fry over high heat for 5 minutes. Remove with a slotted spoon and set aside.

5 Add the mange-touts to the wok and stir-fry over high heat for 2–3 minutes. Return the steak and vegetables to the wok, then pour in the marinade and stir until bubbling and well mixed. Taste and season. Serve immediately.

BOILED BEEF AND CARROTS

SERVES 6

1.6 kg (3½ lb) lean salted silverside or brisket of beef	8 cloves
bouquet garni	2 small turnips, quartered
6 black peppercorns, lightly crushed	2 celery sticks, chopped
	1 leek, chopped
2 small onions, quartered	18 small carrots

1 If necessary, soak the meat in cold water for several hours or overnight, then rinse. Tie up into a neat joint.
2 Place the beef in a large saucepan, add just enough water to cover and bring slowly to the boil. Skim the surface, then add the bouquet garni, peppercorns, onions (each quarter stuck with a clove), turnips, celery and leek. Lower the heat and simmer very gently for about 2 hours.
3 Add the small carrots and simmer gently for a further 30–40 minutes or until the carrots are tender.
4 Carefully transfer the beef and small carrots to a warmed serving plate and keep warm.
5 Skim the fat from the surface of the cooling liquor, then strain. Boil the liquid to reduce slightly, then pour into a warmed sauceboat or jug.
6 Serve the beef surrounded by the carrots, with the sauce served separately.

SPICED BEEF

SERVES 6

1.8 kg (4 lb) salted rolled silverside	100 g (4 oz) dark soft brown sugar
1 medium onion, sliced	2.5 ml (½ tsp) mustard powder
4 medium carrots, sliced	5 ml (1 tsp) ground cinnamon
1 small turnip, sliced	juice of 1 lemon
8 cloves	

1 If necessary, soak the meat in cold water for several hours or overnight, then rinse. Tie up the meat to form a neat joint and put in a large saucepan or flameproof casserole with the vegetables.
2 Cover with water and bring slowly to the boil. Skim the surface, cover and simmer for 3–4 hours or until tender. Leave to cool completely in the liquid for 3–4 hours.
3 Drain the meat well, then put into a roasting tin and stick the cloves into the fat. Mix together the remaining ingredients and spread over the meat.
4 Bake in a preheated oven at 180°C (350°F) mark 4 for 45 minutes to 1 hour or until tender, basting from time to time. Serve hot or cold.

--- **COOK'S TIP** ---

If the meat has not had a prolonged salting it may not need soaking, so check with your butcher when buying. The long cooking ensures that the beef is meltingly tender.

BEEF IN WINE WITH WALNUTS

SERVES 6

900 g (2 lb) shin of beef, cut into 2.5 cm (1 inch) cubes	1 garlic clove, crushed
150 ml (¼ pint) dry red wine	5 ml (1 tsp) ground allspice
3 medium parsnips	30 ml (2 tbsp) plain flour
15 ml (1 tbsp) vegetable oil	150 ml (¼ pint) beef stock
15 g (½ oz) butter	50 g (2 oz) walnut pieces, ground
1 small onion, finely chopped	salt and pepper
	chopped walnuts, to garnish

1 Put the beef in a bowl with the wine and mix well. Cover and leave to marinate overnight, stirring occasionally.

2 Cut the parsnips into 5 cm (2 inch) lengths, about 1 cm (½ inch) wide. Drain the meat from the marinade, reserving the marinade. Heat the oil and butter in a large frying pan, add the beef, a few pieces at a time, and cook over a high heat until browned. Transfer to an ovenproof casserole with a slotted spoon.

3 Add the onion and garlic to the frying pan and fry for 5–10 minutes or until beginning to brown. Stir in the allspice, flour, reserved marinade, stock and ground walnuts. Bring to the boil, stirring constantly.

4 Pour into the casserole and add the parsnips. Season lightly to taste. Cover and cook in a preheated oven at 170°C (325°F) mark 3 for 2½–3 hours or until the meat is really tender.

5 Serve hot, straight from the casserole, sprinkled with the chopped walnuts.

BEEF AND CHESTNUT CASSEROLE

SERVES 4

45 ml (3 tbsp) vegetable oil	30 ml (2 tbsp) mushroom ketchup
1.1 kg (2½ lb) chuck steak, cubed	5 ml (1 tsp) dried mixed herbs
1 medium onion, sliced	salt and pepper
1 garlic clove, crushed	439 g (15½ oz) can whole chestnuts in salted water, drained
30 ml (2 tbsp) plain wholemeal flour	
300 ml (½ pint) dry cider	30 ml (2 tbsp) chopped fresh parsley, to garnish
300 ml (½ pint) beef stock	

1 Heat the oil in a large flameproof casserole, add the beef in batches and fry over brisk heat until browned on all sides. Remove with a slotted spoon and set aside.

2 Add the onion and garlic to the casserole, lower the heat and fry gently for 5 minutes or until soft but not coloured.

3 Return the meat to the casserole and stir in the flour. Cook, stirring, for 1–2 minutes, then stir in the cider, stock and mushroom ketchup. Bring slowly to the boil, then add the herbs and season to taste.

4 Cover the casserole and cook in a preheated oven at 170°C (325°F) mark 3 for 2 hours or until the beef is tender.

5 Ten minutes before the end of the cooking time, remove the casserole from the oven and add the chestnuts. Return to the oven to complete cooking. Taste and adjust the seasoning and sprinkle with the parsley before serving.

BEEF STEW WITH DUMPLINGS

SERVES 4

700 g (1½ lb) stewing steak, cut into cubes	3 medium tomatoes, quartered
15 ml (1 tbsp) plain flour	5 ml (1 tsp) dried mixed herbs
50 g (2 oz) dripping or lard	15 ml (1 tbsp) tomato purée (optional)
3 medium onions, diced	FOR THE DUMPLINGS
450 g (1 lb) carrots, diced	225 g (8 oz) self-raising
450–550 g (1–1¼ lb) potatoes, peeled and diced	flour
4 celery sticks, diced	pinch of salt
600 ml (1 pint) beef stock	75 g (3 oz) margarine
salt and pepper	

1 Put the meat in a plastic bag with the flour and shake until coated. Heat the dripping or lard in a large saucepan, add the meat and cook until browned. Remove the meat from the pan with a slotted spoon.
2 Add the onions, carrots, potatoes and celery to the pan and fry for about 5 minutes or until lightly browned.
3 Remove the pan from the heat and add the stock, seasoning, tomatoes, herbs and tomato purée (if using). Return the meat to the pan, bring to the boil, cover, reduce the heat and simmer gently for 2 hours.
4 To make the dumplings, put the flour and salt in a bowl, add the margarine and rub in until the mixture resembles fine breadcrumbs. Gradually mix in 75–90 ml (5–6 tbsp) water until the mixture forms a light, elastic dough. Turn on to a floured surface and knead lightly. Cut the dough into eight pieces and roll each into a ball.
5 Arrange the dumplings on top of the stew, re-cover and continue cooking for a further 20–25 minutes.

BEEF IN CIDER

SERVES 4–5

15 ml (1 tbsp) vegetable oil	25 g (1 oz) plain flour
450 g (1 lb) braising steak, cut into cubes	300 ml (½ pint) cider
225 g (8 oz) chipolata sausages, halved	5 cloves
1 medium onion, chopped	3 beef stock cubes
2 celery sticks, chopped	salt and pepper
1 Granny Smith apple, cored and sliced	10 ml (2 tsp) chopped parsley, to garnish

1 Heat the oil in a large frying pan, add the meat, sausages and onion and fry for about 10 minutes or until lightly browned.
2 Add the celery and apple and sprinkle in the flour. Stir well, then add the cider and cloves. Crumble in the stock cubes and stir well again.
3 Transfer to an ovenproof casserole, cover and cook in a preheated oven at 180°C (350°F) mark 4 for 2–2½ hours or until the meat is tender. Season to taste and garnish with parsley before serving.

BEEF IN STOUT

SERVES 4–6

15 g (½ oz) butter	salt and pepper
about 15 ml (1 tbsp) vegetable oil	30 ml (2 tbsp) plain flour
900 g (2 lb) stewing steak, cut into 5 cm (2 inch) cubes	300 ml (½ pint) stout
4 medium onions, sliced	1 bay leaf
225 g (8 oz) button mushrooms, halved	5 ml (1 tsp) soft dark brown sugar

1 Heat the butter and oil in a large flameproof casserole and cook the meat for 10 minutes or until browned all over. Remove the meat from the pan with a slotted spoon.
2 Add the onions and mushrooms to the pan, adding more oil if necessary, and fry for about 5 minutes or until softened. Season to taste, add the flour and stir well so that the flour absorbs the fat.
3 Return the meat to the pan, pour in the stout and add the bay leaf and brown sugar. Stir well to mix.
4 Cover and cook gently, either on the hob or in a preheated oven at 180°C (350°F) mark 4 for about 2½ hours or until the meat is tender.

——————— COOK'S TIP ———————

Stout gets its dark colour and bitterness from the roasted malt or barley used in its brewing. It makes a delicious gravy when used in a casserole and is packed with goodness.

MEXICAN BEEF TORTILLAS

SERVES 4

30 ml (2 tbsp) vegetable oil	salt and pepper
2 onions, finely chopped	350 g (12 oz) ripe tomatoes, skinned and roughly chopped
2 garlic cloves, crushed	
2.5–5 ml (½–1 tsp) chilli powder	2 fresh green chillies, seeded and finely chopped
450 g (1 lb) lean minced beef	5 ml (1 tsp) granulated sugar
30 ml (2 tbsp) tomato purée	12 hot tortillas (see below)

1 Heat the oil in a heavy-based saucepan, add half the onions and garlic and fry gently for 5 minutes or until soft and lightly coloured. Add the chilli powder and fry for a further 1–2 minutes, stirring constantly.
2 Add the beef and fry until browned. Add the tomato purée and stir to mix, then add salt and pepper to taste. Fry for a further 10–15 minutes, stirring occasionally.
3 Meanwhile, put the tomatoes in a blender or food processor with the remaining onions and garlic, the chillies, sugar and salt and pepper to taste. Work until quite smooth, then transfer to a sauceboat or jug.
4 Put a spoonful of the beef mixture on a hot tortilla and roll up. Repeat until all the beef and tortillas are used. Serve immediately, with the cold tomato sauce.

——————— COOK'S TIP ———————

To make 12 tortillas, mix 250 g (9 oz) plain flour with 5 ml (1 tsp) salt and rub in 40 g (1½ oz) lard. Gradually add 225 ml (8 fl oz) tepid water and mix to a dough. Knead lightly and shape into 12 pieces. Roll out thinly between sheets of waxed paper. Cook the tortillas for about 30 seconds on each side in an ungreased frying pan until speckled with brown. Stack in foil to keep hot.

14

BOEUF STROGANOFF

SERVES 4

700 g (1½ lb) rump steak, thinly sliced	225 g (8 oz) mushrooms, sliced
45 ml (3 tbsp) plain flour	150 ml (¼ pint) soured cream
salt and pepper	
50 g (2 oz) butter	10 ml (2 tsp) tomato purée (optional)
1 onion, thinly sliced	

1 Put the steak slices between two sheets of greaseproof paper and beat out with a meat mallet or rolling pin.

2 Trim the fat off the steak and discard. Cut the meat across the grain into thin strips. Coat the strips of steak in flour seasoned with salt and pepper.

3 Melt half the butter in a sauté pan, add the meat and fry for 5–7 minutes or until golden brown, tossing constantly.

4 Add the remaining butter, the onion and mushrooms and fry, stirring, for 3–4 minutes. Stir in the soured cream and tomato purée (if liked), and season well, using plenty of pepper. Heat through gently, without boiling. Transfer to a warmed serving dish and serve immediately.

HUNGARIAN GOULASH

SERVES 6

45 ml (3 tbsp) beef dripping or vegetable oil	397 g (14 oz) can tomatoes
	salt and pepper
3 medium onions, chopped	1 green or red pepper, chopped
2 garlic cloves, crushed	
1.1 kg (2½ lb) chuck steak or shin of beef, cut into 4 cm (1½ inch) pieces	550 g (1¼ lb) potatoes, peeled and cut into 2.5 cm (1 inch) chunks
15 ml (1 tbsp) paprika	2 green chillies (optional)
1.25 ml (¼ tsp) caraway seeds	

1 Melt the dripping or heat the oil in a flameproof casserole, add the onions and garlic and cook over moderate heat for 10 minutes or until the onions are soft and golden brown, stirring occasionally.

2 Add the meat and cook over high heat, stirring constantly, until browned slightly. Add the paprika, caraway seeds, tomatoes with their juice, 300 ml (½ pint) water and salt and pepper to taste. Stir well to break up the tomatoes.

3 Bring to the boil, cover and cook in a preheated oven at 170°C (325°F) mark 3 for 1½ hours.

4 Remove the casserole from the oven and stir in the chopped pepper and potatoes, adding the whole chillies if liked. Cover and return to the oven for a further 45 minutes or until the potatoes are tender. The goulash should be of a fairly thin consistency.

5 Remove the chillies, and taste and adjust the seasoning before serving.

BEEF AND SPINACH CURRY

SERVES 4–6

10 black peppercorns	6 garlic cloves, crushed
4 cloves	2.5 cm (1 inch) piece of fresh root ginger, finely chopped
2 bay leaves	
seeds of 6 cardamoms	900 g (2 lb) lean stewing beef, cut into 2.5 cm (1 inch) cubes
10 ml (2 tsp) cumin seeds	
15 ml (1 tbsp) coriander seeds	150 ml (¼ pint) natural yogurt
2.5 ml (½ tsp) chilli powder	900 g (2 lb) fresh spinach, stalks removed, or two 300 g (10.6 oz) packs frozen spinach, thawed and drained
5 ml (1 tsp) salt	
90 ml (6 tbsp) ghee or vegetable oil	
1 large onion, finely chopped	

1 Finely grind the dry spices and salt in a small electric mill or with a pestle and mortar.
2 Heat the ghee or oil in a large heavy-based saucepan or flameproof casserole, add the onion, garlic, ginger and ground spices and cook over a moderate heat for about 5 minutes or until softened and just turning brown.
3 Increase the heat and add the meat. Cook, stirring all the time, until the meat is well browned on all sides. Add the yogurt to the pan, 15 ml (1 tbsp) at a time. Cook each addition over a high heat, stirring constantly, until the yogurt is absorbed.
4 Cover the pan tightly with a lid and turn down the heat to very low. Simmer for 1½ hours or until the meat is tender, stirring occasionally.
5 Add the spinach, mix well and cook over a moderate heat for a further 5–10 minutes, stirring all the time until the liquid has evaporated. Adjust the seasoning and serve.

SPICED MINCE WITH PEAS

SERVES 4–6

30 ml (2 tbsp) ghee or vegetable oil	900 g (2 lb) lean minced beef
1 medium onion, finely chopped	226 g (8 oz) can tomatoes, chopped
2.5 cm (1 inch) piece of fresh root ginger, grated	5 ml (1 tsp) caster sugar
8 garlic cloves, crushed	10 ml (2 tsp) salt
10 ml (2 tsp) ground cumin	350 g (12 oz) frozen peas
15 ml (1 tbsp) ground coriander	45 ml (3 tbsp) chopped coriander, parsley or mint
5 ml (1 tsp) chilli powder	30 ml (2 tbsp) lemon or lime juice
2.5 ml (½ tsp) ground turmeric	5 ml (1 tsp) garam masala

1 Heat the ghee or oil in a heavy-based saucepan or flameproof casserole, add the onion and cook over a high heat for about 5 minutes or until just turning brown. Lower the heat, add the ginger, garlic and spices and cook gently for 2–3 minutes.
2 Add the minced meat, chopped tomatoes with their juice, sugar and salt. Stir well until mixed and bring to the boil. Cover and simmer for 45 minutes.
3 Stir in the peas, herbs and lemon or lime juice. Cover and simmer for 15 minutes, stirring occasionally.
4 To serve, sprinkle with garam masala. Serve hot.

STEAMED BEEF AND TOMATO PUDDING

SERVES 4–6

FOR THE FILLING	
45 ml (3 tbsp) olive oil	2.5 ml (½ tsp) dried oregano
2.5 ml (½ tsp) cumin seeds	15 ml (1 tbsp) paprika
100 g (4 oz) onion, chopped	2.5 ml (½ tsp) black pepper
100 g (4 oz) mixed red, green and yellow peppers, diced	1 beef stock cube
1 garlic clove, crushed	50 g (2 oz) mushrooms, chopped
2.5 ml (½ tsp) salt	FOR THE PASTRY
1 bay leaf	225 g (8 oz) self-raising flour
450 g (1 lb) lean minced beef	50 g (2 oz) shredded beef suet
397 g (14 oz) can tomatoes	50 g (2 oz) potato, grated
30 ml (2 tbsp) tomato purée	2.5 ml (½ tsp) salt
	2.5 ml (½ tsp) baking powder

1 Heat the oil in a pan, add the cumin and fry for 30 seconds. Add the onion and peppers and fry for 5–6 minutes. Add the garlic, salt and bay leaf. Add the beef, stir well and fry for 5 minutes. Drain the tomatoes, reserving the juice, and chop, discarding the seeds.
2 Add the tomatoes, tomato purée, oregano, paprika, pepper, stock cube and tomato juice and cook for 10 minutes. Add the mushrooms, season and cook for 5 minutes.
3 To make the pastry, mix the ingredients and gradually add about 150 ml (¼ pint) water to bind. Roll out to a 35.5 cm (14 inch) round and cut out one quarter for the lid. Use to line a greased 1.4 litre (2½ pint) pudding basin. Spoon in the meat and cover with puding pastry lid. Cover with greaseproof paper and foil and steam for 1½ hours.

CURRIED MINCE AND APPLE BAKE

SERVES 4

50 g (2 oz) slice of bread, crusts removed	700 g (1½ lb) lean minced beef
300 ml (½ pint) milk	30 ml (2 tbsp) raisins
40 g (1½ oz) butter or margarine	25 g (1 oz) flaked almonds
2 medium onions, finely chopped	15 ml (1 tbsp) lemon juice
1 cooking apple, cored and chopped	salt and pepper
	2 bay leaves
15 ml (1 tbsp) mild curry powder	3 eggs

1 Put the bread in a bowl, pour in the milk and leave to soak. Meanwhile, melt the butter in a saucepan, add the onions and fry for 5 minutes or until beginning to soften. Add the apple and curry powder and fry, stirring, for a further 2–3 minutes.
2 Turn the onion mixture into a bowl and add the meat, raisins, almonds, lemon juice and salt and pepper to taste. Mix until well combined.
3 Squeeze the milk from the bread, reserving the milk, and stir the bread into the meat mixture.
4 Place the bay leaves on the bottom of a 1.1 litre (2 pint) pie dish. Fill with the meat mixture, then cover with foil. Bake in a preheated oven at 180°C (350°F) mark 4 for 35 minutes, then remove the foil and break up the meat mixture with a fork.
5 Whisk the eggs together with the reserved milk and pour over the meat, stirring gently to distribute the custard mixture evenly.
6 Return the dish to the oven and cook for a further 35 minutes or until the custard has set and the top browned.

BEEF 'MOUSSAKA'

SERVES 4–6

450 g (1 lb) aubergines, sliced	397 g (14 oz) can tomatoes
salt and pepper	300 ml (10 fl oz) natural yogurt
90 ml (6 tbsp) vegetable oil	2 eggs, size 3, beaten
2 large onions, sliced	1.25 ml (¼ tsp) grated nutmeg
1 garlic clove, chopped	25 g (1 oz) grated Parmesan cheese
700 g (1½ lb) lean minced beef	

1 Layer the aubergine slices in a colander, sprinkling each layer with salt. Cover and leave for about 30 minutes.
2 Meanwhile, heat 30 ml (2 tbsp) oil in a frying pan and fry the onions and garlic for 5 minutes. Add the minced meat and fry for 10 minutes. Add the tomatoes with their juice, season to taste and simmer for 20 minutes.
3 Drain the aubergine slices, rinse and dry well on absorbent kitchen paper. Heat the remaining oil in a separate large frying pan and cook the aubergine slices for 4–5 minutes or until lightly browned, turning once. Add more oil, if necessary.
4 Arrange a layer of aubergine slices in the bottom of a large ovenproof dish and spoon over a layer of the meat mixture. Continue the layers until all the meat and aubergines are used, finishing with a layer of aubergines.
5 Beat the yogurt, eggs and nutmeg together, season to taste and stir in half the Parmesan. Pour over the dish and sprinkle with the remaining cheese. Cook in a preheated oven at 180°C (350°F) mark 4 for 45–60 minutes.

BEEF AND RED BEAN GRATIN

SERVES 4

100 g (4 oz) dried red kidney beans, soaked overnight	225 g (8 oz) tomatoes, skinned and chopped
75 g (3 oz) butter or margarine	15 ml (1 tbsp) tomato purée
1 small onion, thinly sliced	5 ml (1 tsp) chopped fresh mixed herbs or 2.5 ml (½ tsp) dried
225 g (8 oz) lean minced beef	250 ml (9 fl oz) milk
65 g (2½ oz) plain flour	50 g (2 oz) Cheddar cheese, grated
200 ml (7 fl oz) beef stock	1.25 ml (¼ tsp) prepared English mustard
cayenne	
salt and pepper	

1 Drain the beans and put in a saucepan. Cover with water and boil rapidly for 10 minutes, then boil gently for 45 minutes or until tender. Drain.
2 Melt 25 g (1 oz) butter in a saucepan, add the onion and beef and brown over a high heat, stirring. Stir in 40 g (1½ oz) flour, the stock, cayenne, salt and pepper. Cook until very thick. Transfer to an ovenproof dish.
3 Melt another 25 g (1 oz) butter in the pan, add the tomatoes and cook for 10 minutes or until soft. Stir in the beans, tomato purée and herbs and simmer until reduced. Spread over the meat.
4 Melt the remaining butter in a clean pan and add the remaining flour. Cook, stirring, for 2 minutes. Remove from the heat and stir in the milk. Bring to the boil and cook, stirring, until thick.
5 Stir in half the cheese and the mustard and season. Pour the sauce over the bean layer and sprinkle the remaining cheese on top. Bake in a preheated oven at 200°C (400°F) mark 6 for 25 minutes or until golden brown. Serve hot.

MEAT AND POTATO PIE
SERVES 4

FOR THE FILLING	300 ml (½ pint) beef stock
vegetable oil, for frying	150 ml (¼ pint) red wine
225 g (8 oz) baby onions	salt and pepper
1 garlic clove, crushed	5 ml (1 tsp) cornflour
100 g (4 oz) button mushrooms	FOR THE PASTRY
450 g (1 lb) stewing steak, cubed	50 g (2 oz) shredded beef suet
4 large potatoes, peeled and cut into small cubes	100 g (4 oz) self-raising flour
175 g (6 oz) carrots, sliced	pinch of salt
5 ml (1 tsp) dried mixed herbs	milk, to glaze

1 Heat a little oil in a medium saucepan, add the onions, garlic and mushrooms and fry for 3 minutes. Drain and place in a 1.1 litre (2 pint) ovenproof casserole.
2 Add the meat to the pan, a few pieces at a time, and fry until browned, then add to the casserole.
3 Add the potatoes, carrots and herbs to the casserole and pour in the stock and wine. Season well, stir and cook in a preheated oven at 170°C (325°F) mark 3 for 2 hours.
4 Fifteen minutes before the end of the cooking time, blend the cornflour to a paste with a little cold water. Stir into the casserole and continue cooking.
5 Meanwhile, to make the pastry, mix the suet, flour and salt in a bowl and gradually stir in enough water to bind. Roll out the pastry until large enough to cover the casserole and press the edges firmly on to the rim. Brush with a little milk to glaze. Return to the oven and cook at 200°C (400°F) mark 6 for about 30 minutes or until brown.

STEAK AND KIDNEY PIE
SERVES 4

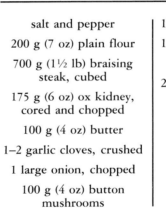

salt and pepper	150 ml (¼ pint) beef stock
200 g (7 oz) plain flour	150 ml (¼ pint) brown ale
700 g (1½ lb) braising steak, cubed	1 bay leaf
175 g (6 oz) ox kidney, cored and chopped	2.5 ml (½ tsp) dried thyme
100 g (4 oz) butter	15 ml (1 tbsp) Worcestershire sauce
1–2 garlic cloves, crushed	15 ml (1 tbsp) tomato purée
1 large onion, chopped	milk, to glaze
100 g (4 oz) button mushrooms	

1 Season 25 g (1 oz) of the flour, then toss the steak and kidney in the flour, shaking off and reserving any excess.
2 Melt 25 g (1 oz) of the butter in a large saucepan and lightly fry the garlic, onion and mushrooms for 3 minutes. Add the steak, kidney and reserved seasoned flour and cook for 5 minutes or until lightly browned.
3 Gradually stir in the stock, ale, bay leaf, thyme, Worcestershire sauce and tomato purée. Cover and simmer for 1¼ hours. Spoon into a 1.7 litre (3 pint) pie dish.
4 Put the remaining flour and a pinch of salt in a bowl. Rub in the remaining butter. Gradually add about 60 ml (4 tbsp) cold water and mix to form a dough.
5 Roll out the dough to 5 cm (2 inches) wider than the pie dish. Cut a 2.5 cm (1 inch) wide strip from the outer edge. Brush the rim of the dish with water and press the pastry strip in place around it. Brush with water and cover with the pastry lid. Garnish with pastry leaves, brush with milk and bake in a preheated oven at 200°C (400°F) mark 6 for 30–45 minutes or until golden brown.

MEAT LOAF WITH ONION SAUCE

SERVES 4

25 g (1 oz) butter	60 ml (4 tbsp) tomato purée
2 medium onions, finely chopped	15 ml (1 tbsp) chopped fresh mixed herbs or 5 ml (1 tsp) dried
5 ml (1 tsp) paprika	
450 g (1 lb) lean minced beef	salt and pepper
75 g (3 oz) fresh breadcrumbs	1 egg, beaten
1 garlic clove, crushed	15 g (½ oz) plain wholemeal flour
	300 ml (½ pint) milk

1 Grease a 900 ml (1½ pint) loaf tin, then line the base with greased greaseproof paper. Melt half the butter in a frying pan. Add half the onions and cook for 5 minutes or until soft. Add the paprika and cook for 1 minute, stirring. Remove from the heat.
2 Add the beef, breadcrumbs, garlic, tomato purée and herbs to the onions and season to taste. Stir thoroughly until evenly mixed, then bind with the beaten egg.
3 Spoon the mixture into the loaf tin, level the surface and cover tightly with foil. Stand the tin in a roasting tin and pour in water to a depth of 2.5 cm (1 inch). Bake in a preheated oven at 180°C (350°F) mark 4 for 1½ hours.
4 Meanwhile, melt the remaining butter in a saucepan. Add the rest of the onion and cook for 10 minutes or until soft but not coloured, stirring occasionally. Add the flour and cook for 1–2 minutes, stirring. Remove from the heat and add the milk, stirring constantly. Simmer for 2–3 minutes or until thick, stirring constantly. Simmer very gently for a further 2–3 minutes. Season to taste.
5 To serve the meat loaf, turn out on to a warmed plate and peel off the paper. Serve with the hot onion sauce.

BEEF WELLINGTON

SERVES 8

1.4 kg (3 lb) fillet of beef	175 g (6 oz) smooth liver pâté
pepper	
15 ml (1 tbsp) vegetable oil	368 g (13 oz) packet frozen puff pastry, thawed
40 g (1½ oz) butter	
225 g (8 oz) button mushrooms, sliced	1 egg, beaten, to glaze

1 Trim and tie up the fillet at intervals so it retains its shape. Season to taste with pepper. Heat the oil and 15 g (½ oz) of the butter in a large frying pan, add the meat and fry briskly on all sides. Press down with a wooden spoon while frying to seal well. Transfer to a roasting tin.
2 Roast the beef in a preheated oven at 220°C (425°F) mark 7 for 20 minutes, then set the beef aside to allow it to cool. Remove the string.
3 Meanwhile, melt the remaining butter in the frying pan and fry the mushrooms for about 5 minutes or until soft. Leave until cold, then blend with the pâté.
4 On a lightly floured surface, roll out the pastry to a large rectangle measuring about 33 x 28 cm (13 x 11 inches) and 0.5 cm (¼ inch) thick.
5 Spread the pâté mixture down the centre of the pastry. Place the meat on top. Brush the pastry edges with egg. Fold the pastry edges over lengthways. Place on a baking sheet with the pastry join underneath and fold the ends under the meat.
6 Decorate with leaves cut from the pastry trimmings, brush with the remaining egg and bake in a preheated oven at 220°C (425°F) mark 7 for 50–60 minutes, depending on how well done you like your beef, covering with foil after 25 minutes. Allow to rest for 10 minutes before serving.

VEAL ESCALOPES IN MUSHROOM SAUCE

SERVES 4

four 175 g (6 oz) veal escalopes	1 small onion, chopped
2 slices of cooked ham, halved	100 g (4 oz) button mushrooms, sliced
50 g (2 oz) butter	25 g (1 oz) plain flour
1 celery stick, chopped	300 ml (½ pint) milk
1 eating apple, peeled, cored and chopped	salt and pepper
25 g (1 oz) Cheddar cheese, grated	30 ml (2 tbsp) fromage frais
	celery leaves, to garnish

1 Put each escalope between two sheets of dampened greaseproof paper and beat until thin with a meat mallet.
2 Place a ham slice on each escalope.
3 Melt 15 g (½ oz) of the butter in a large frying pan, add the celery and apple and fry lightly for 3–4 minutes. Stir in the cheese.
4 Place some of the stuffing on each escalope and roll up, securing with wooden cocktail sticks or fine string.
5 Melt the remaining butter in the pan. Add the veal rolls and cook over a high heat until browned on all sides, then reduce the heat and cook for 10 minutes. Remove from the pan, place on a warmed serving plate and keep hot.
6 Add the onion and mushrooms to the pan and cook for about 5 minutes or until softened. Stir in the flour and cook for 2 minutes, then gradually add the milk, stirring continuously, until the sauce thickens, boils and is smooth. Simmer for 1–2 minutes. Season to taste.
7 Stir the fromage frais into the sauce, pour over the escalopes and garnish with celery leaves. Serve at once.

ESCALOPES FINES HERBES

SERVES 4

four 100 g (4 oz) veal escalopes	30 ml (2 tbsp) chopped herbs (parsley, chervil, tarragon and chives)
salt and pepper	60 ml (4 tbsp) double cream
45 ml (3 tbsp) plain flour	lemon wedges, to serve
25 g (1 oz) butter or margarine	
100 ml (4 fl oz) dry white wine	

1 Place the veal escalopes between two sheets of dampened greaseproof paper and beat until thin with a rolling pin or meat mallet.
2 Season the flour with a little salt and pepper and use to coat the escalopes.
3 Melt the butter or margarine in a large frying pan, add the escalopes and fry over a high heat for 1–2 minutes on each side or until browned. (You may have to fry in two batches, depending on the size of the pan.) Lower the heat and continue to cook for a further 4 minutes on each side or until tender. Transfer the veal to a warmed serving dish, cover and keep hot.
4 Add the white wine to the pan and bring slowly to the boil, stirring to scrape up any sediment left in the pan. Stir in the herbs and cream and season to taste. Simmer very gently for about 5 minutes or until slightly thickened.
5 Pour the sauce over the escalopes and serve immediately, with lemon wedges.

VEAL COBBLER

SERVES 4–6

SAUTÉED VEAL WITH COURGETTES AND GRAPEFRUIT

SERVES 4

25 g (1 oz) butter	225 g (8 oz) button mushrooms, sliced
1 large onion, finely chopped	30 ml (2 tbsp) soured cream
1 garlic clove, crushed	chopped parsley, to garnish
900 g (2 lb) lean pie veal, cut into 2.5 cm (1 inch) cubes	FOR THE TOPPING
	225 g (8 oz) self raising flour
30 ml (2 tbsp) paprika	pinch of salt
salt and pepper	50 g (2 oz) butter
1 red pepper, cut into rings	150 ml (¼ pint) milk
1 green pepper, cut into rings	milk, to glaze
397 g (14 oz) can chopped tomatoes	

1 Melt the butter in a flameproof casserole, add the onion and garlic and sauté for 5 minutes. Add the pie veal and cook for a further 5–7 minutes or until evenly browned.
2 Stir in the paprika, season and cook for a further 2 minutes. Add the pepper rings, tomatoes and mushrooms. Stir well and cook for 5 minutes. Cover and cook in a preheated oven at 190°C (375°F) mark 5 for 1½–2 hours.
3 Meanwhile, make the scone topping. Sift the flour and salt into a bowl, add the butter and rub in until the mixture resembles fine breadcrumbs. Gradually mix in the milk to form a smooth, soft dough. Roll out to 1 cm (½ inch) thick and cut into rounds using a 5 cm (2 inch) cutter.
4 Remove the casserole from the oven and carefully position the scones around the edge of the dish. Brush with milk to glaze, then cook, uncovered, for a final 30–35 minutes. Pour the soured cream over the casserole, avoiding the scones, and sprinkle with parsley.

450 g (1 lb) veal rump or fillet, in one piece	450 g (1 lb) courgettes, thinly sliced
2 grapefruit	a few saffron strands
45 ml (3 tbsp) olive oil	salt and pepper

1 Cut the veal into wafer-thin slices. Place between two sheets of dampened greaseproof paper and beat out with a rolling pin or meat mallet.
2 With a potato peeler, pare the rind off one of the grapefruit. Cut into thin julienne strips. Squeeze the juice from the grapefruit and reserve.
3 With a serrated knife, peel the remaining grapefruit as you would an apple, removing all skin and pith. Slice the grapefruit flesh thinly and set aside.
4 Heat 30 ml (2 tbsp) of the oil in a large frying pan. Add a few slices of veal and sauté for about 2–3 minutes or until well browned on both sides. Transfer to a warmed serving dish, cover and keep warm while sautéeing the remainder.
5 Heat the remaining oil in the pan, add the courgettes and sauté for 2–3 minutes or until beginning to brown. Add the julienne strips of grapefruit rind, the saffron strands and 90 ml (6 tbsp) of the reserved grapefruit juice.
6 Bring to the boil, then lower the heat and simmer for 4–5 minutes or until the liquid is well reduced. Stir in the thinly sliced grapefruit and heat through.
7 Season to taste, pour over the veal and serve.

FRICASSÉE OF VEAL

SERVES 6

900 g (2 lb) stewing veal	salt and pepper
450 g (1 lb) carrots	50 g (2 oz) butter
1 medium onion, sliced	50 g (2 oz) plain flour
15 ml (1 tbsp) chopped fresh thyme or 2.5 ml (½ tsp) dried	2 egg yolks
	150 ml (5 fl oz) single cream
150 ml (¼ pint) dry white wine	chopped parsley, to garnish

1 Cut the veal into 4 cm (1½ inch) cubes, discarding any skin or fat. Put the meat in a saucepan, cover with cold water, bring to the boil and cook for 1 minute. Strain the meat and rinse under cold running water to remove all scum. Rinse out the pan thoroughly and replace the meat.
2 Cut the carrots into finger-sized pieces and add to the pan with the onion, thyme, wine and 900 ml (1½ pints) water. Season to taste. Bring slowly to the boil, cover and simmer gently for about 1¼ hours or until the veal is quite tender.
3 Strain off the cooking liquid, make up to 750 ml (1¼ pints) with stock, if necessary, and reserve. Keep the veal and vegetables warm in a covered serving dish.
4 Melt the butter in a saucepan, stir in the flour and cook gently for 1 minute, stirring. Remove from the heat and gradually stir in the strained cooking liquid and season well. Bring to the boil, stirring all the time, then simmer for 5 minutes.
5 Mix the egg yolks with the cream. Remove the sauce from the heat and stir in the cream mixture. Return to the heat and warm gently, without boiling, until the sauce becomes slightly thicker. Adjust the seasoning and pour over the meat. Serve garnished with parsley.

SPICED VEAL WITH PEPPERS

SERVES 4

550 g (1¼ lb) pie veal	2.5 ml (½ tsp) ground cumin
15 ml (1 tbsp) vegetable oil	2.5 ml (½ tsp) chilli powder
2 medium onions, thinly sliced	1.25 ml (¼ tsp) ground cloves
2 small red peppers, thinly sliced	225 g (8 oz) tomatoes, skinned and roughly chopped
1 garlic clove, crushed	
2.5 ml (½ tsp) ground ginger	300 ml (½ pint) natural yogurt
2.5 ml (½ tsp) ground turmeric	salt and pepper

1 Trim the veal of fat and cut into chunky cubes.
2 Heat the oil in a large saucepan. Add the onions, peppers, garlic and spices and fry for 1 minute. Stir in the chopped tomatoes.
3 Turn the heat to very low and add the yogurt very gradually, stirring well between each addition.
4 Add the veal and season to taste. Cover and simmer gently for 30 minutes.
5 Uncover the pan and cook the veal for a further 30 minutes or until it is tender and the liquid has reduced. Stir occasionally to prevent the meat sticking to the pan. Taste and adjust the seasoning before serving.

VEAL IN MARSALA
SERVES 6

six 75 g (3 oz) veal escalopes	175 g (6 oz) button mushrooms, sliced
salt and pepper	90 ml (6 tbsp) Marsala
plain flour, for coating	90 ml (6 tbsp) chicken stock
60 ml (4 tbsp) vegetable oil	5 ml (1 tsp) arrowroot
50 g (2 oz) butter	lemon wedges, to serve
1 onion, finely chopped	

1 Trim each escalope to remove any skin. Place well apart between two sheets of dampened greaseproof paper and beat out until very thin, using a meat mallet or rolling pin.
2 Season the flour, add the veal and toss until coated. Heat the oil and butter in a large sauté or deep frying pan, add the veal and cook until well browned on all sides.
3 Push the veal to the side of the pan and add the onion and mushrooms to the remaining fat. Cook until browned. Add the Marsala and stock, bring to the boil and season lightly.
4 Cover the pan and cook gently for 5–10 minutes or until the veal is quite tender. Transfer to a warmed serving dish, cover and keep warm.
5 Mix the arrowroot to a smooth paste with a little water. Stir into the pan juices off the heat, then bring slowly to the boil, stirring all the time. Cook for 1 minute, adjust the seasoning and spoon over the veal. Serve with lemon.

VEAL COLLOPS
SERVES 4

four 100 g (4 oz) veal escalopes	10 ml (2 tsp) plain flour
65 g (2½ oz) butter	salt and pepper
1 small onion, chopped	pinch of ground mace
175 ml (6 fl oz) dry white wine	FOR THE GARNISH
400 ml (14 fl oz) veal stock	crisp bacon rolls
5–10 ml (1–2 tsp) mushroom ketchup	button mushroom caps
about 15 ml (1 tbsp) lemon juice	lemon twists
	parsley sprigs

1 Cut each escalope into two pieces and place between two sheets of dampened greaseproof paper. Beat until thin with a rolling pin or meat mallet.
2 Melt 50 g (2 oz) of the butter in a frying pan, add the veal and cook for about 2 minutes on each side. Transfer to a warmed plate and keep warm.
3 Add the onion to the butter remaining in the pan and cook for about 3 minutes or until softened but not browned, stirring frequently. Stir in the wine, bring to the boil and cook until almost evaporated. Stir in the stock, mushroom ketchup and lemon juice, return to the boil and simmer until reduced to 225 ml (8 fl oz).
4 Work the flour into the remaining butter, then gradually whisk into the stock to thicken it slightly. Season with salt, pepper and mace, taste and add more mushroom ketchup and lemon juice if necessary.
5 Arrange the collops, overlapping each other, on a warmed oval serving platter. Spoon some of the sauce down the centre of the collops, garnish and serve the remaining sauce separately.

VEAL AND KIDNEY PIE

SERVES 6

900 g (2 lb) stewing veal, cut into 2.5 cm (1 inch) cubes	40 g (1½ oz) plain flour
juice of 1 lemon	30 ml (2 tbsp) single cream
6.25 ml (1¼ tsp) dried tarragon	FOR THE PASTRY
	100 g (4 oz) plain wholemeal flour
salt and pepper	225 g (8 oz) plain white flour
225 g (8 oz) lamb kidneys	225 g (8 oz) butter or margarine
350 g (12 oz) leeks	
40 g (1½ oz) butter or margarine	1 egg, beaten, to glaze

1 Place the veal in a saucepan with 900 ml (1½ pints) water, 15 ml (1 tbsp) lemon juice and 5 ml (1 tsp) tarragon. Season, cover and simmer for 1–1¼ hours.
2 Meanwhile, skin and core the kidneys and cut into bite-sized pieces. Trim and slice the leeks, rinse and drain.
3 Stir the kidneys and leeks into the saucepan. Cover and simmer for a further 8–10 minutes. Strain off the liquor and reserve. Spoon into a 26.5 cm (10½ inch) pie plate.
4 To make the sauce, melt the butter in a saucepan, stir in the flour and cook for 1–2 minutes. Remove from the heat and stir in 600 ml (1 pint) of the reserved stock. Cook, stirring, until thick. Remove from the heat and stir in 15 ml (1 tbsp) lemon juice, 1.25 ml (¼ tsp) tarragon and the cream. Season, pour over the veal and cool.
5 To make the pastry, mix the flours and rub in the butter. Gradually add about 75 ml (5 tbsp) water. Chill.
6 Roll out the pastry and use to cover the pie. Brush with beaten egg. Bake in a preheated oven at 190°C (375°F) mark 5 for about 40 minutes or until well browned.

VEAL AND HAM PIE

SERVES 8–10

450 g (1 lb) lean minced veal	2 medium onions, finely chopped
100 g (4 oz) boiled ham, minced	salt and pepper
30 ml (2 tbsp) chopped parsley	100 g (4 oz) lard
	350 g (12 oz) plain wholemeal flour
2.5 ml (½ tsp) ground mace	1 egg yolk
1.25 ml (¼ tsp) ground bay leaves	3 eggs, hard-boiled and shelled
finely grated rind of 1 lemon	10 ml (2 tsp) powdered aspic jelly

1 Grease a 1.4 litre (2½ pint) loaf tin and line the base with greased greaseproof paper.
2 Put the first seven ingredients in a bowl and add 5 ml (1 tsp) salt and 1.25 ml (¼ tsp) pepper. Mix well.
3 Put the lard and 200 ml (7 fl oz) water in a saucepan and heat gently to melt. Bring to the boil, remove from the heat and tip in the flour with 2.5 ml (½ tsp) salt. Beat well to form a soft dough. Beat the egg yolk into the dough. Cover with a damp tea towel and rest in a warm place for 20 minutes. Do not allow to cool.
4 Use two thirds of the pastry to line the prepared tin. Press in half the meat and place the eggs down the centre. Fill with the remaining meat.
5 Roll out the remaining pastry and use to cover the pie. Make a hole in the centre of the pie. Bake at 180°C (350°F) mark 4 for 1½ hours. Leave to cool for 3–4 hours.
6 Make up the aspic jelly with 300 ml (½ pint) water and leave to cool for about 10 minutes. Pour the aspic through the hole in the top of the pie. Chill the pie for about 1 hour. Leave at room temperature for 1 hour before turning out.

VEAL WITH TUNA FISH MAYONNAISE

SERVES 4–6

900 g (2 lb) boned, rolled and tied leg or loin of veal	2 cloves
300 ml (½ pint) dry white wine	200 g (7 oz) can tuna in oil, drained
1 carrot, sliced	4 canned anchovy fillets, soaked in milk for 20 minutes and drained
1 celery stick, sliced	
a few parsley sprigs	300 ml (½ pint) thick mayonnaise
2 bay leaves	
a few black peppercorns	15 ml (1 tbsp) capers, roughly chopped
salt and pepper	lemon slices, black olives and lamb's lettuce, to garnish
1 small onion	

1 Put the veal in a large saucepan and add the wine, carrot, celery, parsley, bay leaves, peppercorns and 5 ml (1 tsp) salt. Push the cloves into the onion and add to the pan. Add enough water to cover, then bring to the boil.
2 Lower the heat, cover the pan and simmer gently for 1–1¼ hours or until the veal is tender. Remove the pan from the heat and leave the veal to cool in the liquid.
3 When the meat is cold, remove from the pan, reserving the liquid, and dry with kitchen paper. Untie the meat, slice and arrange on a platter. Cover with cling film.
4 Pound the tuna and anchovies together, then stir into the mayonnaise with the capers and pepper to taste. Thin to a coating consistency with a few spoonfuls of the reserved cooking liquid, taste and adjust the seasoning.
5 Spoon the mayonnaise over the veal, then cover loosely with foil. Chill for 24–48 hours. To serve, leave the veal to stand at room temperature for 1 hour. Uncover and garnish.

PORTMANTEAU LAMB CHOPS

SERVES 4

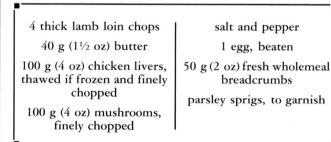

4 thick lamb loin chops	salt and pepper
40 g (1½ oz) butter	1 egg, beaten
100 g (4 oz) chicken livers, thawed if frozen and finely chopped	50 g (2 oz) fresh wholemeal breadcrumbs
	parsley sprigs, to garnish
100 g (4 oz) mushrooms, finely chopped	

1 Using a sharp, pointed knife, make a horizontal cut in each chop, working from the outside fat edge to the bone, to form a pocket.
2 To make the stuffing, melt 15 g (½ oz) of the butter in a frying pan, add the chicken livers and mushrooms and fry for 4–5 minutes or until soft but not brown. Season to taste.
3 Leave the stuffing to cool slightly, then spoon into the cavity in the chops and secure the open edges with wooden cocktail sticks.
4 Dip the chops in the beaten egg, then in the breadcrumbs to coat thoroughly.
5 Put the chops in a roasting tin. Melt the remaining butter and pour over the chops. Bake in a preheated oven at 200°C (400°F) mark 6 for 15 minutes, then turn and bake for a further 15 minutes or until golden brown. Serve hot, garnish with parsley sprigs.

TANGY CHOPS

SERVES 4

30 ml (2 tbsp) vegetable oil	15 ml (1 tbsp) chopped fresh mint or 5 ml (1 tsp) dried
4 lamb chump chops	
salt and pepper	5 ml (1 tsp) sugar
juice and finely grated rind of 1 lemon	150 ml (¼ pint) beef or chicken stock
30 ml (2 tbsp) chopped fresh parsley or 10 ml (2 tsp) dried	

1 Heat the oil in a frying pan, add the chops and fry over a brisk heat until browned on both sides. Lower the heat and season to taste.
2 Mix the lemon juice and rind with the herbs and sugar, then spoon this mixture over the chops and pour in the stock. Cover the pan tightly and simmer gently for 30 minutes or until the meat is tender. Serve hot with the juices poured over.

─────── **VARIATION** ───────

You can vary the herbs used in this dish, depending on what is available. Fresh rosemary is, of course, the classic herb to use with lamb.

LAMB STEAKS WITH CAPER SAUCE

SERVES 4

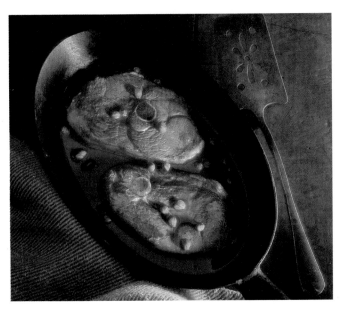

salt and pepper	300 ml (½ pint) lamb or beef stock
four 175 g (6 oz) lamb leg steaks	30 ml (2 tbsp) drained capers
25 g (1 oz) butter	15 ml (1 tbsp) vinegar from the capers
5 ml (1 tsp) plain flour	

1 Season the lamb steaks to taste. Heat the butter in a frying pan and fry the steaks gently for 10–15 minutes or until browned on both sides, turning occasionally. Remove from the pan with a slotted spoon.
2 Stir to loosen any sediment at the bottom of the pan, then stir in the flour and cook for 1–2 minutes. Gradually add the stock, stirring all the time, then cook until the sauce thickens, boils and is smooth. Add the capers and vinegar and simmer for 1–2 minutes.
3 Return the lamb steaks to the pan and simmer for 5 minutes or until cooked to your liking. Serve hot.

SHEPHERD'S PIE

SERVES 4

700 g (1½ lb) potatoes, peeled	15 ml (1 tbsp) Worcestershire sauce
salt and pepper	90 ml (6 tbsp) chopped parsley
450 g (1 lb) cooked lamb	
30 ml (2 tbsp) vegetable oil	5 ml (1 tsp) dried marjoram
1 medium onion, chopped	50 g (2 oz) Cheddar cheese, grated
30 ml (2 tbsp) plain flour	
300 ml (½ pint) lamb or beef stock	chopped parsley, to garnish

1 Cook the potatoes in boiling salted water for 20 minutes or until tender.
2 Meanwhile, trim the excess fat from the lamb and discard. Chop the meat finely or mince coarsely.
3 Heat the oil in a frying pan, add the onion and fry for 5 minutes or until lightly browned. Stir in the flour and fry for 2–3 minutes. Add the stock and simmer, stirring, until thickened.
4 Stir in the lamb, Worcestershire sauce, parsley, marjoram and salt and pepper. Spoon into a 1.1 litre (2 pint) shallow pie dish.
5 Drain the potatoes. Mash well, then beat in the cheese and salt and pepper. Spoon or pipe over the lamb.
6 Bake in a preheated oven at 200°C (400°F) mark 6 for 30 minutes or until well browned. Serve hot, sprinkled with parsley.

--- VARIATION ---
Cottage Pie
Replace the minced lamb with minced beef and omit the marjoram and cheese for a traditional 'Cottage' pie.

LAMB CUTLETS REFORM

SERVES 4

15 g (½ oz) butter	2 blades of mace
1 small onion, finely chopped	1 bay leaf
1 medium carrot, finely chopped	4 juniper berries, crushed
	pinch of dried thyme
50 g (2 oz) lean ham, cut into thin strips	eight 75 g (3 oz) lamb cutlets
60 ml (4 tbsp) red wine vinegar	50 g (2 oz) ham, finely minced
45 ml (3 tbsp) port	50 g (2 oz) fresh breadcrumbs
600 ml (1 pint) lamb or chicken stock	1 egg, beaten
2 cloves	15 ml (1 tbsp) cornflour

1 To make the sauce, melt the butter in a saucepan, add the onion, carrot and ham strips and cook until just turning brown. Add the vinegar and port and boil until almost all the liquid has evaporated.
2 Remove the pan from the heat and add the stock, cloves, mace, bay leaf, juniper berries and thyme. Stir well and bring to the boil. Simmer for 30 minutes.
3 Meanwhile, trim the cutlets to remove most of the surrounding fat. Scrape the bone of each cutlet absolutely clean to within 2.5 cm (1 inch) of the 'eye' of the meat.
4 Mix the minced ham and breadcrumbs together. Brush each cutlet with beaten egg and coat with the ham and breadcrumb mixture. Cover and chill until required.
5 Blend the cornflour with about 30 ml (2 tbsp) water and add to the sauce. Stir well and bring the sauce to the boil, stirring continuously. Simmer until thickened.
6 Cook the cutlets under a preheated grill for 4 minutes on each side. Reheat the sauce and serve separately.

LAMB FILLET WITH REDCURRANT SAUCE

SERVES 3

90 ml (6 tbsp) soured cream	450 g (1 lb) lamb fillet
1 garlic clove, crushed	30 ml (2 tbsp) dry red wine
5 ml (1 tsp) wholegrain mustard	15 ml (1 tbsp) redcurrant jelly
salt and pepper	

1 Mix 30 ml (2 tbsp) of the soured cream with the garlic and mustard. Season to taste.

2 Put the lamb fillet in a roasting tin and spoon the garlic mixture all over. Roast in a preheated oven at 180°C (350°F) mark 4 for 30 minutes or until tender and cooked to your liking. Transfer the lamb to a warmed serving dish and keep warm.

3 Add the wine to the roasting tin, stirring in any sediment from the bottom of the tin. Stir in the redcurrant jelly. Bring to the boil, then stir in the remaining soured cream and boil for 2–3 minutes or until thickened slightly.

4 Slice the lamb and serve with the sauce spooned over.

─────────── **TO MICROWAVE** ───────────

Complete step 1. Put the lamb in a shallow dish and spoon over the garlic mixture. Cook, uncovered, on HIGH for 3 minutes. Cover and cook on MEDIUM for 10–15 minutes, rearranging twice, until cooked to your liking. Transfer the lamb to a warmed serving dish. Stir the remaining soured cream, the wine and redcurrant jelly into the dish. Cook on HIGH for 1–2 minutes, stirring occasionally, until hot. Complete step 4.

HONEYED LAMB NOISETTES

SERVES 6

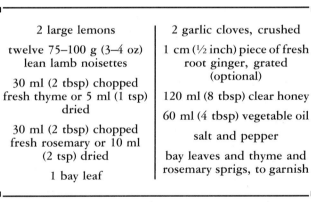

2 large lemons	2 garlic cloves, crushed
twelve 75–100 g (3–4 oz) lean lamb noisettes	1 cm (½ inch) piece of fresh root ginger, grated (optional)
30 ml (2 tbsp) chopped fresh thyme or 5 ml (1 tsp) dried	120 ml (8 tbsp) clear honey
30 ml (2 tbsp) chopped fresh rosemary or 10 ml (2 tsp) dried	60 ml (4 tbsp) vegetable oil
	salt and pepper
1 bay leaf	bay leaves and thyme and rosemary sprigs, to garnish

1 Pare the rind off one lemon and cut into fine strips. Cover and set aside.

2 Place the lamb in a shallow, non-metallic dish. Sprinkle over the herbs and bay leaf.

3 Whisk together the grated rind of the remaining whole lemon, 90 ml (6 tbsp) lemon juice, the crushed garlic, ginger (if using), the honey and oil. Season to taste. Pour over the lamb, cover and leave to marinate in the refrigerator overnight.

4 Drain the marinade from the lamb and strain into a small saucepan. Place the meat on a rack over the grill pan. Cook under a preheated hot grill for 7 minutes on each side. Transfer to an ovenproof serving dish, cover lightly with foil and keep warm.

5 Carefully pour the grill pan juices into the strained marinade. Stir in the strips of lemon rind. Bring to the boil and simmer for 2–3 minutes or until syrupy, stirring occasionally. Adjust the seasoning and spoon over the noisettes. Garnish with bay leaves and sprigs of fresh thyme and rosemary.

LAMB NOISETTES WITH RED WINE SAUCE

SERVES 6

12 lamb noisettes	225 g (8 oz) button mushrooms
flour, for coating	300 ml (½ pint) red wine
25 g (1 oz) butter	150 ml (¼ pint) chicken stock
60 ml (4 tbsp) vegetable oil	15 ml (1 tbsp) tomato purée
2 large onions, sliced	2 bay leaves
1 garlic clove, finely chopped	salt and pepper

1 Lightly coat the lamb noisettes with flour. Heat the butter and oil in a large flameproof casserole. Add the noisettes, a few at a time, and cook over a high heat until browned on both sides. Remove from the casserole with a slotted spoon and set aside.

2 Add the onion and garlic to the casserole and fry for about 5 minutes or until golden. Add the mushrooms and fry for a further 2–3 minutes. Stir in the red wine, stock, tomato purée and bay leaves. Season to taste.

3 Return the noisettes to the casserole and bring to the boil, then cover and simmer gently for about 40 minutes or until tender, turning the meat once during this time.

4 Lift the noisettes out of the sauce and remove the string. Place the noisettes on a warmed serving dish and keep warm. Boil the remaining sauce rapidly for 5–10 minutes to reduce. Taste and adjust the seasoning, remove the bay leaves, then pour over the noisettes. Serve immediately.

MINTED LAMB BURGERS WITH CUCUMBER

SERVES 4

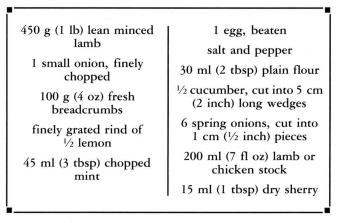

450 g (1 lb) lean minced lamb	1 egg, beaten
1 small onion, finely chopped	salt and pepper
100 g (4 oz) fresh breadcrumbs	30 ml (2 tbsp) plain flour
finely grated rind of ½ lemon	½ cucumber, cut into 5 cm (2 inch) long wedges
45 ml (3 tbsp) chopped mint	6 spring onions, cut into 1 cm (½ inch) pieces
	200 ml (7 fl oz) lamb or chicken stock
	15 ml (1 tbsp) dry sherry

1 Mix the lamb, onion, breadcrumbs and lemon rind with 15 ml (1 tbsp) of the chopped mint and the egg. Season to taste.

2 Shape into eight burgers with floured hands, then completely coat in the flour.

3 Dry-fry the burgers in a large heavy-based non-stick frying pan for about 6 minutes or until lightly browned, turning once. Add the cucumber and spring onions.

4 Pour in the stock and sherry, then add the remaining mint and season to taste. Bring to the boil, cover and simmer gently for about 20 minutes or until the meat is tender. Skim off any excess fat and taste and adjust the seasoning before serving.

EASTERN LAMB KEBABS

SERVES 4–6

CROWN ROAST

SERVES 6

450 g (1 lb) lean minced lamb	5 ml (1 tsp) ground fenugreek
1 large onion, grated	10 ml (2 tsp) ground turmeric
15 ml (1 tbsp) chopped fresh dill or 5 ml (1 tsp) dried	salt and pepper
	30 ml (2 tbsp) sultanas
30 ml (2 tbsp) chopped fresh coriander or 10 ml (2 tsp) dried	1 egg, beaten
	coriander sprigs, to garnish

1 Put the lamb and onion in a medium bowl. Add the remaining ingredients, except the coriander sprigs, and mix well, using your fingers.
2 Divide the mixture into 30 walnut-size pieces. Using dampened hands, form into even round shapes.
3 Thread about five balls on to each of six metal skewers, leaving about 2.5 cm (1 inch) of each skewer exposed at both sides. Place the kebabs on a grill rack as you prepare them.
4 Cook the kebabs under a preheated grill for 5–8 minutes. Turn them over and continue to cook for a further 5–8 minutes or until the meat is cooked. Garnish with coriander sprigs.

——————— **TO MICROWAVE** ———————
Complete steps 1 and 2. Thread the balls on to wooden skewers and arrange on a microwave roasting rack. Microwave on HIGH for 12-15 minutes, re-arranging occasionally. Stand for 2 minutes. Garnish with coriander sprigs.

2 best end necks of lamb, each with 6 cutlets, chined	juice and grated rind of ½ lemon
15 g (½ oz) butter	1 egg, beaten
1 medium onion, chopped	salt and pepper
3 celery sticks, chopped	30 ml (2 tbsp) plain flour
2 eating apples, chopped	450 ml (¾ pint) lamb or beef stock
100 g (4 oz) fresh breadcrumbs	mint sprigs, to garnish
30 ml (2 tbsp) chopped mint	

1 Trim each cutlet bone to a depth of 2.5 cm (1 inch).
2 Bend the joints around, fat side inwards, and sew together using strong cotton or fine string to form a crown. Cover the exposed bones with foil.
3 Melt the butter in a saucepan and cook the onion, celery and apples until brown. Stir in the breadcrumbs, mint, lemon juice and rind and egg. Season to taste and cool, then fill the centre of the joint with the stuffing and weigh. Roast in a preheated oven at 180°C (350°F) mark 4 for 25 minutes per 450 g (1 lb) plus 25 minutes.
4 Transfer the roast to a warmed serving dish and keep warm. Drain off all but 30 ml (2 tbsp) of the fat in the roasting tin, then add the flour and blend well. Cook for 2–3 minutes, stirring continuously. Remove from the heat and gradually add the stock. Boil for 2–3 minutes. Adjust the seasoning and serve with the roast. Garnish with mint.

——————— **VARIATION** ———————
For a 'Guard of Honour', trim the best end necks of lamb and interlace the bones, fat sides outwards, to form an arch. Stuff the cavity and tie as above.

BRAISED SHOULDER OF LAMB WITH APRICOT STUFFING

SERVES 6

25 g (1 oz) butter	2 kg (4½ lb) shoulder of lamb, boned
15 ml (1 tbsp) chopped onion	600 ml (1 pint) beef or lamb stock
60 ml (4 tbsp) fine fresh white breadcrumbs	225 g (8 oz) onions, quartered
15 ml (1 tbsp) chopped parsley	450 g (1 lb) carrots, diced
15–30 ml (1–2 tbsp) milk	6 celery sticks, sliced
75 g (3 oz) no-soak dried apricots, chopped	350 g (12 oz) turnips, quartered
salt and pepper	

1 Melt the butter in a saucepan, add the chopped onion and fry for about 5 minutes or until soft and transparent.
2 Remove the pan from the heat and add the breadcrumbs, parsley, milk and apricots. Season to taste.
3 Sprinkle the cut surface of the lamb with seasoning and spread the stuffing over. Roll up and tie with string. Place the joint in a greased flameproof casserole and cook in a preheated oven at 230°C (450°F) mark 8 for 15 minutes.
4 Remove the casserole from the oven and add half the stock. Reduce the oven temperature to 180°C (350°F) mark 4, re-cover and cook the meat for 45 minutes.
5 Arrange the onions, carrots, celery and turnips round the joint and add the remaining stock. Re-cover and cook for a further 1¼ hours.
6 Remove the casserole from the oven and lift the meat and vegetables on to a warmed serving dish. Skim the fat off the stock in the casserole, then boil fast for 3–5 minutes to reduce by half. Serve with the lamb.

ROLLED STUFFED BREASTS OF LAMB

SERVES 4

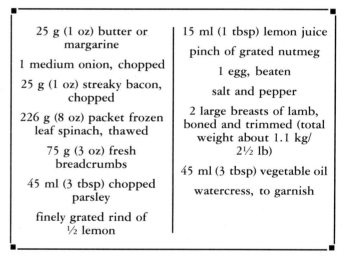

25 g (1 oz) butter or margarine	15 ml (1 tbsp) lemon juice
1 medium onion, chopped	pinch of grated nutmeg
25 g (1 oz) streaky bacon, chopped	1 egg, beaten
	salt and pepper
226 g (8 oz) packet frozen leaf spinach, thawed	2 large breasts of lamb, boned and trimmed (total weight about 1.1 kg/ 2½ lb)
75 g (3 oz) fresh breadcrumbs	45 ml (3 tbsp) vegetable oil
45 ml (3 tbsp) chopped parsley	watercress, to garnish
finely grated rind of ½ lemon	

1 Melt the butter or margarine in a saucepan, add the onion and bacon and fry for about 5 minutes or until lightly browned.
2 Drain the spinach and chop roughly. Place in a bowl with the onion and bacon, breadcrumbs, parsley, lemon rind and juice, nutmeg and egg. Mix together well and season to taste.
3 Lay the breasts of lamb, fat side down, on a work surface and spread the stuffing evenly over them with a palette knife.
4 Roll up the lamb breasts loosely and tie in several places with strong thread or fine string to hold their shape.
5 Weigh each joint and calculate the cooking time, allowing 25 minutes per 450 g (1 lb) plus 25 minutes for each joint. Heat the oil in a roasting tin and place the joints in the tin. Roast in a preheated oven at 180°C (350°F) mark 4 for the calculated cooking time, basting occasionally. Serve hot, garnished with watercress.

LAMB IN TOMATO SAUCE WITH HERB BREAD

SERVES 4

30 ml (2 tbsp) vegetable oil	60 ml (4 tbsp) red wine (optional)
1 kg (2¼ lb) boned lean shoulder of lamb, cubed	salt and pepper
1 medium onion, sliced	lamb or beef stock, if necessary
20 ml (4 tsp) plain flour	40 g (1½ oz) butter
397 g (14 oz) and 227 g (8 oz) cans tomatoes	15 ml (1 tbsp) snipped chives
30 ml (2 tbsp) tomato purée	eight 1 cm (½ inch) slices of French bread
pinch of granulated sugar	
2.5 ml (½ tsp) dried rosemary	

1 Heat the oil in a flameproof casserole, add the lamb and fry over a high heat until browned on all sides. Remove from the casserole with a slotted spoon and set aside.
2 Add the onion to the pan and fry for 5 minutes or until soft. Stir in the flour and cook for 1 minute. Add the tomatoes with their juice, the tomato purée, sugar, rosemary and wine, if using. Bring to the boil, stirring.
3 Return the meat to the pan and add salt and pepper to taste. Add a little stock, if necessary, to cover the meat. Cover the casserole and cook in the oven at 170°C (325°F) mark 3 for about 1¼ hours.
4 Meanwhile, make the herb butter. Beat the butter until soft, then beat in the chives and salt and pepper to taste.
5 Spread the butter on to the slices of French bread. Uncover the casserole and place the bread, butter side up, on top. Cook for a further hour, or until the meat is tender. Serve hot.

PARSON'S 'VENISON'

SERVES 4–6

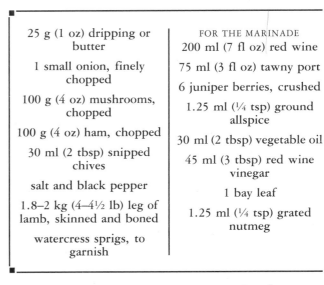

	FOR THE MARINADE
25 g (1 oz) dripping or butter	200 ml (7 fl oz) red wine
1 small onion, finely chopped	75 ml (3 fl oz) tawny port
100 g (4 oz) mushrooms, chopped	6 juniper berries, crushed
100 g (4 oz) ham, chopped	1.25 ml (¼ tsp) ground allspice
30 ml (2 tbsp) snipped chives	30 ml (2 tbsp) vegetable oil
salt and black pepper	45 ml (3 tbsp) red wine vinegar
1.8–2 kg (4–4½ lb) leg of lamb, skinned and boned	1 bay leaf
watercress sprigs, to garnish	1.25 ml (¼ tsp) grated nutmeg

1 Melt half the dripping in a saucepan and cook the onion and mushrooms for 5 minutes or until soft, stirring frequently. Stir in the ham and chives, season and cool.
2 Season the lamb inside and out with black pepper, then spread the onion mixture over the inside. Roll up tightly and tie securely. Place in an ovenproof casserole.
3 Mix the marinade ingredients, pour over the lamb, cover and leave in a cool place for 24 hours, turning occasionally. Remove the meat from the marinade, drain and dry.
4 Melt the remaining dripping in a frying pan. Add the meat and cook until browned. Transfer to a casserole.
5 Pour the marinade into the frying pan, bring to the boil, then pour over the meat. Cover, then cook at 180°C (350°F) mark 4 for 1¾–2 hours, basting occasionally.
6 Transfer the meat to a warmed plate and keep warm. Skim the fat from the surface of the liquid, then boil the liquid rapidly until reduced and slightly thickened. Season to taste. Garnish the meat and serve with the gravy.

LAMB WITH CHERRIES
SERVES 6

225 g (8 oz) streaky bacon rashers, chopped	1 garlic clove, sliced
15 g (½ oz) butter	600 ml (1 pint) dry red wine
1.4 kg (3 lb) boneless leg or shoulder of lamb, cut into 4 cm (1½ inch) cubes	bouquet garni
	pinch of grated nutmeg
1 medium onion, sliced	salt and pepper
1 medium carrot, sliced	450 g (1 lb) fresh red cherries, stoned
1 celery stick, sliced	

1 In a large frying pan, fry the bacon in its own fat until browned. Add the butter to the pan and fry the lamb, a little at a time, until browned. Remove from the pan with the bacon and put in an ovenproof casserole.
2 Add the onion, carrot, celery and garlic to the fat remaining in the pan and fry for about 5 minutes or until lightly browned. Add the vegetables to the casserole.
3 Pour over the wine and add the bouquet garni and nutmeg. Season to taste, cover and cook in a preheated oven at 150°C (300°F) mark 3 for about 2½ hours or until tender.
4 Thirty minutes before the end of the cooking time, stir the cherries into the casserole and continue to cook until the meat is tender and the cherries soft. Serve hot.

—————————— **COOK'S TIP** ——————————
Look for red-skinned sour cherries for this dish. Dark-skinned Morellos are also a good choice.

ORIENTAL LAMB
SERVES 4

1.4 kg (3 lb) lean shoulder of lamb, boned	5 ml (1 tsp) ground ginger
30 ml (2 tbsp) vegetable oil	300 ml (½ pint) chicken stock
25 g (1 oz) butter or margarine	15 ml (1 tbsp) Worcestershire sauce
450 g (1 lb) small new potatoes, scrubbed or scraped	30 ml (2 tbsp) soy sauce
	salt and pepper
225 g (8 oz) small pickling onions, skinned	2 caps canned pimiento, diced
15 ml (1 tbsp) plain flour	

1 Cut the lamb into 2.5 cm (1 inch) pieces about 5 mm (¼ inch) thick, discarding any excess fat.
2 Heat the oil and butter or margarine in a large sauté pan and add the meat, a few pieces at time. Fry until browned on all sides, turning frequently. Remove from the pan with a slotted spoon.
3 Add the potatoes and onions to the fat remaining in the pan and fry until lightly browned, turning frequently.
4 Return the meat to the pan, sprinkle in the flour and ginger and stir well. Cook gently, stirring, for 2 minutes.
5 Add the stock, Worcestershire sauce and soy sauce, and season to taste. Bring to the boil, stirring, then cover and simmer for 30 minutes or until the meat is tender.
6 Add the pimientos and stir over a low heat to heat through. Taste and adjust the seasoning, then transfer the lamb to a warmed serving dish. Serve hot.

BROWN RAGOUT OF LAMB

SERVES 6

75 g (3 oz) butter, diced	salt and pepper
900 g (2 lb) boneless leg of lamb, cut into 2.5 cm (1 inch) pieces	3 carrots, cut into pieces
	12 small onions, skinned
750 ml (1¼ pints) brown stock, preferably veal	100 g (4 oz) button mushrooms
4 cloves	squeeze of lemon juice
1 onion	75 g (3 oz) shelled broad beans, cooked
3 parsley sprigs	FOR THE GARNISH
2 thyme sprigs	flesh of 2 large firm tomatoes, cut into strips
2 bay leaves	30 ml (2 tbsp) finely chopped parsley
1 rosemary sprig	

1 Melt half the butter in a frying pan and cook the lamb until brown. Transfer to a flameproof casserole.

2 Put the stock in a saucepan. Push the cloves into the unskinned onion and add to the stock with the herbs. Season and bring to the boil. Pour over the lamb, cover and cook at 180°C (350°F) mark 4 for 1 hour.

3 Add another 15 g (½ oz) butter to the frying pan and melt. Fry the carrots and small onions until browned. Drain, then stir into the casserole and cook for a further 30 minutes. Cook the mushrooms in the remaining butter with the lemon juice. Drain on kitchen paper.

4 Remove the onion and cloves from the casserole, then stir in the mushrooms and cook, uncovered, for 10 minutes. Lift the meat and vegetables from the dish and keep warm. Boil the liquid until reduced. Arrange the meat on a plate with all the vegetables. Garnish and serve.

LAMB AND ORANGE CASSEROLE WITH CHOUX DUMPLINGS

SERVES 4

45 ml (3 tbsp) vegetable oil	150 ml (¼ pint) chicken stock
900 g (2 lb) lean boneless leg of lamb, cubed	2 bay leaves
1 medium onion, chopped	salt and pepper
2 turnips, roughly chopped	50 g (2 oz) butter
3 carrots, roughly chopped	2 eggs, beaten
75 g (3 oz) plain flour	finely grated rind of 2 oranges
15 ml (1 tbsp) tomato purée	15 ml (1 tbsp) chopped parsley
300 ml (½ pint) unsweetened orange juice	

1 Heat the oil in a flameproof casserole and fry the lamb until brown. Remove and set aside. Fry the onion for 5 minutes. Add the turnips and carrots and fry for 5 minutes.

2 Stir in 15 g (½ oz) of the flour, then add the tomato purée. Add the orange juice and stock and boil, stirring.

3 Return the meat, add the bay leaves, season and stir well. Cover and cook at 180°C (350°F) mark 4 for 1½ hours.

4 To make the dumplings, sift together the remaining flour and a pinch of salt. Put the butter in a medium saucepan, add 150 ml (¼ pint) water and heat gently until the butter has melted. Bring to a rolling boil and tip in the flour and salt. Immediately take the pan off the heat and beat vigorously until the mixture forms a ball. Turn into a bowl and cool slightly, then beat in the eggs, a little at a time. The paste should be quite stiff.

5 Beat the orange rind and parsley into the choux paste. Remove the bay leaves from the casserole, then pipe or spoon eight choux balls on top. Bake, uncovered, at 200°C (400°F) mark 6 for 1 hour.

LANCASHIRE HOT POT

SERVES 4

8 middle neck lamb chops	5 ml (1 tsp) dried thyme
2 lamb's kidneys, halved and cored	salt and pepper
8 shelled oysters (optional)	450 g (1 lb) potatoes, peeled and thinly sliced
2 medium onions, sliced	450 ml (¾ pint) lamb or beef stock
100 g (4 oz) mushrooms, sliced	25 g (1 oz) lard or dripping

1 Remove any excess fat from the lamb. Select a large, deep casserole. If it is not deep enough to hold the meat, chop the ends off the bones.

2 Cut each kidney half into three or four pieces.

3 Layer the meat in the casserole with the oysters (if using), the kidneys, onions and mushrooms. Sprinkle each layer with thyme and seasoning to taste. If the casserole has a narrow top, add some of the potatoes at this stage. Pour in the stock.

4 Arrange a layer of overlapping potato slices on top. Melt the lard or dripping and brush over the potatoes. Cover and cook in a preheated oven at 170°C (325°F) mark 3 for 2 hours or until both the meat and the potatoes are tender when tested with a skewer.

5 Remove the lid carefully, increase the oven temperature to 220°C (425°F) mark 7 and continue cooking for about 20 minutes or until the potatoes are golden brown and crisp.

LAMB AND MAÎTRE D'HÔTEL BUTTER

SERVES 4

4 large lamb loin chops	salt and pepper
50 g (2 oz) butter	1 egg, beaten
50 g (2 oz) button mushrooms, finely chopped	15 ml (1 tbsp) vegetable oil
	FOR THE BUTTER
50 g (2 oz) ham, finely chopped	100 g (4 oz) butter, softened
grated rind of 1 small lemon	30 ml (2 tbsp) finely chopped parsley
25 g (1 oz) fresh breadcrumbs	squeeze of lemon juice
	salt and cayenne

1 To make the maître d'hôtel butter, beat the butter until very soft, then add the parsley, lemon juice and salt and cayenne to taste. Shape into a roll, wrap in greaseproof paper and chill in the refrigerator until required.

2 Using a sharp knife, slit the lean 'eye' of each chop horizontally through the fat edge.

3 Melt 25 g (1 oz) of the butter in a small saucepan, add the mushrooms and fry lightly until soft. Add the ham, lemon rind and breadcrumbs, season to taste and bind with a little beaten egg. Allow to cool, then stuff the mixture into the incisions in the chops. Secure each chop with strong thread or fine string.

4 Heat the oil and remaining butter in a large frying pan, add the chops and fry over a high heat, until well browned on both sides. Reduce the heat and continue to cook for 20 minutes. Remove the chops from the pan and remove the string.

5 Cut the maître d'hôtel butter into pats and place several on each of the chops to serve.

BLANQUETTE D'AGNEAU
SERVES 4

700 g (1½ lb) boneless lean shoulder of lamb, diced	300 ml (½ pint) stock or water
100 g (4 oz) carrots, sliced	25 g (1 oz) butter, softened
1 onion, sliced	45 ml (3 tbsp) plain flour
2 celery sticks, sliced	1 egg yolk
1 small bay leaf	150 ml (5 fl oz) single cream
5 ml (1 tsp) dried thyme	chopped parsley, to garnish
salt and pepper	

1 Put the meat, carrots, onion, celery, bay leaf and thyme in a large saucepan. Season to taste. Cover with stock or water, cover and simmer for 1½ hours or until the meat is tender. Remove the bay leaf.
2 Blend together the softened butter and flour and add to the stew in small knobs, stirring after each addition until the stew is thickened. Simmer for 10 minutes, adding more liquid if necessary.
3 Blend together the egg yolk and cream, add to the stew and reheat without boiling. Garnish with parsley.

——— VARIATION ———
Blanquette de Veau
This classic creamy stew can also be made with 700 g (1½ lb) pie veal. Substitute a bouquet garni for the bay leaf and thyme.

SPICED LAMB
SERVES 4

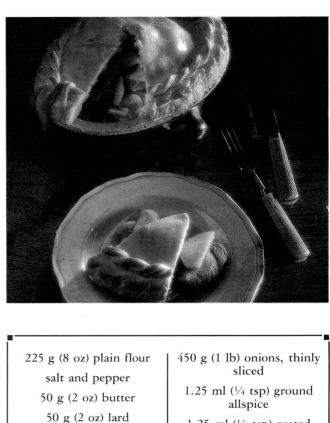

225 g (8 oz) plain flour	450 g (1 lb) onions, thinly sliced
salt and pepper	1.25 ml (¼ tsp) ground allspice
50 g (2 oz) butter	
50 g (2 oz) lard	1.25 ml (¼ tsp) grated nutmeg
700 g (1½ lb) lamb neck fillets, sliced into 12 pieces	150 ml (¼ pint) lamb or beef stock
1 large cooking apple, peeled, cored and sliced	milk, to glaze

1 Put the flour and a pinch of salt in a bowl. Rub in the butter and lard until the mixture resembles fine breadcrumbs. Add enough cold water to mix to a firm dough. Knead lightly until smooth, then chill until required.
2 Place half the lamb in the base of a 900 ml (1½ pint) pie dish. Arrange half the apple slices and half the onion slices over the top. Sprinkle over the allspice and nutmeg and season to taste. Repeat the layers, then pour over the stock.
3 Roll out the pastry to fit the dish and use to cover the pie, moistening the edges so the pastry is well sealed. Use any pastry trimmings to decorate.
4 Brush the pastry with milk and bake in a preheated oven at 200°C (400°F) mark 6 for 20 minutes. Reduce the temperature to 180°C (350°F) mark 4 and cook for a further 1¼ hours. Cover the pastry with greaseproof paper if it shows signs of becoming too brown. Serve hot.

CHILLI LAMB AND COCONUT CURRY

SERVES 4–6

50 g (2 oz) desiccated coconut	2.5 ml (½ tsp) chilli powder
200 ml (7 fl oz) milk	5 ml (1 tsp) ground cinnamon
60 ml (4 tbsp) vegetable oil	60 ml (4 tbsp) plain flour
1.4 kg (3 lb) boneless shoulder of lamb, cut into 2.5 cm (1 inch) cubes	400 ml (¾ pint) chicken stock
4 celery sticks, cut into 5 cm (2 inch) pieces	salt and pepper
1 onion, sliced	chopped parsley, to garnish
225 g (8 oz) cooking apples, peeled, cored and sliced	

1 Put the coconut in a saucepan with the milk and 200 ml (7 fl oz) water. Bring to the boil, then remove from the heat and leave to infuse for 30 minutes. Strain into a jug, pressing the coconut to extract all the juice.
2 Heat the oil in a flameproof casserole, add the lamb and cook until browned. Remove the meat with a slotted spoon.
3 Add the celery, onion and apple to the oil in the pan and cook for about 10 minutes or until browned.
4 Stir in the spices and flour, then gradually stir in the stock and coconut milk. Season to taste and bring to the boil.
5 Return the meat to the casserole, cover and cook in a preheated oven at 180°C (350°F) mark 4 for about 1¼ hours. Garnish with parsley before serving.

LAMB AND AUBERGINE MOUSSAKA

SERVES 4

900 g (2 lb) aubergines, sliced	2.5 ml (½ tsp) dried oregano
salt and pepper	2.5 ml (½ tsp) dried basil
vegetable oil, for frying	30 ml (2 tbsp) flour
350 g (12 oz) lean minced lamb	75 g (3 oz) fresh breadcrumbs
2 medium onions, chopped	15 g (½ oz) butter
45 ml (3 tbsp) tomato purée	300 ml (½ pint) milk
150 ml (¼ pint) dry white wine	75 g (3 oz) Cheddar cheese, grated
227 g (8 oz) can tomatoes	1 egg yolk

1 Put the aubergine slices in a colander, sprinkling each layer generously with salt. Leave to drain for 30 minutes.
2 Heat 15 ml (1 tbsp) oil in a saucepan, add the lamb and cook until well browned. Stir in the onion, tomato purée, wine, tomatoes with their juice, herbs and 15 ml (1 tbsp) flour. Boil, cover and simmer for 30 minutes. Season.
3 Rinse the aubergine slices and pat dry on absorbent kitchen paper. Heat some oil in a large frying pan and fry the aubergine slices, in batches, until browned on both sides. Drain well. Layer the aubergines in a shallow ovenproof dish with the lamb and 50 g (2 oz) breadcrumbs.
4 To make the sauce, melt the butter in a saucepan, stir in the remaining flour and cook for 1 minute, stirring. Remove from the heat and gradually stir in the milk. Bring to the boil and cook, stirring, until thick. Stir in 50 g (2 oz) of the cheese and the egg yolk.
5 Spoon the sauce over the moussaka, then sprinkle with the remaining cheese and breadcrumbs. Bake at 180°C (350°F) mark 4 for 45 minutes or until golden.

LAMB AND WATERCRESS BAKE

SERVES 4–6

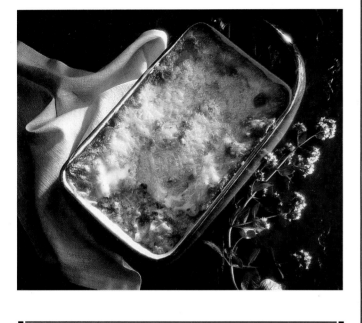

450 g (1 lb) lean minced lamb	50 ml (2 fl oz) dry white wine
2 large onions, finely chopped	salt and pepper
2 bunches of watercress, finely chopped	25 g (1 oz) butter
10 ml (2 tsp) dried oregano	568 ml (1 pint) milk
105 ml (7 tbsp) plain flour	175 g (6 oz) Lancashire cheese, crumbled
300 ml (½ pint) lamb or chicken stock	225 g (8 oz) oven-ready lasagne verdi

1 Put the lamb in a large, preferably non-stick saucepan and fry in its own fat until well browned, stirring constantly. Pour off excess fat. Add the onion and cook for 5 minutes, stirring occasionally. Add the watercress, oregano and 30 ml (2 tbsp) of the flour. Cook for 1–2 minutes, then gradually stir in the stock and wine. Season to taste. Bring to the boil, then simmer gently, uncovered, for 45 minutes, stirring occasionally.

2 Put the butter, remaining flour and milk in a saucepan. Heat, whisking continously, until the sauce thickens, boils and is smooth. Simmer for 1–2 minutes. Remove the pan from the heat and add 100 g (4 oz) of the cheese, stirring until melted. Season to taste.

3 Layer the mince mixture with the uncooked lasagne in a fairly deep ovenproof serving dish. Spoon over the cheese sauce and sprinkle with the remaining cheese.

4 Bake in a preheated oven at 190°C (375°F) mark 5 for about 40 minutes in a preheated oven or until browned. Serve hot straight from the dish.

SPICED LENTIL BAKE

SERVES 4

45 ml (3 tbsp) vegetable oil	75 g (3 oz) red lentils
8 middle neck lamb chops (total weight about 1.1 kg/ 2½ lb)	salt and pepper
2 medium onions, thinly sliced	450 g (1 lb) potatoes, peeled and thinly sliced
15 ml (1 tbsp) ground turmeric	450 g (1 lb) swede, thinly sliced
5 ml (1 tsp) paprika	300 ml (½ pint) lamb or chicken stock
5 ml (1 tsp) ground cinnamon	

1 Heat the oil in a large sauté or frying pan, add the chops and fry until well browned on both sides. Remove from the pan with a slotted spoon.

2 Add the onions to the pan with the turmeric, paprika, cinnamon and lentils. Fry for 2–3 minutes, then add plenty of salt and pepper and spoon into a shallow 2 litre (3½ pint) ovenproof dish.

3 Place the chops on top of the onion and lentil mixture. Arrange the vegetable slices on top of the chops, then season to taste and pour over the stock.

4 Cover the dish tightly and cook in a preheated oven at 180°C (350°F) mark 4 for about 1½ hours, or until the chops are tender. Uncover and cook for a further 30 minutes, or until lightly browned on top. Serve hot.

COOK'S TIP

There are many different types of lentil available. The red lentils used in this recipe are the most common kind, sometimes also described as 'split red lentils' or even 'Egyptian lentils'. They do not need soaking and are quick-cooking, but they tend to lose their shape.

LAMB CRUMBLE

SERVES 4

350 g (12 oz) leftover roast lamb	salt and pepper
1 medium onion	50 g (2 oz) butter
115 g (4½ oz) flour	50 g (2 oz) Cheshire or Cheddar cheese, grated
15 ml (1 tbsp) tomato purée	2.5 ml (½ tsp) dried mixed herbs
300 ml (½ pint) beef stock	

1 Mince together the meat and onion. Mix in 15 g (½ oz) flour, the tomato purée and the stock. Season to taste. Turn into a shallow ovenproof dish.

2 Put the remaining flour in a bowl and rub in the butter until the mixture resembles fine breadcrumbs. Stir in the grated cheese, herbs and seasoning. Spoon the crumble over the meat.

3 Bake in a preheated oven at 190°C (375°F) mark 5 for 45 minutes–1 hour. Serve immediately.

--- **VARIATION** ---

Beef Crumble

Substitute 350 g (12 oz) leftover roast beef for the lamb.

LAMB KEBABS IN SPICY YOGURT DRESSING

SERVES 4

1 large corn-on-the-cob	15 ml (1 tbsp) coriander seeds
salt and pepper	700 g (1½ lb) boned leg of lamb, cut into 2.5 cm (1 inch) cubes
8 shallots	
150 ml (5 fl oz) natural yogurt	225 g (8 oz) courgettes, cut into 0.5 cm (¼ inch) slices
1 garlic clove, crushed	
2 bay leaves, crumbled	4 tomatoes, halved
15 ml (1 tbsp) lemon juice	lemon wedges, to garnish
5 ml (1 tsp) ground allspice	

1 Blanch the corn in boiling salted water for 1 minute, drain well, then cut into eight pieces and set aside. Blanch the shallots in boiling salted water for 1 minute, skin and set aside.

2 To make the marinade, pour the yogurt into a shallow dish and stir in the garlic, bay leaves, lemon juice, allspice, coriander seeds and salt and pepper to taste.

3 Thread the lamb cubes on to eight skewers with the courgettes, tomatoes, corn and shallots. Place in the dish, spoon over the marinade, cover and leave for 2–3 hours, turning occasionally to ensure even coating.

4 Cook the kebabs under a preheated grill for 15–20 minutes, turning and brushing with the marinade occasionally. To serve, spoon the remaining marinade over the kebabs and garnish with lemon wedges.

ROAST PORK WITH APPLES

SERVES 6–8

1.6 kg (3½ lb) loin of pork	150 ml (¼ pint) dry white wine (optional)
40 g (1½ oz) butter	150 ml (¼ pint) chicken stock
coarse salt	
fresh rosemary sprig	fresh watercress sprigs, to garnish
6 large Cox's apples, cored	
salt and pepper	

1 Score the pork rind all over with a sharp knife. Rub with the butter, then sprinkle with coarse salt.
2 Place the rosemary on a rack in a roasting tin, put the pork on top and roast in a preheated oven at 180°C (350°F) mark 4 for 2 hours.
3 Season the apples to taste inside and make a shallow cut through the skin around the apples about one third of the way down. Place in a tin or ovenproof dish and baste with some of the fat from the pork. Cook on a lower shelf for the last 30 minutes of the meat roasting time.
4 Transfer the pork, still on the rack, to a plate and keep warm. Drain off most of the fat from the roasting tin, leaving the meat juices. Stir in the wine, if using, loosening the sediment at the bottom of the pan. Boil until almost completely evaporated. Stir in the stock and boil for 2–3 minutes. Strain into a sauceboat.
5 Put the pork on a warmed serving plate. Arrange the apples around the pork, garnish with watercress and serve accompanied by the gravy.

DANISH ROAST LOIN OF PORK

SERVES 6

1.5 kg (3–3½ lb) boned, rolled and tied loin of pork	18 no-soak prunes, stoned
salt and pepper	15 g (½ oz) plain flour
2 cooking apples, peeled, cored and cut into eighths	50 ml (2 fl oz) double cream

1 Score the rind of the pork with a very sharp knife, if the butcher has not already done so. Weigh the joint and calculate the cooking time, allowing 40 minutes per 450 g (1 lb).
2 Dry the rind thoroughly with absorbent kitchen paper, then rub with 10 ml (2 tsp) salt. Place the joint, rind side uppermost, on a rack in a roasting tin.
3 Roast the pork in a preheated oven at 220°C (425°F) mark 7 for 40 minutes, then remove from the oven and pour 300 ml (½ pint) water into the roasting tin, underneath the rack. Return the pork to the oven, lower the temperature to 180°C (350°F) mark 4, and roast for the remaining cooking time, adding the apples and prunes to the water for the last 45 minutes. Do not baste.
4 Transfer the pork to a warmed carving dish and leave to settle for about 15 minutes before carving. Remove the fruit from the water with a slotted spoon and keep hot.
5 Make a gravy from the pan juices. In a measuring jug, mix the flour to a paste with a little cold water. Stir in more cold water up to the 300 ml (½ pint) mark.
6 Remove the rack from the roasting tin and transfer the tin to the hob. Stir the flour mixture into the liquid in the tin, a little at a time, then bring to the boil. Simmer, stirring, until thickened, then stir in the cream and season to taste. Heat through, then pour into a gravyboat. Serve the pork with the fruit and the gravy.

POT ROAST OF PORK AND RED CABBAGE

SERVES 4

45 ml (3 tbsp) red wine vinegar	15 ml (1 tbsp) plain flour
450 g (1 lb) red cabbage	salt and pepper
225 g (8 oz) cooking apple	700 g (1½ lb) boned shoulder of pork, rinded
15 ml (1 tbsp) demerara sugar	coriander sprigs, to garnish

1 Bring a large saucepan of water to the boil, to which 15 ml (1 tbsp) of the vinegar has been added.
2 Meanwhile, shred the red cabbage. When the water is boiling, add the cabbage, bring back to the boil, then drain well.
3 Peel, core and slice the apple and place with the cabbage in a casserole just wide enough to take the pork joint.
4 Add the sugar, the remaining vinegar and the flour. Season to taste and stir well together.
5 Slash the fat side of the joint several times and sprinkle with plenty of salt and pepper. Place on top of the cabbage and cover the casserole.
6 Cook in a preheated oven at 190°C (375°F) mark 5 for about 1¾ hours or until the pork is tender. Slice the pork and serve on a warmed platter surrounded by cabbage. Garnish with coriander and serve the remaining cabbage in a separate serving dish.

CHILLI PORK AND BEANS

SERVES 4–6

30 ml (2 tbsp) vegetable oil	175 g (6 oz) red kidney beans, soaked in cold water overnight
900 g (2 lb) boneless pork shoulder, cut into cubes	15 ml (1 tbsp) black treacle
1 large onion, roughly chopped	15 ml (1 tbsp) French mustard
2 celery sticks, sliced	5 ml (1 tsp) chilli powder
1–2 garlic cloves, crushed	salt and pepper

1 Heat 15 ml (1 tbsp) of the oil in a flameproof casserole, add the pork in batches and fry over a high heat until coloured on all sides. Remove with a slotted spoon and drain on absorbent kitchen paper.
2 Lower the heat, then add the remaining oil to the pan with the onion, celery and garlic. Fry gently for 10 minutes or until softened.
3 Drain the kidney beans and add to the pan with 1.1 litres (2 pints) fresh water. Bring to the boil, stirring, then boil rapidly for 10 minutes.
4 Lower the heat, return the pork to the pan and add the black treacle, mustard, chilli powder and pepper to taste. Stir well to mix.
5 Cover the casserole and cook in a preheated oven at 150°C (300°F) mark 2 for 3 hours. Stir the pork and beans occasionally during the cooking time and add more water if dry. Add 5 ml (1 tsp) salt halfway through, then taste and adjust the seasoning before serving, adding more chilli powder if a hotter flavour is preferred.

PORK IN PLUM SAUCE

SERVES 4

450 g (1 lb) plums	25 g (1 oz) butter
300 ml (½ pint) rosé wine	1 large onion, chopped
salt and pepper	175 g (6 oz) white cabbage, shredded
25 g (1 oz) plain wholemeal flour	30 ml (2 tbsp) natural yogurt
700 g (1½ lb) pork fillet (tenderloin), cubed	

1 Put the plums and wine in a saucepan and simmer for 5 minutes or until tender. Strain, reserving the juice. Remove the stones from the plums and purée half in a blender or food processor.

2 Season the flour, add the pork and toss until coated.

3 Melt the butter in a large saucepan or flameproof casserole and lightly fry the onion and cabbage for 3–4 minutes. Add the meat and fry until brown on all sides.

4 Pour in the reserved plum juice and puréed plums, then simmer, uncovered, for 10–15 minutes or until tender. Add the remaining plums and yogurt and reheat gently.

--------- **TO MICROWAVE** ---------

Put the plums and wine in a large bowl and cook on HIGH for 3–4 minutes. Complete the remainder of step 1 and step 2. Melt the butter in a large bowl on HIGH for 45 seconds. Add the onion and cabbage and cook on HIGH for 7 minutes, stirring occasionally. Add the pork and cook on HIGH for 3 minutes. Pour in 200 ml (7 fl oz) plum juice and the puréed plums and cook on HIGH for 3–4 minutes or until boiling, stirring occasionally. Cook on LOW for 7–8 minutes or until the pork is tender. Stir in the remaining plums and yogurt. Stand, covered, for 5 minutes.

PORK ESCALOPES WITH JUNIPER

SERVES 4

450 g (1 lb) pork fillet (tenderloin)	4 juniper berries, lightly crushed
salt and pepper	150 ml (¼ pint) double cream
40 g (1½ oz) plain flour	chopped fresh parsley, to garnish
25 g (1 oz) butter	
75 ml (5 tbsp) dry white wine	

1 Trim any fat from the pork fillet and cut the meat into 5 mm (¼ inch) slices. Place the slices between two sheets of dampened greaseproof paper and beat out into even thinner slices, using rolling pin or meat mallet.

2 Season the flour, then dip each pork escalope in the flour, turning to coat and shaking off any excess.

3 Melt the butter in a large frying pan and fry the escalopes over a high heat for 2 minutes on each side. Remove and keep warm while making the sauce.

4 Add the wine and juniper berries to the pan and boil rapidly, scraping the bottom of the pan to loosen any sediment, until reduced by half. Pour in the cream, season to taste and bring to the boil. Boil rapidly for 1 minute, stirring. Pour over the escalopes and serve immediately, garnished with chopped parsley.

--------- **COOK'S TIP** ---------

Juniper berries are small purple-black berries with an aromatic scent and pine-like tang. They should be crushed before being added to a dish to release maximum flavour. They are now readily available in supermarkets.

PORK STEAKS WITH PEPPERS

SERVES 4

15 ml (1 tbsp) vegetable oil	1 red pepper, thinly sliced
15 g (½ oz) butter	1 green pepper, thinly sliced
1 medium onion, chopped	45 ml (3 tbsp) dry sherry
2.5 cm (1 inch) piece of fresh root ginger, finely grated	30 ml (2 tbsp) soy sauce
1 garlic clove, crushed	150 ml (¼ pint) unsweetened pineapple juice
four 150 g (5 oz) boneless pork loin steaks	salt and pepper

1 Heat the oil and butter in a large frying pan, add the onion, ginger and garlic and fry gently for 5 minutes or until soft. Push to one side of the pan.

2 Add the steaks to the pan and cook until brown on both sides, then add the remaining ingredients and mix thoroughly together.

3 Cover tightly and simmer gently for 8–10 minutes or until the steaks are tender and the peppers are soft. Transfer the steaks and peppers to warmed serving plates. Bring the remaining liquid in the pan to the boil and boil for 2–3 minutes or until reduced slightly. Spoon over the steaks and serve immediately.

FRUITY STUFFED PORK CHOPS

SERVES 4

4 thick pork loin chops	juice and finely grated rind of 1 large orange
60 ml (4 tbsp) vegetable oil	50 g (2 oz) no-soak prunes
1 small onion, finely chopped	50 g (2 oz) no-soak dried apricots
2 celery sticks, finely chopped	50 g (2 oz) blanched almonds
25 g (1 oz) Italian risotto rice	5 ml (1 tsp) ground cinnamon
450 ml (¾ pint) chicken stock	salt and pepper

1 Using a sharp knife, make a horizontal cut in each pork chop, working from the outside edge to the bone.

2 To make the stuffing, heat 30 ml (2 tbsp) of the oil in a heavy-based saucepan, add the onion and celery and fry gently for 5 minutes or until soft and lightly coloured.

3 Add the rice and stir well, then add 150 ml (¼ pint) of the stock and half of the orange juice. Bring to the boil, stirring all the time. Lower the heat and simmer for 15–20 minutes, stirring frequently and adding more stock if necessary. When cooked, turn into a bowl and cool.

4 Meanwhile, stone the prunes and chop finely with the apricots and almonds. Add to the rice mixture with the cinnamon. Season to taste. Spoon the stuffing into the cavities in the chops, then secure the open edges with wooden cocktail sticks. Reserve any remaining stuffing.

5 Heat the remaining oil in a flameproof casserole, add the chops and fry until browned on both sides. Pour in the remaining stock and orange juice, add any reserved stuffing, season and bring to the boil. Cover and simmer for 40 minutes or until the chops are tender, basting frequently.

6 Transfer the chops to a warmed serving dish, pour over the pan juices and sprinkle with the grated orange rind.

CRUMB-TOPPED PORK CHOPS

SERVES 4

4 lean pork loin chops	pinch of dried thyme
50 g (2 oz) fresh white breadcrumbs	finely grated rind of 1 lemon
15 ml (1 tbsp) chopped fresh parsley or 5 ml (1 tsp) dried	2.5 ml (½ tsp) coriander seeds, crushed
5 ml (1 tsp) chopped fresh mint or 2.5 ml (½ tsp) dried	1 egg, beaten
	salt and pepper

1 Cut the rind off the chops and put them in one layer in a baking tin.
2 Mix the remaining ingredients together and season to taste. Spread this mixture evenly over the chops with a palette knife.
3 Bake in a preheated oven at 200°C (400°F) mark 6 for 45–50 minutes or until golden. Serve hot.

––––––––––– VARIATION –––––––––––
Crumb-topped Lamb Chops
Substitute four lamb chump chops for the pork and use rosemary instead of thyme in the crumb topping. Omit the coriander, if preferred.

PARCELLED PORK

SERVES 4

4 medium pork chops	90 ml (6 tbsp) dry cider
25 g (1 oz) butter	30 ml (2 tbsp) lemon juice
1 medium onion, finely chopped	150 ml (5 fl oz) soured cream
225 g (8 oz) mushrooms, sliced	salt and pepper

1 Trim the chops of any rind and excess fat. Melt the butter in a large frying pan, add the chops and cook until well browned. Remove the chops from the pan and place each one on a piece of foil about 20 cm (8 inches) square.
2 Add the onion and mushrooms to the butter remaining in the pan and cook for 5 minutes.
3 Stir in the cider and lemon juice and bring to the boil. Boil the liquid over a high heat until reduced by half, then remove from the heat and stir in the soured cream. Season well.
4 Place a quarter of the mushroom mixture on top of each chop, then shape the foil into neat parcels and seal well.
5 Place the parcels in a small ovenproof dish and bake in a preheated oven at 180°C (350°F) mark 4 for about 50 minutes or until the chops are tender.
6 To serve, place each parcel on a warmed plate and open carefully so that no juices escape.

PORK FILLET WITH WHITE WINE AND MUSHROOMS

SERVES 6

1 kg (2¼ lb) pork fillet (tenderloin)	150 ml (¼ pint) beef stock
vegetable oil, for frying	150 ml (¼ pint) dry white wine
65 g (2½ oz) butter or margarine	salt and pepper
2 medium onions, chopped	twelve 1 cm (½ inch) slices of French bread
225 g (8 oz) button mushrooms	chopped fresh parsley, to garnish
45 ml (3 tbsp) plain flour	

1 Cut the pork fillet into slices, place between two sheets of dampened greaseproof paper and beat out with a rolling pin or meat mallet. Heat 30 ml (2 tbsp) of the oil in a frying pan, add the pork and cook over a high heat until browned. Remove from the pan and set aside.
2 Melt 50 g (2 oz) of the butter or margarine in the frying pan, add the onions and fry for 5 minutes. Add the mushrooms to the pan, increase the heat and fry for 1–2 minutes, tossing constantly.
3 Blend the flour into the juices in the pan, with the remaining butter or margarine. Cook, stirring, for 1–2 minutes, then gradually blend in the stock and wine. Season to taste and simmer for 2–3 minutes.
4 Return the meat to the pan, cover and cook for 20–25 minutes or until the pork is tender.
5 Meanwhile, heat some oil in a frying pan, add the French bread slices and fry until golden brown on both sides. Drain well on absorbent kitchen paper.
6 Serve the pork hot with the French bread and sprinkled liberally with chopped parsley.

PORK WITH CIDER AND CORIANDER

SERVES 4

450 g (1 lb) pork fillet (tenderloin)	15 ml (1 tbsp) ground coriander
30 ml (2 tbsp) oil	15 ml (1 tbsp) plain flour
50 g (2 oz) butter	150 ml (¼ pint) dry cider
1 green pepper, cut into rings	150 ml (¼ pint) chicken or vegetable stock
225 g (8 oz) celery, sliced	salt and pepper
100 g (4 oz) onion, chopped	

1 Trim excess fat from the pork fillet and slice into 0.5 cm (¼ inch) thick pieces. Place between two sheets of dampened greaseproof paper and beat out until thin with a rolling pin or meat mallet.
2 Heat the oil with half the butter in a large frying pan. Add the green pepper and celery and fry gently for 2–3 minutes. Lift out with a slotted spoon and keep warm on a serving plate.
3 Add the remaining butter to the pan, increase the heat to high, then add the pork, a few pieces at a time. Cook the pork until browned on all sides, then remove from the pan.
4 Add the onion to the fat remaining in the pan and fry until golden brown. Stir in the coriander and flour and cook for 1 minute. Gradually add the cider and stock and bring quickly to the boil, stirring constantly. Return the pork to the pan, season to taste and simmer for about 5 minutes. Serve hot, with the green pepper and celery.

SWEET AND SOUR PORK

SERVES 2–3

	FOR THE SAUCE
350 g (12 oz) lean boneless pork	15 ml (1 tbsp) cornflour
15 g (½ oz) plain flour	10 ml (2 tsp) soy sauce
198 g (7 oz) can pineapple pieces	45 ml (3 tbsp) vinegar
15 ml (1 tbsp) vegetable oil	30 ml (2 tbsp) sugar
1 dessert apple, cored and sliced	150 ml (¼ pint) chicken stock
1 green pepper, chopped	

1 Cut the pork into 2.5 cm (1 inch) cubes, add to the flour and toss until coated.
2 Drain the pineapple, reserving 60 ml (4 tbsp) juice.
3 Heat the oil in a pan, add the pork and fry until lightly browned. Lower the heat and add the apple, pepper and pineapple pieces.
4 To make the sauce, put all the ingredients in a small basin and mix thoroughly, adding the reserved pineapple juice.
5 Add the sauce to the pork, bring to the boil, cover and simmer for 25–35 minutes or until the pork is tender. Serve immediately.

BARBECUED SPARE RIBS

SERVES 4–6

30 ml (2 tbsp) vegetable oil	2.5 ml (½ tsp) black pepper
1 large onion, finely chopped	2.5 ml (½ tsp) dried sage or rosemary
1 garlic clove, crushed	10 ml (2 tsp) mustard powder
150 ml (¼ pint) tomato purée	60 ml (4 tbsp) light soft brown sugar
45 ml (3 tbsp) lemon juice	100 ml (4 floz) beef stock
60 ml (4 tbsp) Worcestershire sauce	1.4 kg (3 lb) pork spare ribs, cut into serving pieces
2.5 ml (½ tsp) salt	

1 Heat the oil in a large saucepan, add the onion and garlic and cook for 5–10 minutes or until transparent.
2 Add the tomato purée, lemon juice, Worcestershire sauce, salt, pepper, sage or rosemary, mustard and sugar. Pour in the stock and simmer for 10 minutes, stirring.
3 Put the spare ribs on a rack in a roasting tin and pour the sauce over them. Roast in a preheated oven at 200°C (400°F) mark 6 for 1 hour or until crisp, basting every 15 minutes with sauce from the bottom of the pan.

─ TO MICROWAVE ─
Honeyed Spare Ribs
For an alternative sauce, mix together 100 g (4 oz) clear honey, 60 ml (4 tbsp) dark brown soft sugar, 60 ml (4 tbsp) tomato ketchup, 30 ml (2 tbsp) Worcestershire sauce, 30 ml (2 tbsp) prepared English mustard and 30 ml (2 tbsp) red wine vinegar. Roast the ribs for 30 minutes, then pour over the sauce and continue roasting until the ribs are tender and the sauce syrupy.

GOURMET PORK ROLLS

SERVES 4

350 g (12 oz) pork fillet (tenderloin)	4 slices Gruyère cheese
4 thin slices of lean cooked ham	salt and pepper
1 garlic clove, crushed	45 ml (3 tbsp) plain flour
30 ml (2 tbsp) pine nuts	15 ml (1 tbsp) vegetable oil
100 g (4 oz) fresh wholemeal breadcrumbs	200 ml (7 fl oz) dry white wine
50 g (2 oz) no-soak dried apricots, chopped	200 ml (7 fl oz) unsweetened apple juice
45 ml (3 tbsp) chopped fresh parsley or 15 ml (1 tbsp) dried	15 g (½ oz) butter
	apple slices and parsley sprigs, to garnish

1 Cut the pork into four equal pieces. Place between two sheets of dampened greaseproof paper and beat with a rolling pin or meat mallet to flatten to about 0.5 cm (¼ inch) thick. Lay a slice of ham on each escalope.

2 Mix the garlic, pine nuts, breadcrumbs, apricots and 30 ml (2 tbsp) fresh parsley or 10 ml (2 tsp) dried. Spread over each escalope and lay a slice of Gruyère cheese on top.

3 Roll up each escalope and secure with a wooden cocktail stick. Season 30 ml (2 tbsp) of the flour and use to dust the pork rolls. Heat the oil in a frying pan and cook the rolls for 5–7 minutes, turning frequently.

4 Pour in the wine and apple juice. Bring to the boil and simmer for 20–25 minutes or until the meat is tender.

5 Using a slotted spoon, transfer the rolls to a warmed dish. Remove the cocktail sticks and keep the rolls warm.

6 Increase the heat and reduce the liquor in the pan to about 150 ml (¼ pint). Mix the butter with the remaining flour and gradually whisk in until thickened. Stir in the remaining parsley, pour over the sauce and garnish.

STUFFED CABBAGE PARCELS

SERVES 4

350 g (12 oz) lean minced pork	16 large Savoy cabbage leaves
1 medium onion, finely chopped	40 g (1½ oz) butter
227 g (8 oz) can tomatoes	40 g (1½ oz) plain flour
salt and pepper	450 ml (¾ pint) milk
282 g (10 oz) can red kidney beans, drained and rinsed	50 g (2 oz) mature Cheddar cheese, grated
	pinch of cayenne

1 Put the pork in a saucepan and cook in its own fat until beginning to brown, stirring from time to time. Drain off excess fat.

2 Add the onion and fry until softened and lightly coloured. Add the tomatoes with their juice and bring to the boil, stirring. Season to taste, then simmer over a moderate heat for 20 minutes or until the pork is cooked and the sauce thick and well reduced, stirring occasionally. Stir in the kidney beans and remove the pan from the heat.

3 Blanch the cabbage for 3 minutes, in batches of four leaves at a time, in a large pan of boiling salted water. Drain the leaves, rinse and pat dry, then cut out and discard the thick central stalks.

4 Put 15–25 ml (1–1½ tbsp) filling mixture at the stalk end of each cabbage leaf. Fold the two sides inwards to cover the filling, then roll into neat parcels. Arrange, seam sides down, in a single layer in a well-buttered heatproof serving dish.

5 Heat the butter, flour and milk, whisking continuously, until the sauce thickens, boils and is smooth. Simmer for 1–2 minutes, then season. Pour over the cabbage parcels.

6 Sprinkle the parcels with cheese and cayenne and place under a preheated grill until golden brown and bubbling.

CANADIAN PORK AND VEAL PIE

SERVES 6

50 g (2 oz) butter	about 25 g (1 oz) fresh breadcrumbs
2 large onions, finely chopped	60–90 ml (4–6 tbsp) chopped fresh parsley and thyme, mixed
450 g (1 lb) lean boneless pork	150 g (5 oz) frozen shortcrust pastry, thawed
450 g (1 lb) pie or stewing veal	225 g (8 oz) frozen puff pastry, thawed
150 ml (¼ pint) dry white wine or chicken stock	beaten egg, to glaze
5 ml (1 tsp) ground allspice	
salt and pepper	

1 Melt the butter in a large frying pan and fry the onions very gently for 10–15 minutes or until soft.
2 Meanwhile, cut the pork and veal into fine dice. Add to the onions and fry for 10 minutes.
3 Stir in the wine or stock, then add the allspice. Season, cover and cook for 30 minutes, stirring occasionally.
4 Remove the meat and onions from the cooking liquid and set aside. Boil the liquid in the pan to reduce slightly, then pour over the meat. Add enough breadcrumbs to absorb the liquid, then stir in the herbs. Leave to cool.
5 Meanwhile, roll out the shortcrust pastry on a floured surface and use to line a 23 cm (9 inch) pie plate. Pile the cooled meat mixture on top, doming it in the centre.
6 Roll out the puff pastry to a circle slightly larger than the first. Moisten the rim of shortcrust pastry with water, then place the puff pastry lid on top. Press to seal.
7 Decorate the top of the pie with pastry trimmings and make a hole in the centre. Brush with egg.
8 Bake in a preheated oven at 200°C (400°F) mark 6 for 30 minutes or until the pastry is golden brown. Serve hot.

BAKED HAM

SERVES 8–10

1.8 kg (4 lb) middle gammon joint	1 bay leaf
2 medium onions, quartered	5 black peppercorns
	cloves
2 medium carrots, thickly sliced	demerara sugar, to glaze

1 Weigh the gammon and calculate the cooking time, allowing 20 minutes per 450 g (1 lb) plus 20 minutes. Place the gammon in a large saucepan and cover with cold water. Bring slowly to the boil, then drain.
2 Return the gammon to the saucepan. Add the vegetables, bay leaf and peppercorns, cover with cold water and bring slowly to the boil. Skim the surface with a slotted spoon. Cover and boil for half the calculated cooking time.
3 Drain the gammon and wrap in foil. Place in a roasting tin and bake in a preheated oven at 180°C (350°F) mark 4 until 30 minutes before the cooking time is completed.
4 Remove the foil and rind from the gammon. Score the fat in diamonds and stud with cloves. Sprinkle the surface with demerara sugar and pat in.
5 Bake at 220°C (425°F) mark 7 for 30 minutes or until crisp and golden. Serve hot or cold.

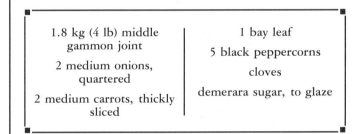

———————————— COOK'S TIP ————————————

Ham generally refers to the leg of a pig that is cured separately and sold cooked. However, this recipe uses a gammon joint, which is cured as part of the whole side of the pig and sold uncooked.

GLAZED GAMMON STEAKS

SERVES 4

15 ml (1 tbsp) soy sauce	garlic salt
2.5 ml (½ tsp) mustard powder	black pepper
15 ml (1 tbsp) golden syrup	15 ml (1 tbsp) cornflour
1.25 ml (¼ tsp) ground ginger	15 ml (1 tbsp) lemon juice
90 ml (6 tbsp) orange juice	8 bacon chops or 4 gammon steaks

1 In a small saucepan, combine the first five ingredients and add garlic salt and pepper to taste.
2 Blend the cornflour with the lemon juice, stir in a little of the mixture from the pan and then return it all to the pan. Bring to the boil, stirring all the time, until the mixture has thickened to a glaze. Remove from the heat.
3 Cut most of the fat from the bacon chops or gammon steaks and then brush half of the glaze on one side.
4 Cook under a preheated moderate grill for 15 minutes or until the meat is cooked right through, brown and bubbling. Turn several times and brush with the remaining glaze during cooking. Serve hot.

BACON CHOPS IN CIDER

SERVES 4

four 175 g (6 oz) bacon chops	15 g (½ oz) butter
15 ml (1 tbsp) prepared English mustard	25 ml (1½ tbsp) plain flour
25 g (1 oz) demerara sugar	salt and pepper
300 ml (½ pint) dry cider	chopped fresh parsley, to garnish

1 Put the chops side by side in a large ovenproof dish. Mix the mustard and sugar with enough cider to make a smooth paste. Spread over the chops and leave for 30 minutes.
2 Bake the chops in a preheated oven at 200°C (400°F) mark 6 for 15 minutes.
3 Meanwhile, put the butter, flour and remaining cider in a saucepan. Heat, whisking continuously, until the sauce thickens, boils and is smooth. Simmer for 1–2 minutes. Season to taste.
4 Pour the sauce over the chops. Bake for a further 15 minutes or until cooked. Serve garnished with parsley.

───────────── COOK'S TIP ─────────────

For a stronger cider flavour, use one third to one half more cider than the recipe states and reduce it by boiling to concentrate the flavour before using.

BACON AND LIVER ROULADES

SERVES 3–4

4 rashers streaky bacon (about 100 g/4 oz total weight)	30 ml (2 tbsp) brandy
225 g (8 oz) lamb's liver	15 ml (1 tbsp) chopped fresh marjoram or oregano or 5 ml (1 tsp) dried
60 ml (4 tbsp) orange juice	salt and pepper

1 Cut the rind off each rasher and stretch the rashers with a blunt-edged knife. Cut each rasher across into three pieces.
2 Divide the liver into 12 even-sized pieces, removing any skin and ducts.
3 Roll a piece of bacon around each piece of liver and secure with a cocktail stick. Place in the base of a foil-lined grill pan.
4 Mix the orange juice, brandy, herbs and seasoning together and spoon over the bacon rolls. Leave to marinate in a cool place for at least 1 hour.
5 Cook under a moderate grill for 12–15 minutes, turning and basting occasionally. Remove the cocktail sticks before serving, replacing them with fresh ones if liked. Serve hot.

BACON CHOPS WITH GOOSEBERRY SAUCE

SERVES 4

15 ml (1 tbsp) dark soft brown sugar	15 g (½ oz) butter
5 ml (1 tsp) mustard powder	1 large onion, chopped
pepper	150 ml (¼ pint) vegetable stock
four 175 g (6 oz) bacon chops	100 g (4 oz) gooseberries, topped and tailed

1 Mix together the brown sugar, mustard and pepper to taste and rub into both sides of the bacon chops.
2 Melt the butter in a large frying pan or flameproof casserole, add the onion and cook for 2 minutes, then add the bacon chops, half the stock and the gooseberries. Simmer gently for 15 minutes
3 Remove the chops from the pan. Purée the onions and gooseberries in a blender or food processor until smooth.
4 Return the chops and purée to the pan with the remaining stock. Simmer gently for 10 minutes or until the chops are cooked through and tender. Serve at once.

SAUSAGE YORKSHIRES WITH ONION SAUCE

SERVES 4

350 g (12 oz) pork sausagemeat	2 eggs
175 g (6 oz) cooking apple, peeled and cored	568 ml (1 pint) milk
	lard
5 ml (1 tsp) chopped parsley	175 g (6 oz) onions, sliced
salt and pepper	15 g (½ oz) butter
100 g (4 oz) plus 15 ml (1 tbsp) flour	

1 Place the sausagemeat in a bowl and grate in the apple. Stir in the parsley and season to taste. Work the ingredients together and form into 16 small balls.

2 Make a batter from the 100 g (4 oz) flour, the eggs, and 300 ml (½ pint) milk.

3 Put a little lard in the base of each of four 300 ml (½ pint) individual ramekin dishes and heat in a preheated oven at 220°C (425°F) mark 7 until sizzling hot. Divide the sausage balls between the dishes and cook in the oven for 10 minutes.

4 Pour the batter over the sausage balls and return to the oven for 35–40 minutes or until risen and golden.

5 Meanwhile, put the onion in a saucepan with the remaining milk, bring to the boil and cook until the onion is soft. To make the sauce, melt the butter in a pan, stir in the 15 ml (1 tbsp) flour and cook gently for 1 minute, stirring. Remove the pan from the heat and gradually stir in the onions and milk. Bring to the boil and continue to cook, stirring, until the sauce thickens, then season to taste.

6 When the popovers are baked, turn them out on to warmed serving plates and pour a little onion sauce into the centre of each. Serve immediately.

BACON AND APPLE PIE

SERVES 4

250 g (9 oz) plain flour	225 g (8 oz) cooking apples, peeled, cored and roughly chopped
salt and pepper	
100 g (4 oz) butter, diced	15 ml (1 tbsp) chopped parsley
225 g (8 oz) back bacon, roughly chopped	150 ml (¼ pint) medium-dry cider
1 medium onion, roughly chopped	1 egg, beaten, to glaze

1 To make the pastry, sift 225 g (8 oz) of the flour and a pinch of salt into a bowl. Rub in the butter until the mixture resembles breadcrumbs. Add just enough water to mix to a firm dough.

2 Gather the dough into a ball and knead lightly. Wrap the dough in foil and chill in the refrigerator for 30 minutes.

3 Meanwhile, combine the bacon, onion and apples in a 600 ml (1 pint) pie dish. Add the parsley and season to taste.

4 Blend the remaining flour with the cider, a little at a time, then pour into the pie dish.

5 Roll out the pastry on a lightly floured surface to 5 cm (2 inches) wider than the dish. Cut a 2.5 cm (1 inch) strip from the outer edge and use to line the dampened rim of the pie dish.

6 Moisten the strip of pastry, then place the lid on top and press to seal. Knock up and flute the edge.

7 Make a diagonal cross in the centre almost to the edges of the dish, then fold the pastry back to reveal the filling.

8 Brush the pastry with the egg. Bake in a preheated oven at 190°C (375°F) mark 5 for about 45 minutes or until the pastry is golden and the filling is cooked through. Serve the pie hot or cold.

BACON IN CIDER WITH SAGE AND ONION DUMPLINGS

SERVES 6

1.1 kg (2½ lb) smoked collar of bacon	50 g (2 oz) shredded suet
4 cloves	5 ml (1 tsp) rubbed sage
300 ml (½ pint) dry cider	25 g (1 oz) butter or margarine
1 bay leaf	2 medium onions, skinned
100 g (4 oz) fresh white breadcrumbs	salt and pepper
175 g (6 oz) self raising flour	parsley sprigs, to garnish

1 Place the bacon in a saucepan and cover with cold water. Bring slowly to the boil. Drain off the water. Pat the bacon dry.

2 Slice or peel off the bacon rind. Stud the fat with cloves.

3 Put the bacon in a shallow casserole with the cider and bay leaf. Cover tightly and cook in a preheated oven at 180°C (350°F) mark 4 for 2¼ hours.

4 Meanwhile, mix the breadcrumbs, flour, suet and sage together in a bowl. Rub in the butter. Coarsely grate in the onions. Bind to a soft dough with water, then add a little salt and pepper.

5 Shape the dough into 12 dumplings. Forty-five minutes before the end of the cooking time, add the dumplings to the juices surrounding the bacon. Cover again and finish cooking. Serve the bacon sliced, with a little of the cooking liquid spooned over, surrounded by the dumplings. Garnish with parsley sprigs.

LIKKY PIE

SERVES 4

225 g (8 oz) leeks, sliced	75 ml (3 fl oz) single cream
salt and pepper	2 eggs, lightly beaten
450 g (1 lb) lean boneless pork, cut into 2.5 cm (1 inch) cubes	212 g (7½ oz) packet frozen puff pastry, thawed
150 ml (¼ pint) milk	

1 Parboil the leeks in salted water for about 5 minutes. Drain well. Fill a 1.1 litre (2 pint) pie dish with the leeks and pork. Season to taste and pour in the milk.

2 Cover with foil and bake in a preheated oven at 200°C (400°F) mark 6 for about 1 hour. (Don't worry if it looks curdled.)

3 Stir the cream into the eggs, then pour into the dish. Allow the pie to cool.

4 Roll out the pastry on a lightly floured surface to 5 cm (2 inches) wider than the dish. Cut a 2.5 cm (1 inch) strip from the outer edge and use to line the dampened rim of the pie dish. Dampen the pastry rim with water, cover with the pastry lid and seal the edges well, then knock up and flute. Make a hole in the centre of the pie and use pastry trimmings to decorate.

5 Bake in a preheated oven at 220°C (425°F) mark 7 for about 25–30 minutes or until risen and golden brown.

SAUSAGE AND EGG PIE

SERVES 4–6

275 g (10 oz) frozen shortcrust pastry, thawed	150 ml (¼ pint) single cream or milk
3 eggs, hard-boiled	5 ml (1 tsp) chopped fresh sage or 2.5 ml (½ tsp) dried
10 ml (2 tsp) horseradish sauce	
225 g (8 oz) pork sausagemeat	salt and pepper
2 eggs, beaten	

1 Roll out two thirds of the pastry on a lightly floured surface and use to line a 20.5 cm (8 inch) flan ring placed on a baking sheet.
2 Shell the hard-boiled eggs and halve lengthways. Mix the horseradish sauce with the sausagemeat, divide into six and mould over the white of each egg half. Place yolk sides down in the flan case.
3 Reserve 10 ml (2 tsp) of the beaten eggs for glazing, then mix the remainder with the cream or milk and sage. Season to taste and pour into the flan case.
4 Roll out the remaining pastry and use to cover the pie, sealing the edges well. Decorate with pastry trimmings.
5 Brush the pie with the remaining beaten egg and bake in a preheated oven at 170°C (325°F) mark 3 for about 1 hour. Serve hot or cold.

CHIPOLATAS AND BEANS

SERVES 4

30 ml (2 tbsp) vegetable oil	430 g (15 oz) can red kidney beans, drained and rinsed
450 g (1 lb) pork chipolata sausages	
1 large onion, sliced	150 ml (¼ pint) beef stock
4 rashers of streaky bacon, chopped	salt and pepper
	chopped fresh parsley, to garnish

1 Heat the oil in a flameproof casserole, add the sausages and fry until browned on all sides. Remove the sausages from the pan with a slotted spoon and set aside.
2 Add the onion and bacon to the pan and fry for about 5 minutes or until they begin to turn brown, stirring occasionally.
3 Cut each sausage into four and return to the pan with the kidney beans and beef stock. Season to taste, cover and cook gently for about 15 minutes or until the sausages are tender. Serve hot, garnished with parsley.

TOAD IN THE HOLE

SERVES 3–4

450 g (1 lb) pork sausages	100 g (4 oz) plain flour
25 g (1 oz) lard or dripping	pinch of salt
225 ml (8 fl oz) milk	1 egg

1 Prick the sausages all over with a fork. Put the lard or dripping in a small roasting tin and add the sausages.
2 Bake in the oven at 220°C (425°F) mark 7 for 10 minutes or until the fat is hot.
3 Meanwhile, make the batter. Mix the milk and 50 ml (2 fl oz) water together in a jug. Put the flour and salt in a bowl. Make a well in the centre and break in the egg.
4 Mix the flour and egg together gradually, then add the milk and water, a little at a time, and beat until the mixture is smooth.
5 Pour the batter into the tin. Bake for about 30 minutes or until the batter is golden brown and well risen. Do not open the oven door during baking or the batter might sink. Serve at once.

─────── **VARIATION** ───────
Kidney Toad in the Hole
Skin, core and slice three lambs' kidneys and cook with the sausages before pouring in the batter.

ITALIAN LIVER

SERVES 4

350 g (12 oz) lamb's liver	30 ml (2 tbsp) tomato purée
salt and pepper	1 garlic clove, finely chopped
25 g (1 oz) plain flour	
40 g (1½ oz) butter or margarine	1.25 ml (¼ tsp) dried mixed herbs
450 g (1 lb) onions, thinly sliced	30 ml (2 tbsp) double cream
150 ml (¼ pint) beef stock	chopped parsley
300 ml (½ pint) milk	

1 Cut the liver into small pieces. Season the flour, add the liver and toss until coated.
2 Melt the butter or margarine in a frying pan and add the liver. Fry until browned on all sides, then remove from the pan and set aside.
3 Add the onions to the butter remaining in the pan and fry slowly for about 5 minutes or until soft. Gradually stir in the stock, milk, tomato purée, garlic and herbs. Bring the sauce to the boil, stirring continuously.
4 Add the liver to the sauce. Cover the pan and cook gently for 10–15 minutes or until the liver is tender. Adjust the seasoning to taste.
5 Replace the liver and sauce on a hot serving dish. Trickle the cream over the sauce, sprinkle with chopped parsley and serve immediately.

LIVER GOUJONS WITH ORANGE SAUCE

SERVES 4

350 g (12 oz) lamb's liver, sliced	300 ml (½ pint) lamb or beef stock
75 ml (5 tbsp) plain flour	juice and finely grated rind of 1 medium orange
salt and pepper	5 ml (1 tsp) dried sage
1 egg, beaten	a few drops of gravy browning
100 g (4 oz) medium oatmeal	60 ml (4 tbsp) vegetable oil
50 g (2 oz) butter or margarine	
1 medium onion, sliced	

1 Cut the liver into 5 cm (2 inch) pencil-thin strips. Put 45 ml (3 tbsp) of the flour in a bowl, season with salt and pepper, add the liver and toss until coated.
2 Dip the liver in the beaten egg, then roll in the oatmeal to coat. Chill in the refrigerator while preparing the sauce.
3 Melt 25 g (1 oz) of the butter or margarine in a saucepan, add the onion and fry gently for about 10 minutes or until golden brown. Add the remaining flour and cook gently, stirring, for 1–2 minutes.
4. Gradually blend in the stock, orange rind and juice and sage. Season to taste. Bring to the boil, then simmer for 10–15 minutes, stirring constantly. Add the gravy browning and taste and adjust the seasoning.
5 Heat the remaining butter or margarine and the oil in a frying pan, add the liver goujons and fry gently for 1–2 minutes or until tender.
6 Arrange the goujons on a warmed serving platter and pour over a little of the sauce. Serve the remaining sauce separately in a warmed sauceboat or jug.

LIVER IN STROGANOFF SAUCE

SERVES 4

450 g (1 lb) lamb's liver, sliced	450 g (1 lb) tomatoes, skinned and quartered, or 397 g (14 oz) can tomatoes, drained
salt and pepper	10 ml (2 tsp) dried sage
30 ml (2 tbsp) plain flour	150 ml (5 fl oz) soured cream, beaten
75 g (3 oz) butter or margarine	
225 g (8 oz) onions, thinly sliced	

1 Slice the lamb's liver into thin strips. Season the flour with salt and pepper, add the liver and toss until coated.
2 Melt the butter or margarine in a frying pan, add the onions and cook for 5–10 minutes or until lightly browned. Add the tomatoes, push to the side of the pan, then add the liver and cook over a high heat for about 5 minutes.
3 Sprinkle over the sage. Reduce the heat and stir in the soured cream.
4 Combine all the ingredients in the pan, taste and adjust the seasoning. Heat gently, but do not boil, and serve hot.

LIVER SAUTÉ

SERVES 5

salt and pepper	1 onion, thinly sliced
40 g (1½ oz) plain flour	300 ml (½ pint) beef stock
350 g (12 oz) lamb's liver, thinly sliced	15 ml (1 tbsp) tomato purée
30 ml (2 tbsp) vegetable oil	75 g (3 oz) frozen peas

1 Season the flour with salt and pepper, add the liver and toss until coated. Shake off and reserve any excess flour. Heat the oil in a frying pan and lightly fry the liver for 1 minute on each side. Remove the liver from the pan with a slotted spoon and keep hot.

2 Add the onion to the oil remaining in the pan and fry for about 5 minutes or until soft. Stir in any remaining flour and cook for 1 minute, then gradually add the stock. Bring to the boil, stirring constantly, and cook for 5 minutes.

3 Stir in the tomato purée, taste and adjust the seasoning. Return the liver to the pan with the frozen peas and cook for a further 5 minutes. Serve hot.

VARIATION

Kidney Sauté
Substitute 350 g (12 oz) lambs' kidneys for the liver. Skin, core and slice before tossing in the seasoned flour.

LAMB'S LIVER AND MUSHROOMS

SERVES 3

15 g (½ oz) butter or margarine	150 ml (¼ pint) beef stock
1 medium onion, sliced	4 tomatoes, skinned and roughly chopped
450 g (1 lb) lamb's liver, sliced	30 ml (2 tbsp) Worcestershire sauce
15 ml (1 tbsp) plain flour	salt and pepper
100 g (4 oz) button mushrooms	150 ml (5 fl oz) soured cream

1 Melt the butter or margarine in a large frying pan and gently fry the onion for 5 minutes or until soft.

2 Cut the liver into thin strips, add to the flour and toss until coated. Add to the pan with the mushrooms. Fry for 5 minutes, stirring well, then add the stock and bring to the boil.

3 Stir in the tomatoes and Worcestershire sauce. Season to taste, then simmer for 3–4 minutes. Stir in the soured cream and reheat without boiling. Serve hot.

TO MICROWAVE

Cut the butter into small pieces and melt in a large bowl on HIGH for 30 seconds. Add the onion, cover and cook on HIGH for 5–7 minutes or until softened. Coat the liver in the flour and add to the bowl with the mushrooms. Cover and cook on HIGH for 2–3 minutes or until the liver just changes colour, stirring once. Add the stock, tomatoes, Worcestershire sauce and salt and pepper, re-cover and cook on HIGH for 2–3 minutes or until boiling, stirring once. Stir in the soured cream and serve immediately.

CHICKEN LIVERS IN SHERRY CREAM SAUCE

SERVES 2

salt and pepper	75 ml (3 fl oz) sherry
25 g (1 oz) plain flour	50 ml (2 fl oz) chicken stock
225 g (8 oz) chicken livers, thawed if frozen	50 g (2 oz) black or green seedless grapes, halved
25 g (1 oz) butter or margarine	150 ml (5 fl oz) soured cream

1 Season the flour with salt and pepper, add the chicken livers and toss until coated. Shake off and reserve any excess flour.

2 Melt the butter or margarine in a medium frying pan and fry the livers with any remaining flour for about 4 minutes, stirring once or twice. Gradually stir in the sherry and stock and simmer for 1–2 minutes.

3 Add the grapes and soured cream. Heat through without boiling and serve hot.

───────────── **TO MICROWAVE** ─────────────

Complete step 1. Melt the butter or margarine in a large shallow dish on HIGH for 45 seconds. Add the livers with any remaining flour and cook on HIGH for 2 minutes, stirring occasionally. Gradually add the sherry and stock and cook on HIGH for 3 minutes, stirring occasionally. Add the grapes and cream and cook on HIGH for 1 minute before serving hot.

───────────── **VARIATION** ─────────────

If grapes are not available, substitute 25 g (1 oz) sultanas for the fresh grapes.

KIDNEYS IN BATTER

SERVES 4

225 g (8 oz) plain flour	1 large onion, very finely chopped
pinch of salt	350 g (12 oz) mushrooms, finely chopped
2 eggs	
568 ml (1 pint) milk	1 garlic clove, crushed
75 g (3 oz) butter or margarine	2 glasses of dry sherry
8 lambs' kidneys, skinned, cored and chopped	150 ml (5 fl oz) double cream
	salt and pepper

1 Sift the flour and salt into a bowl. Make a well in the centre, add the eggs and gradually blend in the flour. Gradually add the milk and whisk until smooth.

2 Melt 50 g (2 oz) of the butter or margarine in a frying pan, add the kidneys and onion and sauté for about 5 minutes or until the onion is transparent. Add the mushrooms, garlic and sherry. Cook gently for a few minutes, then add the cream.

3 Simmer gently until the sauce is reduced and thick, then season to taste.

4 Heat the remaining butter in an ovenproof dish in a preheated oven at 200°C (400°F) mark 6. Add the batter and pour the kidney mixture in the centre. Bake in the oven for 35 minutes or until the batter is crisp, golden and well risen. Serve at once.

KIDNEYS À LA CRÈME
SERVES 4

25 g (1 oz) butter or margarine	30 ml (2 tbsp) plain flour
8 lambs' kidneys, skinned, cored and halved	150 ml (¼ pint) beef stock
1 small onion, chopped	150 ml (5 fl oz) double cream
1 garlic clove, crushed	salt and pepper

1 Melt the butter or margarine in a frying pan, add the kidneys, onion and garlic and cook for 3–4 minutes or until the kidneys are evenly browned.
2 Push the kidneys to one side of the pan, stir in the flour and cook for 2 minutes, gradually adding the stock and cream. Stir gently and reheat without boiling.
3 Season to taste and serve immediately.

CREAMED KIDNEYS IN WINE
SERVES 4

25 g (1 oz) butter or margarine	25 g (1 oz) plain flour
12 lambs' kidneys, skinned, halved and cored	300 ml (½ pint) dry red wine
225 g (8 oz) mushrooms, sliced	5 ml (1 tsp) mustard powder
3 celery sticks, diced	salt and pepper
1 medium onion, finely chopped	150 ml (5 fl oz) double cream

1 Melt the butter or margarine in a medium saucepan. Add the kidneys, mushrooms, celery and onion and fry gently for 10 minutes or until tender.
2 Stir in the flour and cook for 1–2 minutes. Gradually stir in the wine and mustard, then season to taste. Cook for a further 5 minutes. Stir in the cream and reheat gently without boiling.

———— TO MICROWAVE ————
Melt the butter in a large bowl on HIGH for 45 seconds. Add the kidneys, mushrooms, celery and onion. Cook, covered, on HIGH for 10 minutes. Stir in the flour and cook on HIGH for 1 minute. Gradually stir in the wine, mustard and salt and pepper. Cook on HIGH for 3 minutes or until boiling and thickened, stirring occasionally. Stir in the cream and cook on HIGH for 30 seconds.

KIDNEY AND MUSHROOM SAUTÉ

SERVES 3–4

CREAMED SWEETBREADS

SERVES 4

450 g (1 lb) lambs' kidneys, skinned, halved and cored	10 ml (2 tsp) whole grain mustard
15 ml (1 tbsp) vegetable oil	1 garlic clove, crushed
25 g (1 oz) butter	salt and pepper
225 g (8 oz) large flat mushrooms, sliced	chopped parsley, to garnish
30 ml (2 tbsp) single cream	

1 Cut the kidney halves in half again.
2 Heat the oil and butter in a large frying pan, add the kidney pieces and fry quickly until browned on all sides, turning frequently.
3 Stir in the mushrooms and cook for 1 minute, shaking the pan from time to time. Lower the heat and add the cream, mustard and garlic. Season to taste and heat through gently. Serve immediately, garnished with parsley.

450 g (1 lb) lambs' sweetbreads, thawed if frozen	40 g (1½ oz) butter or margarine
1 small onion, chopped	60 ml (4 tbsp) plain flour
1 medium carrot, chopped	300 ml (½ pint) milk
a few fresh parsley stalks	a squeeze of lemon juice
1 bay leaf	chopped parsley, to garnish
salt and pepper	

1 Rinse and soak the sweetbreads in cold water for 2 hours. Drain and remove any fat.
2 Put the sweetbreads, vegetables and herbs in a saucepan with water to cover, season to taste, then simmer gently for about 15 minutes or until the sweetbreads are tender. Drain, reserving 300 ml (½ pint) of the cooking liquid, and keep hot.
3 Put the butter or margarine, flour, milk and reserved stock in a saucepan. Heat, whisking continuously, until the sauce thickens, boils and is smooth. Simmer for 1–2 minutes. Season to taste and add the lemon juice.
4 Add the sweetbreads to the sauce and simmer gently for 5–10 minutes. Garnish with parsley and serve at once.

COOK'S TIP

Sweetbreads, although considered a great delicacy, are not always readily available, so you may have to order them from your butcher. Soaking sweetbreads before use helps to keep them white.

CALF'S LIVER WITH GREEN GRAPES AND MADEIRA

SERVES 4

50 g (2 oz) butter	24 large green grapes, peeled, halved and seeded
50 g (2 oz) onion or shallot skinned and finely chopped	4 slices of calf's liver – each weighing about 75–100 g (3–4 oz), trimmed
175 ml (6 fl oz) chicken stock	
100 ml (4 fl oz) Madeira	4 sage leaves, thinly sliced
salt and freshly ground pepper	4 sage sprigs for garnish

1 Melt half the butter in a frying pan and fry the onion until golden. Add the stock and Madeira, season and bring to the boil. Boil rapidly for 4–5 minutes or until reduced and of a slightly syrupy consistency. Add the grape halves and warm through gently. Taste and adjust the seasoning.
2 Melt the remaining butter in a large frying pan. Season the liver, and fry with the sliced sage leaves for 3–5 minutes, turning once.
3 Remove the liver from the pan and serve at once with the Madeira sauce. Garnish with sprigs of fresh sage.

SWEETBREADS WITH MUSHROOMS AND WHITE WINE

SERVES 4

1½ pounds lambs' sweetbreads, thawed if frozen	2 tablespoons butter
	1 tablespoon olive oil
salt and pepper	½ pound button mushrooms, halved or sliced if large
1 onion, chopped	
1 carrot, sliced	⅔ cup heavy cream
1 celery stalk, sliced	4 teaspoons chopped fresh basil or 1 teaspoon dried
1 bouquet garni	
1¼ cups dry white wine	basil sprigs, for garnish

1 Soak the sweetbreads in salted water for about 4 hours to remove traces of blood. Change the water frequently until the sweetbreads turn white. Drain and rinse.
2 Plunge the sweetbreads into a pan of boiling salted water and blanch for 2–3 minutes. Drain and cool.
3 Peel off the skin from the sweetbreads, then cut away all gristle and stringy tissue. Slice thinly and put in a saucepan with the onion, carrot, celery and bouquet garni. Pour in the wine and season.
4 Bring to a boil, then lower the heat, cover and simmer for 10 minutes or until the sweetbreads feel tender. Remove the sweetbreads from the pan, discard the vegetables and bouquet garni, then boil the liquid to reduce to ⅔ cup.
5 Heat the butter and oil in a heavy-based skillet and sauté the mushrooms for 2 minutes.
6 Add the sweetbreads to the pan and toss to mix with the mushrooms. Pour in the cooking liquid and bring to a boil, stirring. Lower the heat and slowly stir in the cream. Heat through gently, then stir in the basil and season. Transfer to a warmed serving dish, garnish and serve.

BRAISED OXTAIL

SERVES 4

salt and pepper	15 ml (1 tbsp) tomato purée
30 ml (2 tbsp) plain flour	
2 small oxtails (total weight about 1.4 kg/3 lb)	finely grated rind of ½ lemon
15 g (½ oz) butter	2 bay leaves
15 ml (1 tbsp) vegetable oil	225 g (8 oz) carrots, thickly sliced
2 large onions, sliced	
900 ml (1½ pints) beef stock	450 g (1 lb) parsnips, cut into chunks
150 ml (¼ pint) dry red wine	chopped parsley, to garnish

1 Season the flour with salt and pepper, add the oxtail pieces and toss until coated. Shake off and reserve any excess flour. Heat the butter and oil in a large flameproof casserole, add the oxtail pieces, a few at a time and fry until browned. Remove with a slotted spoon.

2 Add the onions to the fat remaining in the casserole and fry for 5 minutes or until lightly browned. Stir in any remaining flour, the stock, red wine, tomato purée, lemon rind and bay leaves and season well. Bring to the boil and replace the meat. Cover and simmer for 3 hours, then skim well.

3 Stir the carrots and parsnips into the casserole. Re-cover the casserole and simmer for a further 30 minutes or until the meat is quite tender.

4 Skim all the fat from the surface of the casserole, remove the bay leaves, adjust the seasoning and garnish with chopped parsley.

ORANGE OXTAIL STEW

SERVES 4

2 oranges	30 ml (2 tbsp) vegetable oil
30 ml (2 tbsp) plain flour	1 onion, roughly chopped
10 ml (2 tsp) dried mixed herbs	2 celery sticks, sliced
	3 medium carrots, sliced
salt and pepper	300 ml (½ pint) dry cider
1.4 kg (3 lb) oxtail, cut into pieces	2 bay leaves

1 Cut the rind of one orange into thin matchstick strips with a cannelle knife. Blanch in boiling water for 2 minutes, then drain and reserve. Finely grate the rind of the remaining orange. Squeeze the juice from both oranges.

2 Put the flour in a large polythene bag with the herbs and salt and pepper to taste. Shake well to mix. Add the oxtail, a few pieces at a time, and shake until evenly coated.

3 Heat the oil in a large flameproof casserole, add as many pieces of oxtail as will fit on the base of the pan and fry over moderate heat until well browned. Remove with a slotted spoon and drain. Repeat with the remaining oxtail.

4 Add the onion, celery and carrots to the oil remaining in the casserole and fry gently for about 10 minutes or until softened, stirring frequently. Pour in the cider, add the grated orange rind and orange juice and bring to the boil.

5 Return the oxtail pieces to the casserole and pour in enough water to cover. Add the bay leaves, bring to the boil, then cover and cook in a preheated oven at 150°C (300°F) mark 2 for 3 hours. Cool, then chill overnight.

6 Next day, skim the fat from the casserole and remove the bay leaves. Simmer on the hob until heated through, taste and season. Garnish with the reserved orange rind.

POULTRY AND GAME

Chicken is always popular, whether cooked as a roast or as tender breast fillets in a flavoursome sauce; turkey is almost as versatile and the ideal choice for entertaining, at any time of year. Game, such as pheasant, rabbit and venison, makes a welcome change.

GOLDEN BAKED CHICKEN

SERVES 4

4 chicken portions	15 ml (1 tbsp) chopped fresh parsley and thyme or 5 ml (1 tsp) dried mixed herbs
salt and pepper	
50 g (2 oz) fresh white breadcrumbs	
1 small onion, finely chopped	50 g (2 oz) butter or margarine, melted

1 Wipe the chicken portions and season well with salt and pepper.
2 Mix the breadcrumbs with the onion and herbs.
3 Brush the chicken joints all over with the butter or margarine, add them to the herbed breadcrumbs and turn until coated. Place in a buttered ovenproof dish.
4 Bake in a preheated oven at 190°C (375°F) mark 5 for about 1 hour or until golden. Baste occasionally during cooking. Serve hot, straight from the dish.

STIR-FRIED CHICKEN WITH COURGETTES

SERVES 4

30 ml (2 tbsp) vegetable oil	1 red pepper, cut into thin strips
1 garlic clove, crushed	
450 g (1 lb) chicken breast fillets, skinned and cut into thin strips	45 ml (3 tbsp) dry sherry
	15 ml (1 tbsp) soy sauce
450 g (1 lb) courgettes, cut into thin strips	60 ml (4 tbsp) natural yogurt
	pepper

1 Heat the oil in a large frying pan or wok, add the garlic and fry for 1 minute. Add the chicken and cook for 3–4 minutes, stirring continuously.
2 Add the courgettes and pepper and continue frying for 1–2 minutes or until the chicken is cooked and the vegetables are tender but still crisp.
3 Stir in the sherry and soy sauce and cook for 1 minute or until hot. Stir in the yogurt and season to taste with pepper. Serve immediately.

CORNISH CAUDLE CHICKEN PIE

SERVES 4

50 g (2 oz) butter	150 ml (¼ pint) soured cream
1 onion, finely chopped	100 g (4 oz) puff pastry, thawed if frozen
four 100 g (4 oz) chicken legs, boned	beaten egg, to glaze
20 g (¾ oz) chopped parsley	150 ml (¼ pint) double cream
4 spring onions, chopped	1 egg, beaten
salt and pepper	
150 ml (¼ pint) milk	

1 Melt half the butter and cook the onion until soft. Transfer to a 1.1 litre (2 pint) dish.
2 Add the remaining butter to the pan, add the chicken and cook until browned. Arrange on top of the onion.
3 Stir the parsley, spring onions, salt and pepper to taste, milk and soured cream into the pan and bring to the boil. Simmer for 2–3 minutes, then pour over the chicken.
4 Cover the pie dish with foil and cook at 180°C (350°F) mark 4 for about 30 minutes. Leave to cool.
5 Roll out the pastry and use to cover the pie dish. Crimp the edges, make a small hole in the top and insert a funnel of aluminium foil.
6 Brush the top of the pie with beaten egg and bake at 220°C (425°F) mark 7 for 15–20 minutes or until brown. Reduce the temperature to 180°F (350°F) mark 4.
7 Beat the cream into the egg, then strain into a jug and pour into the pie through the foil funnel. Remove the funnel, shake the dish to distribute the cream and return the pie to the oven for about 5 minutes.
8 Leave the pie to stand in a warm place for 5–10 minutes before serving warm, or leave to cool and serve cold.

SPICED ROAST CHICKEN

SERVES 4

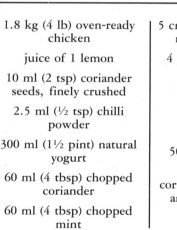

1.8 kg (4 lb) oven-ready chicken	5 cm (2 inch) piece of fresh root ginger, crushed
juice of 1 lemon	4 garlic cloves, crushed
10 ml (2 tsp) coriander seeds, finely crushed	5 ml (1 tsp) paprika
2.5 ml (½ tsp) chilli powder	5 ml (1 tsp) ground turmeric
300 ml (1½ pint) natural yogurt	5 ml (1 tsp) salt
60 ml (4 tbsp) chopped coriander	50 ml (2 fl oz) ghee or melted butter
60 ml (4 tbsp) chopped mint	coriander and mint sprigs and lemon wedges, to garnish

1 Prick the skin of the chicken all over with a fine skewer. Mix together the lemon juice, coriander seeds and chilli powder and brush over the chicken. Leave for 30 minutes.
2 Meanwhile, mix together the remaining ingredients, except the ghee or butter and the garnish.
3 Stand the chicken, breast side up, in a roasting tin. Brush with one quarter of the yogurt mixture. Roast in a preheated oven at 200°C (400°F) mark 6 for about 30 minutes or until the yogurt dries.
4 Turn the chicken over on its side and brush with another quarter of the yogurt mixture. Return to the oven for a further 30 minutes or until the yogurt dries again. Continue turning the chicken and brushing with yogurt twice more, until the chicken has been cooking for 2 hours.
5 Stand the chicken breast side up again, and brush with the ghee or butter. Increase the oven temperature to 200°C (425°F) mark 7 and roast the chicken for a further 15 minutes or until the juices run clear. Transfer to a warmed dish, garnish and serve.

STOVED CHICKEN

SERVES 4

25 g (1 oz) butter	2 large onions, sliced
15 ml (1 tbsp) vegetable oil	salt and pepper
4 chicken quarters, halved	10 ml (2 tsp) chopped fresh thyme or 2.5 ml (½ tsp) dried
100 g (4 oz) lean back bacon, chopped	
1.1 kg (2½ lb) floury potatoes, such as King Edwards, peeled and cut into 0.5 cm (¼ inch) slices	600 ml (1 pint) chicken stock
	snipped chives, to garnish

1 Heat half the butter and the oil in a large frying pan and fry the chicken and bacon for 5 minutes or until lightly browned.

2 Place a thick layer of potato slices in the base of a large ovenproof casserole and cover with a layer of onion slices. Season well, add the thyme and dot with half the remaining butter.

3 Add the chicken and bacon, season to taste and dot with the remaining butter. Cover with the remaining onions and finally another layer of potatoes. Season and dot with butter. Pour over the stock.

4 Cover the casserole and bake in a preheated oven at 150°C (300°F) mark 2 for about 2 hours or until the chicken is tender and the potatoes are cooked, adding a little more hot stock if necessary.

5 Just before serving, sprinkle with snipped chives.

CHICKEN THIGHS WITH SPICY TOMATO SAUCE

SERVES 4

15 g (½ oz) butter	8 chicken thighs
15 ml (1 tbsp) vegetable oil	397 g (14 oz) can tomatoes
1 medium onion, chopped	15 ml (1 tbsp) tomato purée
1 garlic clove, crushed	salt and pepper
5 ml (1 tsp) ground cumin	30 ml (2 tbsp) chopped fresh parsley
5 ml (1 tsp) ground coriander	
large pinch of chilli powder	

1 Heat the butter and oil in a large frying pan, add the onion and garlic, cover and cook for 4–5 minutes or until the onion is softened. Add the cumin, coriander and chilli powder and cook for 1 minute, stirring continuously.

2 Push the onions to one side of the pan, then add the chicken and brown on both sides. Stir in the tomatoes and the tomato purée and season to taste.

3 Bring to the boil, stirring continuously. Cover and simmer gently for about 30 minutes or until the chicken is tender. Stir in the parsley and serve immediately.

── TO MICROWAVE ──

Put all the ingredients, except the butter, oil, chicken and parsley, in a large bowl. Cover and cook on HIGH for 10 minutes. Meanwhile, melt the butter and oil in a frying pan and brown the chicken on both sides. Add the chicken to the sauce, re-cover and cook on HIGH for 15 minutes or until the chicken is tender, stirring occasionally. Stir in the parsley and serve immediately.

SHREDDED CHICKEN WITH MUSHROOMS AND WALNUTS

SERVES 4

four 100 g (4 oz) chicken breast fillets, skinned and cut into thin strips	45 ml (3 tbsp) vegetable oil
5 cm (2 inch) piece of fresh root ginger, thinly sliced	100 g (4 oz) mushrooms, halved
45 ml (3 tbsp) soy sauce	¼ cucumber, cut into chunks
60 ml (4 tbsp) dry sherry	75 g (3 oz) walnut pieces, roughly chopped
5 ml (1 tsp) five-spice powder	pepper

1 Put the chicken in a bowl with the ginger, soy sauce, sherry and five-spice powder. Stir well to mix, then cover and leave to marinate for at least 1 hour.
2 Remove the chicken from the marinade with a slotted spoon, reserving the marinade.
3 Heat the oil in a large frying pan or wok. Add the chicken and cook for 3–4 minutes, stirring continuously.
4 Add the mushrooms, cucumber and walnuts and continue to cook for 1–2 minutes or until the chicken is cooked and the vegetables are tender but still crisp.
5 Stir in the reserved marinade and cook for 1 minute or until hot. Season to taste with pepper. Serve immediately.

––––––––– **TO MICROWAVE** –––––––––

Complete steps 1 and 2. Put the chicken, oil, mushrooms, cucumber and walnuts in a large bowl. Cook on HIGH for 5–6 minutes, stirring frequently. Stir in the reserved marinade and cook on HIGH for 1 minute or until hot. Season to taste with pepper. Serve immediately.

GINGERED JAPANESE CHICKEN

SERVES 4

1.4 kg (3 lb) oven-ready chicken	1 red pepper, sliced
15 ml (1 tbsp) plain flour	150 ml (¼ pint) chicken stock
15 ml (1 tbsp) ground ginger	45 ml (3 tbsp) soy sauce
60 ml (4 tbsp) vegetable oil	45 ml (3 tbsp) medium dry sherry
1 onion, sliced	salt and pepper
283 g (10 oz) can bamboo shoots, drained	100 g (4 oz) mushrooms, sliced

1 Cut all the flesh off the chicken and slice into chunky 'fingers', discarding the skin.
2 Mix the flour and ginger together in a polythene bag, add the chicken and toss to coat.
3 Heat the oil in a very large sauté or deep frying pan and fry the chicken and sliced onion together for 10–15 minutes or until golden.
4 Cut the canned bamboo shoots into 1 cm (½ inch) strips. Add to the pan, together with the sliced pepper, then stir in the stock, soy sauce and sherry. Season to taste. Bring to the boil, cover and simmer for 15 minutes.
5 Add the sliced mushrooms, cover again and cook for a further 5–10 minutes or until the chicken is tender.

––––––––– **COOK'S TIP** –––––––––

Bamboo shoots are used extensively in oriental cooking, although the Chinese and Japanese use fresh shoots rather than the canned version specified above. Canned bamboo shoots are available from specialist oriental food stores, large supermarkets and delicatessens. Look for those canned in water rather than vinegar as they have a milder flavour.

CHICKEN JULIENNE

SERVES 4

175 g (6 oz) long grain rice	100 g (4 oz) green beans, cooked
40 g (1½ oz) butter or margarine	pinch of dried thyme
40 g (1½ oz) plain flour	salt and pepper
300 ml (½ pint) chicken stock	15 ml (1 tbsp) chopped parsley
300 ml (½ pint) milk	100 g (4 oz) carrot, cut into julienne strips, blanched and drained
350 g (12 oz) cooked chicken, cut into long narrow strips	25 g (1 oz) flaked almonds, toasted
30 ml (2 tbsp) lemon juice	

1 Cook the rice in boiling salted water for about 10 minutes or until tender but not soft. Drain, set aside and keep hot.

2 Melt the butter or margarine in a pan, stir in the flour and cook gently for 1 minute, stirring. Remove from the heat and gradually stir in the stock and milk. Bring to the boil and continue to cook, stirring, until the sauce thickens.

3 Gently stir in the chicken, lemon juice, green beans and thyme. Season to taste and cook for 5–10 minutes or until heated through.

4 Add the parsley to the cooked rice and toss lightly. Make a border of rice on a serving dish and spoon the chicken into the centre. Sprinkle with carrots and almonds.

VARIATION
Turkey Julienne

This is a good recipe for using up leftover cooked turkey. Substitute the same amount of turkey for the chicken in the above recipe.

CHICKEN VÉRONIQUE

SERVES 4

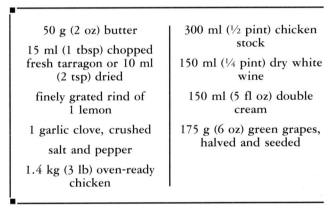

50 g (2 oz) butter	300 ml (½ pint) chicken stock
15 ml (1 tbsp) chopped fresh tarragon or 10 ml (2 tsp) dried	150 ml (¼ pint) dry white wine
finely grated rind of 1 lemon	150 ml (5 fl oz) double cream
1 garlic clove, crushed	175 g (6 oz) green grapes, halved and seeded
salt and pepper	
1.4 kg (3 lb) oven-ready chicken	

1 Beat the butter in a bowl until soft, then mix in the tarragon, lemon rind and garlic. Season to taste. Put half the mixture in the cavity of the bird.

2 Truss the chicken. Spread the remaining butter mixture over the outside of the bird, then stand the bird on a rack in a roasting tin. Pour the chicken stock under the rack.

3 Roast the chicken in a preheated oven at 200°C (400°F) mark 6 for about 1¼ hours or until the juices run clear when the thickest part of a thigh is pierced with a skewer. Turn the bird and baste every 15 minutes.

4 Carve the chicken into neat portions, then arrange on a warmed serving platter, cover and keep warm.

5 To make the sauce, blot off any excess fat from the roasting tin with absorbent kitchen paper, then place the tin on the hob. Pour in the wine, then boil to reduce to about half, stirring to dislodge sediment.

6 Stir in the cream and continue simmering and stirring until thick, smooth and glossy. Add the grapes and heat through, then taste and adjust the seasoning.

7 Pour a little of the sauce over the chicken. Serve immediately, with the remaining sauce and grapes served in a warmed sauceboat.

CHICKEN WITH LEMON AND ALMONDS

SERVES 4

1.4 kg (3 lb) oven-ready chicken	450 ml (¾ pint) chicken stock
50 g (2 oz) blanched almonds	100 g (4 oz) button mushrooms, sliced
1 lemon, thinly sliced	15 ml (1 tbsp) cornflour
1 garlic clove	60 ml (4 tbsp) single cream
25 g (1 oz) butter, softened	watercress, to garnish
salt and pepper	

1 Wipe the chicken and loosen the skin all over the breast with your fingertips. Slip the almonds under the skin.

2 Stuff the lemon into the chicken cavity with the garlic. Truss or tie the bird securely.

3 Place the chicken in a roasting tin and spread the butter all over its surface. Season to taste. Pour the stock around the bird and roast in a preheated oven at 200°C (400°F) mark 6 for 1 hour, basting frequently.

4 Add the mushrooms to the roasting tin. Lay a piece of foil over the bird and continue cooking for a further 20 minutes or until the bird is tender.

5 Drain the bird and discard the lemon and garlic. Joint the chicken neatly so that each person has a breast and leg or thigh portion.

6 Blend the cornflour to a smooth paste with a little water and pour into the pan juices. Heat, stirring, until thickened. Add the cream and heat through without re-boiling. Adjust the seasoning and spoon over the bird just before serving. Garnish with watercress.

CHICKEN WITH APRICOTS AND BRANDY

SERVES 4–6

4 or 6 chicken breast fillets, with skin on	300 ml (½ pint) chicken stock
45 ml (3 tbsp) plain flour, plus extra for dusting	salt and pepper
	3 juniper berries (optional)
100 g (4 oz) butter	100 g (4 oz) no-soak dried apricots
60 ml (4 tbsp) dry white wine	1 bay leaf
15–30 ml (1–2 tbsp) brandy	4–6 thick round slices of bread
100 g (4 oz) bacon, chopped	150 ml (¼ pint) single cream
100 g (4 oz) mushrooms, sliced	fresh parsley, to garnish
100 g (4 oz) onion, chopped	

1 Dust the chicken with flour. Melt 40 g (1½ oz) butter in a frying pan, add the chicken and cook gently until browned. Transfer to a casserole. Add the wine and brandy to the pan, boil, then pour over the chicken.

2 Melt a further 40 g (1½ oz) butter in the pan and fry the bacon, mushrooms and onion for 5–10 minutes. Blend in 45 ml (3 tbsp) flour, then gradually stir in the stock. Season and add the juniper berries, apricots and bay leaf.

3 Pour the sauce over the chicken, cover and cook at 170°C (325°F) mark 3 for about 1½ hours or until tender.

4 Melt the remaining butter in the pan and fry the bread until crisp. Drain and keep hot.

5 When the chicken is cooked, remove from the casserole and keep hot. Remove the bay leaf, then purée the sauce. Add the cream, adjust the seasoning and reheat.

6 Arrange a chicken breast on each croûton and place on a warmed serving platter. Spoon over some sauce and garnish.

CHICKEN WITH MUSHROOMS AND BACON

SERVES 4

30 ml (2 tbsp) vegetable oil	300 ml (½ pint) chicken stock
100 g (4 oz) streaky bacon, chopped	400 g (14 oz) can chopped tomatoes
1 medium onion, chopped	1 bay leaf
1 garlic clove, crushed	salt and pepper
175 g (6 oz) button mushrooms, sliced	30 ml (2 tbsp) chopped parsley, to garnish
4 chicken quarters, skinned	

1 Heat the oil in a large saucepan, add the bacon and fry for 5 minutes or until crisp.

2 Add the onion, garlic and mushrooms to the pan and fry gently for 3–5 minutes or until the onion has softened. Add the chicken and fry for 8–10 minutes or until evenly browned, turning once.

3 Pour over the stock. Add the tomatoes with their juice and the bay leaf. Season to taste. Gradually bring to the boil, stirring occasionally. Simmer for 35–40 minutes or until tender.

4 Remove the bay leaf, transfer to a warmed serving dish and sprinkle with the chopped parsley.

───────────── **TO MICROWAVE** ─────────────

Place the oil, bacon, onion and garlic in a large bowl, cover and microwave on HIGH for 5 minutes or until softened, stirring occasionally. Add the mushrooms, chicken, tomatoes, bay leaf and 300 ml (½ pint) boiling stock. Cover and microwave on HIGH for 20–25 minutes or until the chicken is tender and the juices run clear. Turn and rearrange the chicken portions twice during cooking. Complete step 4.

LEMON AND TURMERIC CHICKEN

SERVES 4

4 chicken breast fillets, skinned	300 ml (½ pint) milk
pared rind and juice of 1½ lemons	40 g (1½ oz) plain flour
1 onion, chopped	5 ml (1 tsp) ground turmeric, or to taste
2.5 ml (½ tsp) dried thyme	salt and pepper
150 ml (¼ pint) chicken stock	lemon slices and fresh parsley, to garnish

1 Place the chicken breasts in a roasting tin. Sprinkle with a few curls of lemon rind, the onion and thyme. Add the lemon juice to the stock and pour around the chicken. Cover with foil and bake in a preheated oven at 190°C (375°F) mark 5 for about 45 minutes or until tender.

2 Remove the chicken from the tin and keep warm. Strain the stock into a measuring jug and add the milk. Blend the flour and turmeric with a little of the milk and stock mixture in a saucepan, then gradually add all the liquid. Bring slowly to the boil, stirring constantly, until the sauce thickens. Season to taste.

3 Place the chicken on a warmed serving dish and pour over the sauce. Garnish with lemon slices and parsley.

CHICKEN WITH TARRAGON SAUCE

SERVES 6

75 g (3 oz) butter or margarine	5 ml (1 tsp) chopped fresh tarragon or 2.5 ml (½ tsp) dried
6 chicken breast fillets, skinned	45 ml (3 tbsp) grated Parmesan cheese
25 g (1 oz) plain flour	salt and pepper
450 ml (¾ pint) chicken stock	150 ml (5 fl oz) single cream
30 ml (2 tbsp) tarragon vinegar	tarragon sprigs, to garnish
10 ml (2 tsp) French mustard	

1 Melt 50 g (2 oz) butter or margarine in a frying pan, add the chicken, cover and cook gently for about 20 minutes or until tender, turning once. Drain.

2 Meanwhile, melt the remaining butter or margarine in a saucepan, stir in the flour and gradually add the stock and vinegar. Stir in the mustard, tarragon and cheese, then bring to the boil. Season to taste and simmer for 3 minutes.

3 Remove from the heat and add the cream. Heat gently without boiling. To serve, place the chicken on a warmed serving dish, spoon over the sauce and garnish.

CHICKEN WITH SAFFRON

SERVES 6

salt and pepper	30 ml (2 tbsp) dry white wine
30 ml (2 tbsp) plain flour	large pinch of saffron strands
six 175 g (6 oz) chicken breast fillets, skinned	2 egg yolks
40 g (1½ oz) butter	60 ml (4 tbsp) single cream
200 ml (7 fl oz) chicken stock	vegetable julienne, to garnish

1 Season the flour, add the chicken and turn until coated. Shake off and reserve any excess flour.

2 Melt the butter in a medium flameproof casserole, add the chicken pieces, half at a time, and fry for 5–10 minutes or until golden brown.

3 Return all the chicken pieces to the pan with any remaining flour and pour in the chicken stock and white wine.

4 Sprinkle in the saffron, pushing it down under the liquid. Bring to the boil, cover tightly and cook in a preheated oven at 180°C (350°F) mark 4 for about 50 minutes or until cooked

5 Lift the chicken out of the juices and place in a warmed serving dish. Cover and keep warm.

6 Strain the cooking juices into a small saucepan. Mix the egg yolks and cream together and stir into the cooking juices until evenly mixed.

7 Cook gently, stirring all the time, until the juices thicken slightly. Do not boil. To serve, adjust the seasoning of the sauce, spoon over the chicken and garnish with vegetable julienne. Serve immediately.

SPICED CHICKEN

SERVES 4

40 g (1½ oz) plain wholemeal flour	450 ml (¾ pint) milk
5 ml (1 tsp) curry powder	60 ml (4 tbsp) apple chutney
2.5 ml (½ tsp) cayenne	100 g (4 oz) sultanas
350 g (12 oz) boneless chicken, skinned and diced	150 ml (5 fl oz) soured cream
40 g (1½ oz) butter	2.5 ml (½ tsp) paprika
1 medium onion, chopped	

1 Mix the flour, curry powder and cayenne, add the chicken and toss until coated. Reserve any excess flour.

2 Melt the butter in a large saucepan, add the chicken and onion and fry for 5–6 minutes or until the chicken is brown and the onion is lightly coloured.

3 Stir in the remaining flour, then gradually blend in the milk. Heat gently, stirring continuously, until the sauce thickens, boils and is smooth.

4 Add the chutney and sultanas and simmer gently for 30–35 minutes or until the chicken is tender.

5 Remove the pan from the heat and drizzle with the cream. Sprinkle with the paprika and serve at once

---
TO MICROWAVE

Complete step 1. Cube the butter and melt in a large bowl on HIGH for 1 minute. Add the onion and cook on HIGH for 5 minutes. Add the chicken and cook on HIGH for 3–4 minutes, stirring occasionally. Stir in the flour. Gradually blend in the milk and cook on HIGH for 7–8 minutes, whisking frequently, until boiling and thickened. Add the chutney and sultanas and cook on MEDIUM for 12–15 minutes or until the chicken is tender. Drizzle with the cream. Serve at once.

CHICKEN AND REDCURRANT CURRY

SERVES 4

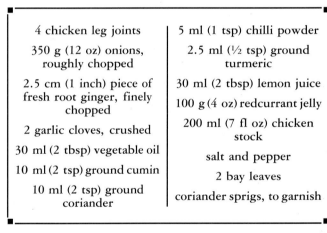

4 chicken leg joints	5 ml (1 tsp) chilli powder
350 g (12 oz) onions, roughly chopped	2.5 ml (½ tsp) ground turmeric
2.5 cm (1 inch) piece of fresh root ginger, finely chopped	30 ml (2 tbsp) lemon juice
2 garlic cloves, crushed	100 g (4 oz) redcurrant jelly
30 ml (2 tbsp) vegetable oil	200 ml (7 fl oz) chicken stock
10 ml (2 tsp) ground cumin	salt and pepper
10 ml (2 tsp) ground coriander	2 bay leaves
	coriander sprigs, to garnish

1 Cut the chicken legs into thighs and drumsticks. Remove skin and fat.

2 Put the onions, ginger and garlic in a blender or food processor and process until fairly smooth.

3 Heat the oil in a large heavy-based pan, add the onion paste and fry gently until golden. Add the chicken joints and fry until golden on all sides.

4 Add the cumin, coriander, chilli, turmeric and lemon juice. Cook for 5 minutes or until the chicken pieces are evenly coated with spices, then stir in the redcurrant jelly and stock. Season to taste, bring to the boil, add the bay leaves, cover and simmer for 45–50 minutes or until the chicken is tender.

5 Taste and adjust the seasoning, remove the bay leaves and garnish with coriander just before serving.

HONEY BARBECUED CHICKEN

SERVES 4

50 g (2 oz) butter	15 ml (1 tbsp) honey
100 g (4 oz) onions, finely chopped	salt and pepper
1 garlic clove, finely chopped (optional)	100 g (4 oz) long grain rice
	4 chicken drumsticks
397 g (14 oz) can tomatoes	grilled mushrooms and tomatoes and parsley sprigs, to garnish
30 ml (2 tbsp) Worcestershire sauce	

1 To make the barbecue sauce, combine the butter, onions, garlic (if using), tomatoes with their juice, Worcestershire sauce and honey in a saucepan. Season to taste and cook gently for 30 minutes.

2 Meanwhile, cook the rice in boiling salted water for about 10 minutes or until tender but not soft. Drain, set aside and keep hot.

3 Place the chicken drumsticks in the grill pan and brush liberally with the barbecue sauce. Cook under a preheated grill for 10 minutes on each side, brushing frequently with more sauce.

4 Serve on a bed of rice garnished with grilled mushrooms and tomatoes and sprigs of parsley. Serve the remaining sauce separately.

CHEESE AND ANCHOVY GRILLED CHICKEN BREASTS

SERVES 6

50 g (2 oz) can anchovy fillets in oil	6 chicken breast fillets, with skin on
30 ml (2 tbsp) finely chopped onion	vegetable oil, for brushing
5 ml (1 tsp) lemon juice	225 g (8 oz) Mozzarella cheese, sliced

1 Drain 15 ml (1 tbsp) of the oil from the anchovy can into a small saucepan. Chop the anchovies finely.

2 Heat the anchovy oil, add the anchovies and onion and cook for about 5 minutes or until a paste forms. Stir in the lemon juice, then remove from the heat and leave to cool.

3 Lift the skin from each chicken breast and rub 5 ml (1 tsp) of the anchovy mixture on the flesh underneath the skin.

4 Put the chicken pieces, skin side down, on to a rack placed over a grill pan. Cook under a preheated moderate grill for 35–40 minutes or until tender, turning once. Brush with oil occasionally during cooking, to moisten.

5 Cover the chicken breasts with slices of cheese and grill for a further 5 minutes, or until the cheese bubbles.

─────────── COOK'S TIP ───────────

If you find anchovies rather salty, soak them in milk for about 30 minutes, then drain before use.

CHICKEN SUPREMES IN WINE AND CREAM

SERVES 6

45 ml (3 tbsp) red wine vinegar	15 ml (1 tbsp) tomato purée
50 g (2 oz) unsalted butter	1 large garlic clove, crushed
six 175 g (6 oz) French-style chicken supremes (with the wing bone attached), wiped and trimmed of excess skin	150 ml (¼ pint) dry white wine
	300 ml (½ pint) chicken stock
	salt and pepper
1 small onion, roughly chopped	150 ml (5 fl oz) double cream
225 g (8 oz) tomatoes, skinned and roughly chopped	chopped parsley, to garnish

1 Place the vinegar in a small saucepan and boil to reduce by half. Heat the butter in a large sauté or deep frying pan. Add the chicken pieces and cook until browned well on all sides. Remove from the pan with a slotted spoon.
2 Add the onion, tomatoes, tomato purée and garlic to the butter remaining in the pan, cover and cook gently for about 5 minutes.
3 Add the wine and cook, uncovered, over a high heat for 5–10 minutes or until the wine reduces by half. Add the vinegar and stock, season to taste and bring to the boil.
4 Replace the chicken, covering it with the sauce. Simmer gently, covered, for about 25 minutes or until the chicken is quite tender. Lift the chicken out of the pan with a slotted spoon and keep warm.
5 Boil the sauce until it is reduced by half, then stir in the cream. Continue reducing the sauce until a thin pouring consistency is obtained.
6 Adjust the seasoning, pass the sauce through a sieve and spoon over the chicken just before serving. Garnish with chopped parsley.

CHICKEN KIEV

SERVES 4

100 g (4 oz) butter, softened	4 large chicken breast fillets, skinned
finely grated rind of ½ lemon	25 g (1 oz) plain flour
15 ml (1 tbsp) lemon juice	1 egg, beaten
15 ml (1 tbsp) chopped parsley	100 g (4 oz) fresh white breadcrumbs
1 garlic clove, crushed	vegetable oil, for deep-frying
salt and pepper	

1 Beat the butter until soft, then work in the lemon rind and juice, the parsley, garlic and salt and pepper to taste.
2 Place the butter on a sheet of non-stick or waxed paper and form into a roll. Refrigerate until firm.
3 Meanwhile, place the chicken breasts on a wooden board and pound them to an even thickness with a meat mallet or rolling pin.
4 Cut the butter into four pieces and place one piece on each of the flattened chicken breasts. Roll up the chicken, folding the ends in to enclose the butter completely. Secure with wooden cocktail sticks.
5 Season the flour with salt and pepper, add the chicken and turn until coated. Dip in beaten egg, then in breadcrumbs. Pat the crumbs firmly so that the chicken is well coated. Chill for at least 1 hour or until required.
6 Heat the oil to 170°C (325°F). Place two chicken portions in a frying basket and carefully lower into the oil. Deep-fry for about 15 minutes, then drain on absorbent kitchen paper while frying the rest. Serve immediately.

CHICKEN AND BROCCOLI PIE

SERVES 4–6

25 g (1 oz) butter	450 g (1 lb) boneless cooked chicken, cut into strips
2 carrots, diced	
8 button onions, skinned	175 g (6 oz) broccoli, blanched
100 g (4 oz) button mushrooms	grated rind of ½ lemon
25 g (1 oz) plain wholemeal flour	30 ml (2 tbsp) single cream
	salt and pepper
450 ml (¾ pint) milk, plus extra to glaze	225 g (8 oz) frozen puff pastry, thawed

1 Melt the butter in a large saucepan, add the carrots, onions and mushrooms and fry lightly for 8 minutes, stirring occasionally.

2 Stir in the flour and cook for 1–2 minutes. Gradually add the milk, stirring continuously, until the sauce thickens, boils and is smooth. Simmer for 3–4 minutes.

3 Add the chicken, broccoli, lemon rind and cream to the sauce. Season to taste and pour into a 1.1 litre (2 pint) pie dish.

4 Roll out the pastry on a lightly floured surface large enough to fit the dish. Cover the pie with the pastry and moisten the edges so the pastry is well sealed. Use any pastry trimmings to decorate. Brush with milk to glaze.

5 Bake in a preheated oven at 200°C (400°F) mark 6 for 25 minutes or until the pastry is golden brown.

CHICKEN POT PIES

SERVES 4

1 lemon	175 g (6 oz) button onions, skinned
1.1 kg (2½ lb) oven-ready chicken, with separate giblets	
	175 g (6 oz) button mushrooms, halved or sliced if large
a few sprigs of fresh tarragon	
	45 ml (3 tbsp) plain flour
1 bay leaf	60 ml (4 tbsp) double cream
salt and pepper	
2 leeks, sliced	368 g (13 oz) packet frozen puff pastry, thawed
2 large carrots, thinly sliced	a little beaten egg, to glaze
40 g (1½ oz) butter	

1 Prick the lemon all over with a skewer, then place inside the chicken. Put the chicken in a saucepan with the tarragon, bay leaf and seasoning. Add the giblets (except the liver), then pour in water to cover and bring to the boil. Simmer for 1¼ hours or until tender.

2 Thirty minutes before the end of cooking, add the leeks and carrots. Remove from the heat and leave to cool.

3 Remove the chicken from the cooking liquid. Cut the flesh from the bird, dice and set aside.

4 Melt the butter and lightly brown the onions.

5 Strain the chicken cooking liquid and reserve 300 ml (½ pint). Add the mushrooms, leeks and carrots to the onions. Fry gently for 1–2 minutes, then add the chicken.

6 Mix the flour to a paste with the cream. Gradually blend in the reserved cooking liquid, then add to the chicken. Season. Simmer, stirring, for 2–3 minutes, then turn into four 300 ml (½ pint) pie dishes.

7 Use the pastry to cover the pies. Brush with beaten egg. Bake at 200°C (400°F) mark 6 for 25 minutes or until the pastry is golden brown.

CORONATION CHICKEN

SERVES 8

2.3 kg (5 lb) chicken, cooked	juice of ½ lemon
25 g (1 oz) butter	4 canned apricots, drained and finely chopped
1 small onion, finely chopped	300 ml (½ pint) mayonnaise
15 ml (1 tbsp) curry paste	150 ml (5 fl oz) whipping cream
15 ml (1 tbsp) tomato purée	salt and pepper
100 ml (4 fl oz) red wine	sliced cucumber, to garnish
1 bay leaf	

1 Remove all the flesh from the chicken and dice. Discard all skin and bones.

2 Heat the butter in a small saucepan, add the onion and cook for 3 minutes or until softened. Add the curry paste, tomato purée, wine, bay leaf and lemon juice. Simmer, uncovered, for about 10 minutes or until well reduced. Strain and cool.

3 Sieve the chopped apricots to produce a purée. Beat the cooked sauce into the mayonnaise with the apricot purée.

4 Whip the cream until softly stiff and fold into the mixture. Season to taste, adding a little more lemon juice if necessary.

5 Toss the chicken pieces into the sauce and garnish with sliced cucumber.

DEVILLED POUSSINS

SERVES 6

15 ml (1 tbsp) mustard powder	15 ml (1 tbsp) lemon juice
15 ml (1 tbsp) paprika	75 g (3 oz) butter, melted
20 ml (4 tsp) ground turmeric	three 700 g (1½ lb) poussins
20 ml (4 tsp) ground cumin	15 ml (1 tbsp) poppy seeds
60 ml (4 tbsp) tomato ketchup	

1 Measure the mustard powder, paprika, turmeric and cumin into a small bowl. Add the tomato ketchup and lemon juice and beat well to form a thick, smooth paste. Slowly pour in the melted butter, stirring all the time.

2 Place the poussins on a chopping board, breast side down. With a small sharp knife, cut right along the backbone of each bird through skin and flesh.

3 With scissors, cut through the backbone to open the birds up. Turn the birds over, breast side up.

4 Continue cutting along the breast bone, splitting the birds into two equal halves.

5 Lie the birds, skin side uppermost, on a large edged baking sheet. Spread the spice paste evenly over the surface of the birds and sprinkle with the poppy seeds. Cover loosely with cling film and leave in a cool place for at least 1–2 hours.

6 Cook the poussins (uncovered on the baking sheet) in a preheated oven at 220°C (425°F) mark 7 for 15 minutes.

7 Remove the poussins from the oven and place under a preheated hot grill until the skin is well browned and crisp.

8 Return to the oven, reduce the temperature to 180°C (350°F) mark 4 and cook for a further 20 minutes or until the poussins are tender. Serve immediately.

BONED STUFFED POUSSINS

SERVES 6

ROAST TURKEY

SERVES 6–12

three 700 g (1½ lb) double poussins, boned (bones reserved)	175 g (6 oz) fresh white breadcrumbs
2 large onions, skinned	juice and grated rind of 1 lemon
1 carrot	2 eggs, size 6, beaten
1 bay leaf	pepper
6 black peppercorns	150 ml (¼ pint) dry white wine
salt	15 ml (1 tbsp) cornflour
100 g (4 oz) butter	a dash of gravy browning
175 g (6 oz) chopped nuts	
two 227 g (8 oz) packets frozen chopped spinach, thawed	

	FOR THE HERB STUFFING
2.7–3.5 kg (6–8 lb) oven-ready turkey, thawed if frozen	3 large onions, skinned and chopped
1 onion, skinned	75 g (3 oz) butter
1 lemon wedge	175 g (6 oz) fresh breadcrumbs
butter	45 ml (3 tbsp) chopped fresh parsley
salt and pepper	salt and pepper
lemon juice	

1 To make the stock, place the bones, one onion, quartered, the carrot, bay leaf, peppercorns and a little salt in a pan. Add 1 litre (1¾ pints) water and simmer, uncovered, for 30 minutes. Strain and reserve 600 ml (1 pint).
2 Chop the remaining onion. Heat 50 g (2 oz) butter, fry the onion and nuts for 2–3 minutes, then add the spinach. Cool slightly, then add the breadcrumbs, lemon juice and rind, egg to bind and seasoning.
3 Lay the birds flesh side up and divide the stuffing between them. Fold the skin over and sew up. Push a skewer through the leg and wing joints and tie the knuckle ends together. Place in a roasting tin and spread over the remaining butter. Pour over half the stock and the wine. Roast at 200°C (400°F) mark 6 for 1 hour.
4 Remove the skewers and string and cut each bird in half lengthways. Place on a serving dish. Mix the cornflour with a little water and add to the tin with the stock. Cook for 2 minutes, season, brown and serve.

1 Wash the turkey inside and out, and dry thoroughly.
2 To make the stuffing, fry the onion in the butter until softened, then stir in the remaining ingredients and mix well. Use to stuff the neck end only of the turkey. Fold the neck skin over and truss to secure.
3 Place the bird in a large roasting tin and place the onion, lemon wedge and a knob of butter inside the body. Spread butter over the turkey skin and season well with salt, pepper and a squeeze of lemon juice. Roast in the oven at 180°C (350°F) mark 4 for 2–3 hours. To test if the turkey is cooked, pierce the deepest part of the thigh with a skewer. If the juices that run out are colourless, the bird is cooked; if pink-tinged cook a little longer.
4 Transfer the turkey to a warmed serving platter and leave to rest before carving. Serve with gravy and bread sauce. Small sausages, rolls of bacon and watercress may be used to garnish the turkey. Cranberry sauce is also a traditional accompaniment.

ROAST TURKEY WITH LEMON STUFFING

3.6–5 kg (8–11¼ lb) SERVES 10–15; 5–6.8 kg (11¼–15 lb)
SERVES 15–20; 6.8–9 kg (15–20¼ lb) SERVES 20–30

25 g (1 oz) butter	finely grated rind of 2 lemons
2 medium onions, finely chopped	salt and pepper
2 celery sticks, finely chopped	1 egg, beaten
225 g (8 oz) fresh wholemeal breadcrumbs	1 oven-ready turkey, thawed if frozen
60 ml (4 tbsp) chopped parsley	streaky bacon rashers

1 To make the stuffing, melt the butter in a large saucepan, add the onions and celery, cover and cook gently for about 10 minutes or until very soft, stirring occasionally.
2 Remove from the heat and add the breadcrumbs, parsley and lemon rind. Season to taste and stir in the egg.
3 Wash the inside of the bird and stuff at the neck end only before folding the neck skin over. Make the turkey plump and as even in shape as possible, then truss it with the wings folded under the body and the legs tied together.
4 Weigh the turkey and calculate the cooking time, allowing 20 minutes per 450 g (1 lb) plus 20 minutes.
5 Place the turkey in a roasting tin, then sprinkle with salt and pepper.
6 Place the streaky bacon rashers over the breast to prevent it from becoming dry. Roast in a preheated oven at 180°C (350°F) mark 4, basting occasionally. Put a piece of foil over the bird if it shows signs of becoming too brown.
7 Leave the turkey to rest for 10 minutes, then carve. Serve with the traditional accompaniments of thin gravy, bread sauce, small sausages and bacon rolls.

TURKEY BREAST WITH ASPARAGUS

SERVES 4

225 g (8 oz) thin asparagus stalks	300 ml (½ pint) chicken stock
two 225 g (8 oz) turkey breast fillets, skinned and halved	5 ml (1 tsp) chopped fresh sage or 2.5 ml (½ tsp) dried
30 ml (2 tbsp) plain flour	60 ml (4 tbsp) dry white wine
salt and pepper	150 ml (5 fl oz) soured cream
15 g (½ oz) butter	
15 ml (1 tbsp) vegetable oil	

1 Cut off the ends of the asparagus if they are tough and woody. Trim them all to the same length, cut off the tips and cut the stalks into three pieces.
2 Put the turkey pieces on a wooden board and beat out slightly with a rolling pin or meat mallet. Season the flour with salt and pepper, add the turkey pieces and turn until coated. Shake off any excess flour. Heat the butter and oil in a large frying pan, add the turkey and fry until lightly browned on both sides. Add the chicken stock, asparagus stalks, reserving the tips, the sage and wine, cover and cook gently for 15–20 minutes or until tender.
3 Five minutes before the end of the cooking time, add the reserved asparagus tips and the cream. Season to taste.

TURKEY ESCALOPES WITH DAMSONS

SERVES 4

two 225 g (8 oz) turkey breast fillets, skinned and cut widthways into 5 cm (2 inch) slices	5 ml (1 tsp) chopped fresh thyme or 1.25 ml (¼ tsp) dried
75 ml (3 fl oz) unsweetened apple juice	15 g (½ oz) butter
	15 ml (1 tbsp) vegetable oil
45 ml (3 tbsp) soy sauce	225 g (8 oz) damsons, halved and stoned
45 ml (3 tbsp) dry sherry	
1 small garlic clove, crushed	pepper

1 Place the turkey slices between two sheets of dampened greaseproof paper and beat out with a rolling pin or meat mallet until about 2.5 cm (1 inch) thick.

2 Place the turkey slices in a large shallow dish and pour over the apple juice, soy sauce, sherry, garlic and thyme. Cover and leave in the refrigerator to marinate for 3–4 hours or overnight.

3 Remove the turkey from the marinade, reserving the marinade. Heat the butter and oil in a frying pan, add the turkey and fry quickly until browned on both sides. Add the damsons, reserved marinade and pepper to taste.

4 Cover and simmer gently for 10–15 minutes or until tender, stirring occasionally.

─── **VARIATION** ───
Turkey Escalopes with Plums
Substitute plums for damsons in the above recipe if damsons are not available.

TURKEY ESCALOPES WITH HAZELNUT CREAM SAUCE

SERVES 4

450 g (1 lb) turkey breast fillets, thinly sliced	25 g (1 oz) hazelnuts, finely chopped
50 g (2 oz) butter	salt and pepper
60 ml (4 tbsp) sweet sherry	paprika, to garnish
60 ml (4 tbsp) double cream	

1 Place the turkey slices between two sheets of dampened greaseproof paper and beat out with a rolling pin or meat mallet into small escalopes.

2 Melt the butter in a frying pan and cook the escalopes quickly for 4–5 minutes, turning once. Remove from the pan and keep warm.

3 Reduce the heat and stir the sherry, cream and hazelnuts into the pan. Season to taste and cook, stirring, for 1 minute. Pour over the escalopes and serve immediately with a light dusting of paprika.

TURKEY ESCALOPES WITH CRANBERRY AND COCONUT

SERVES 4

450 g (1 lb) turkey breast fillets, skinned	1 egg, beaten
salt and pepper	15 g (½ oz) desiccated coconut
20 ml (4 tsp) Dijon mustard	40 g (1½ oz) fresh breadcrumbs
60 ml (4 tbsp) cranberry sauce	50 g (2 oz) butter or margarine
15 g (½ oz) plain flour	

I Thinly slice the turkey breasts to give four portions.
2 Place the turkey pieces between two sheets of dampened greaseproof paper and beat out with a rolling pin or meat mallet to make thin escalopes. Season to taste, then spread each portion with mustard and cranberry sauce.
3 Roll up the escalopes, starting from the thin end, and secure with a cocktail stick. Dust each portion with flour, then brush with egg. Combine the coconut and bread-crumbs, then coat the turkey escalopes with the mixture.
4 Melt the butter or margarine in a frying pan, add the turkey portions, and fry until brown on both sides. Transfer to a baking tin just large enough to take the turkey in a single layer and baste with more fat. Bake in a preheated oven at 180°C (350°F) mark 4 for about 40 minutes or until the turkey is tender.

COOK'S TIP

Cranberry sauce is traditionally associated with turkey. Cultivated mainly in America, the fresh fruit have a limited season, but they can also be bought frozen or canned throughout the year. The sauce is available bottled, from supermarkets.

TURKEY SAUTÉ WITH LEMON AND WALNUTS

SERVES 4

450 g (1 lb) turkey breast fillets, skinned	60 ml (4 tbsp) chicken stock
30 ml (2 tbsp) cornflour	30 ml (2 tbsp) lemon juice
30 ml (2 tbsp) vegetable oil	45 ml (3 tbsp) lemon marmalade
1 green pepper, thinly sliced	5 ml (1 tsp) white wine vinegar
40 g (1½ oz) walnut halves or pieces	1.25 ml (¼ tsp) soy sauce
25 g (1 oz) butter or margarine	salt and pepper

I Cut the turkey flesh into 5 cm (2 inch) pencil thin strips. Add to the cornflour and toss until coated.
2 Heat the oil in a large sauté or deep frying pan, add the pepper strips and walnuts and fry for 2–3 minutes. Remove from the pan with slotted spoon.
3 Add the butter or margarine to the oil remaining in the pan and fry the turkey strips for 10 minutes or until golden. Add the stock and lemon juice, stirring well to scrape up any sediment at the bottom of the pan. Add the lemon marmalade, vinegar and soy sauce. Season to taste.
4 Return the walnuts and green pepper to the pan. Cook gently for a further 5 minutes or until the turkey is tender. Taste and adjust the seasoning and serve immediately.

VARIATION

Turkey Sauté with Orange and Walnuts
Substitute 30 ml (2 tbsp) orange juice and 45 ml (3 tbsp) orange marmalade for the lemon juice and marmalade in the above recipe. Garnish with thin slices or wedges of orange.

CASSEROLED TURKEY IN RED WINE

SERVES 4

25 g (1 oz) butter	1 bay leaf
30 ml (2 tbsp) vegetable oil	150 ml (¼ pint) red wine
450–700 g (1–1½ lb) turkey casserole meat	salt and pepper
100 g (4 oz) lean streaky bacon, diced	12 small onions or shallots, skinned
30 ml (2 tbsp) plain flour	chopped fresh parsley and pastry crescents or croûtons, to garnish
good pinch of dried thyme	

1 Heat half the butter with half the oil in a large frying pan. When foaming, add the turkey meat and fry until well browned. Remove with a slotted spoon and place in a casserole.

2 Add the bacon to the fat remaining in the frying pan and fry until beginning to brown. Remove the bacon with a slotted spoon and add to the turkey.

3 Stir the flour, thyme and bay leaf into the fat in the frying pan and cook gently for a few minutes. Slowly stir in the red wine and 300 ml (½ pint) water. Season to taste. Bring to the boil, stirring, then pour over the turkey.

4 Cover the casserole tightly and cook in a preheated oven at 150°C (300°F) mark 2 for about 2 hours.

5 Thirty minutes before the end of the cooking time, melt the remaining butter and oil in a frying pan. Add the onions or shallots and cook slowly until golden brown and tender. Add the onions to the casserole, re-cover and cook for a further 20 minutes. Garnish with parsley and pastry crescents or croûtons and serve hot.

TURKEY IN SPICED YOGURT

SERVES 6

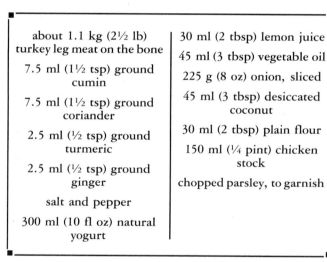

about 1.1 kg (2½ lb) turkey leg meat on the bone	30 ml (2 tbsp) lemon juice
7.5 ml (1½ tsp) ground cumin	45 ml (3 tbsp) vegetable oil
7.5 ml (1½ tsp) ground coriander	225 g (8 oz) onion, sliced
2.5 ml (½ tsp) ground turmeric	45 ml (3 tbsp) desiccated coconut
2.5 ml (½ tsp) ground ginger	30 ml (2 tbsp) plain flour
salt and pepper	150 ml (¼ pint) chicken stock
300 ml (10 fl oz) natural yogurt	chopped parsley, to garnish

1 Cut the turkey meat off the bone into large fork-sized pieces, discarding the skin. There should be about 900 g (2 lb) meat.

2 In a large bowl, mix the spices with the seasoning, yogurt and lemon juice. Stir well until evenly blended

3 Fold the turkey meat into the yogurt mixture, turning until coated. Cover tightly with cling film and refrigerate for several hours.

4 Heat the oil in a medium flameproof casserole, add the onion and fry for 5–10 minutes or until lightly browned. Add the coconut and flour and fry gently, stirring, for about 1 minute.

5 Remove from the heat and stir in the turkey with its marinade and the stock. Return to the heat and bring slowly to the boil, stirring all the time. Cover tightly and cook in a preheated oven at 170°C (325°F) mark 3 for 1–1¼ hours or until the turkey is tender.

6 Adjust the seasoning and serve garnished with parsley.

QUICK TURKEY CURRY

SERVES 4–6

30 ml (2 tbsp) vegetable oil	2.5 ml (½ tsp) chilli powder
3 bay leaves	salt and pepper
2 cardamom pods, crushed	50 g (2 oz) unsalted cashew nuts
1 cinnamon stick, broken into short lengths	700 g (1½ lb) turkey breast fillets, skinned and cut into bite-sized pieces
1 medium onion, thinly sliced	2 medium potatoes, blanched, peeled and cut into chunks
1 green pepper, chopped (optional)	4 tomatoes, skinned and chopped
10 ml (2 tsp) paprika	bay leaves, to garnish
7.5 ml (1½ tsp) garam masala	
2.5 ml (½ tsp) ground turmeric	

1 Heat the oil in a flameproof casserole, add the bay leaves, cardamom and cinnamon and fry over a moderate heat for 1–2 minutes. Add the onion and green pepper (if using), with the spices and salt and pepper to taste. Pour in enough water to moisten, then stir to mix for 1 minute.

2 Add the cashews and turkey, cover and simmer for 20 minutes. Turn the turkey occasionally during this time to ensure even cooking.

3 Add the potatoes and tomatoes and continue cooking for a further 20 minutes or until the turkey and potatoes are tender. Taste and adjust the seasoning before serving. Garnish with bay leaves.

TURKEY TETRAZZINI

SERVES 6

225 g (8 oz) spaghetti	1.25 ml (¼ tsp) grated nutmeg
75 g (3 oz) butter or margarine	salt and pepper
45 ml (3 tbsp) plain flour	100 g (4 oz) button mushrooms, sliced
300 ml (½ pint) hot turkey or chicken stock	350–450 g (12–16 oz) cooked turkey, sliced or cut into bite-sized pieces
100 ml (4 fl oz) double cream	30 ml (2 tbsp) grated Parmesan cheese
45 ml (3 tbsp) dry sherry	

1 Cook the spaghetti in boiling salted water for about 11 minutes or until just tender.

2 Meanwhile, make the sauce. Melt half the butter or margarine in a heavy-based saucepan, sprinkle in the flour and stir over gentle heat for 1–2 minutes. Gradually stir in the hot stock, then bring to the boil. Simmer, stirring all the time, until thick and smooth.

3 Remove the sauce from the heat and leave to cool for about 5 minutes, then stir in the cream, sherry and nutmeg. Season to taste.

4 Melt the remaining butter or margarine in a separate pan. Add the mushrooms and fry gently until soft.

5 Drain the spaghetti and arrange half of it in the base of a greased baking dish.

6 Arrange the turkey and mushrooms over the top. Cover with the remaining spaghetti, then coat with the sauce.

7 Sprinkle with the Parmesan and bake in a preheated oven at 190°C (375°F) mark 5 for 30 minutes or until golden and bubbling.

STUFFED TURKEY LEGS

SERVES 6

2 turkey legs (drumsticks) (at least 900 g/2 lb total weight)	25 g (1 oz) plain flour
225 g (8 oz) pork sausagemeat	1 egg white, beaten
15 ml (1 tbsp) chopped fresh tarragon or 2.5 ml (½ tsp) dried	175 g (6 oz) fresh white breadcrumbs
10 ml (2 tsp) chopped parsley	100 g (4 oz) butter or margarine, softened
salt and pepper	15 ml (1 tbsp) French mustard
50 g (2 oz) button mushrooms, sliced	watercress, to garnish

1 Skin the turkey legs, slit the flesh and carefully ease out the bone and large sinews.

2 Mix the sausagemeat and herbs, season to taste and spread one quarter of the mixture over each boned leg. Cover with a layer of sliced mushrooms, then top with more sausagemeat stuffing.

3 Reshape the stuffed turkey legs, then sew them up neatly, using fine string.

4 Dip the legs in flour, brush with beaten egg white and place, seam side down, in a greased roasting tin.

5 Beat together the breadcrumbs, butter or margarine and mustard. Spread over the tops and sides only of the legs.

6 Bake in a preheated oven at 190°C (375°F) mark 5 for about 1 hour 40 minutes or until the turkey is tender with a crisp, golden crust. Remove the string, slice, and serve garnished with watercress.

TURKEY BALLS WITH CRANBERRY AND ORANGE SAUCE

SERVES 4

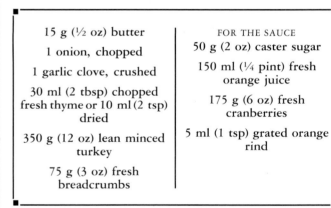

	FOR THE SAUCE
15 g (½ oz) butter	50 g (2 oz) caster sugar
1 onion, chopped	150 ml (¼ pint) fresh orange juice
1 garlic clove, crushed	175 g (6 oz) fresh cranberries
30 ml (2 tbsp) chopped fresh thyme or 10 ml (2 tsp) dried	5 ml (1 tsp) grated orange rind
350 g (12 oz) lean minced turkey	
75 g (3 oz) fresh breadcrumbs	

1 Melt the butter in a small saucepan. Add the onion, garlic and thyme and sauté for 3–5 minutes, then leave to cool.

2 Place the turkey and breadcrumbs in a medium bowl, add the onion mixture and mix thoroughly.

3 Divide the mixture into walnut-sized balls and place on a lightly greased baking sheet. Bake in a preheated oven at 200°C (400°F) mark 6 for 30–40 minutes or until cooked through.

4 Meanwhile, to make the sauce, place the sugar and fresh orange juice in a medium saucepan and heat gently, stirring, until the sugar has dissolved. Add the cranberries and grated orange rind and bring to the boil. Cover and simmer for 5–10 minutes or until the cranberries have softened. Serve with the turkey balls.

TURKEY AND BACON KEBABS

SERVES 4

30 ml (2 tbsp) cranberry sauce	salt and pepper
90 ml (6 tbsp) vegetable oil	700 g (1½ lb) boneless turkey escalopes
45 ml (3 tbsp) fresh orange juice	1 small onion
1 garlic clove, crushed	6 streaky bacon rashers, halved
2.5 ml (½ tsp) ground allspice	1 large red pepper, cut into chunks

1 Put the cranberry sauce, oil and orange juice in a shallow dish with the garlic, allspice and seasoning to taste. Whisk with a fork until well combined.

2 Cut the turkey into bite-sized pieces and place in the dish. Stir to coat in the oil and orange juice mixture, then cover and leave to marinate for at least 4 hours, stirring occasionally.

3 Cut the onion into squares or even-sized chunks. Form the bacon rashers into small rolls. Drain the turkey from the marinade, reserving the marinade.

4 Thread the turkey, onion and red pepper on to oiled skewers with the bacon, dividing the ingredients as evenly as possible.

5 Cook under a preheated moderate grill for about 20 minutes, turning the skewers frequently and basting with the remaining marinade. Serve hot.

─────────── COOK'S TIP ───────────

Don't be tempted to reduce the marinating time suggested above as the longer the turkey is marinated the more tender and succulent it will be. If marinating in the refrigerator overnight, allow the turkey to come to room temperature before grilling.

MARINATED TURKEY WITH ASPARAGUS

SERVES 4–6

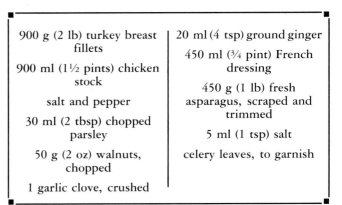

900 g (2 lb) turkey breast fillets	20 ml (4 tsp) ground ginger
900 ml (1½ pints) chicken stock	450 ml (¾ pint) French dressing
salt and pepper	450 g (1 lb) fresh asparagus, scraped and trimmed
30 ml (2 tbsp) chopped parsley	5 ml (1 tsp) salt
50 g (2 oz) walnuts, chopped	celery leaves, to garnish
1 garlic clove, crushed	

1 Put the turkey fillets in a large saucepan and add enough chicken stock to cover. Season to taste. Poach for about 20 minutes or until tender. Leave to cool in the liquid.

2 Meanwhile, to make the marinade, stir the parsley, walnuts, garlic and ginger into the French dressing.

3 Tie the asparagus stalks into two neat bundles. Wedge upright in a large deep saucepan and cover the tips with foil.

4 Pour in enough boiling water to come three-quarters of the way up the asparagus stalks. Add salt, return to the boil and simmer gently for about 10 minutes.

5 Lift the bundles carefully out of the water, place in a dish and remove the string. Whilst still hot, pour over half the dressing. Leave the asparagus to cool.

6 Cut the turkey into 0.5 cm (¼ inch) wide strips. Marinate in the remaining dressing for 3–4 hours.

7 To serve, arrange the turkey strips and asparagus in a serving dish and garnish with celery leaves. Serve chilled.

DUCKLING WITH GREEN PEAS

SERVES 4

2 kg (4½ lb) oven-ready duckling	450 g (1 lb) fresh or frozen peas
salt and pepper	few sprigs of fresh herbs, such as savory, thyme or mint
16 pickling or small onions, chopped	
50 g (2 oz) smoked streaky bacon, diced	60 ml (4 tbsp) chicken stock

1 Weigh the duckling, prick the skin all over with a sharp skewer or fork and rub with salt. Place the duckling on a wire rack or trivet in a roasting tin and roast in a preheated oven at 180°C (350°F) mark 4 for 30–35 minutes per 450 g (1 lb).
2 Thirty minutes before the end of the cooking time, drain off the fat from the roasting tin, transferring 30 ml (2 tbsp) of it to a saucepan, and discarding the remainder. Add the onions to the pan and cook, turning frequently, until lightly browned. Add the bacon and cook for 2 minutes or until the fat starts to run.
3 If using fresh peas, blanch them for 3 minutes in boiling water, then refresh and drain well. Do not blanch frozen peas. Mix the peas with the onions, bacon and herbs and season to taste with pepper.
4 Stir the stock into the sediment in the roasting tin, then stir in the pea mixture. Return the duckling to the roasting tin, still on the rack, and continue cooking for the remaining 30 minutes. Serve the duckling on a larger platter surrounded by the vegetables and cooking juice.

ROAST DUCK WITH APPLE STUFFING

SERVES 4

15 g (½ oz) butter	salt and pepper
1 celery stick, finely chopped	1 egg, beaten
2 small onions, chopped	1.8 kg (4 lb) oven-ready duck (with separate giblets)
100 g (4 oz) fresh white breadcrumbs	1 bay leaf
1 small eating apple, peeled, cored and grated	15 ml (1 tbsp) plain flour
15 ml (1 tbsp) chopped fresh sage or 5 ml (1 tsp) dried	watercress, to garnish

1 Melt the butter in a saucepan, add the celery and half the chopped onions and fry gently for about 5 minutes.
2 Mix the breadcrumbs, apple, sage, celery and onion. Season, then bind with egg. Cool for 15 minutes.
3 Stuff the neck cavity of the duck with the apple stuffing, then sew or truss the duck to keep in the stuffing.
4 Weigh the stuffed duck and calculate the cooking time, allowing 30–35 minutes per 450 g (1 lb). Put the duck on a wire rack in a roasting tin. Prick the skin of the duck all over and sprinkle with salt and pepper. Roast at 180°C (350°F) mark 4 for the calculated time.
5 To make the gravy, put the giblets in a saucepan with the remaining onion, 600 ml (1 pint) water, the bay leaf and seasoning. Simmer for 1 hour, then strain.
6 When the duck is cooked, remove from the tin and keep warm. Pour off any excess fat from the tin, leaving about 30 ml (2 tbsp). Transfer to the hob and blend in the flour. Cook until browned, stirring continuously. Stir in the stock and boil, stirring. Taste and season.
7 To serve, joint the duck into four portions and arrange on a warmed dish. Pour gravy round, garnish and serve.

DUCKLING ROULADES WITH PEACHES

SERVES 6

six 350 g (12 oz) duckling wing portions, skinned	25 g (1 oz) chopped hazelnuts
slices of onion and carrot	2 firm, ripe peaches, skinned and chopped
1 bay leaf	30 ml (2 tbsp) brandy
salt and pepper	50 g (2 oz) fresh wholemeal breadcrumbs
65 g (2½ oz) butter	
1 small onion, finely chopped	30 ml (2 tbsp) plain flour

1 Carefully fillet the duckling flesh in one piece away from the breastbone. Place the breast meat between two sheets of dampened greaseproof paper and beat out thinly. Cut any meat off the wings, chop finely and set aside.
2 To make the stock, place the wing bones in a saucepan together with the slices of onion and carrot, the bay leaf and seasoning. Just cover with water and bring to the boil. Simmer, uncovered, for 30–40 minutes or until about 300 ml (½ pint) stock remains. Strain the stock.
3 To make the stuffing, melt 25 g (1 oz) butter in a frying pan and fry the onion, chopped duckling flesh and hazelnuts for 3–4 minutes, turning frequently. Stir in the peaches and fry until soft. Remove from the heat, stir in the brandy, breadcrumbs and seasoning, and cool.
4 Divide the stuffing between the duckling fillets and roll up tightly. Secure with wooden cocktail sticks, then sprinkle with flour.
5 Melt the remaining butter in a large flameproof casserole and cook the duckling rolls until lightly browned. Sprinkle in any remaining flour, then pour in 300 ml (½ pint) stock. Season to taste. Bring to the boil, cover and bake in the oven at 180°C (350°F) mark 4 for 40 minutes. Adjust the seasoning and skim before serving.

DUCKLING WITH BRANDY AND GREEN PEPPERCORN SAUCE

SERVES 6

6 duckling portions	30 ml (2 tbsp) plain flour
salt and pepper	300 ml (½ pint) chicken stock
3 large oranges	
45 ml (3 tbsp) vegetable oil	30 ml (2 tbsp) brandy
1 onion, chopped	a dash of gravy browning
30 ml (2 tbsp) green peppercorns, lightly crushed	

1 Wipe the duckling portions all over and pat dry with absorbent kitchen paper. Place on a rack in a roasting tin.
2 Prick the skin well with a fork and sprinkle with salt. Roast in a preheated oven at 180°C (350°F) mark 4 for about 1 hour or until the juices run clear, basting occasionally.
3 Meanwhile, to make the sauce, remove the rind from one orange and cut it into fine shreds. Blanch in boiling water for 1 minute, then drain. Squeeze the juice from the orange and reserve. Thinly slice the remaining oranges.
4 Heat the oil in a medium saucepan, add the chopped onion and fry gently until golden.
5 Stir in the lightly crushed peppercorns and flour and cook gently, stirring, for 1–2 minutes. Blend in the stock with the orange juice. Season to taste and bring to the boil, stirring all the time, then simmer for about 4 minutes.
6 Warm the brandy slightly in a small saucepan, ignite and, when the flames die down, add to the sauce with a dash of gravy browning and a few orange shreds. Adjust the seasoning.
7 Heat the sauce to boiling point and pour into a warmed sauceboat. Garnish the duck portions with orange slices and the remaining orange shreds.

DUCK WITH CUMBERLAND SAUCE

SERVES 4

4 duckling portions	60 ml (4 tbsp) redcurrant jelly
salt and pepper	10 ml (2 tsp) cornflour
finely shredded rind and juice of 1 large orange	60 ml (4 tbsp) port
finely shredded rind and juice of 1 lemon	30 ml (2 tbsp) brandy
	lemon balm sprigs, to garnish

1 Prick the duckling portions all over with a sharp skewer or fork, then sprinkle with salt and pepper.
2 Place the duckling portions on a wire rack in a roasting tin and roast in a preheated oven at 190°C (375°F) mark 5 for 45–60 minutes or until the skin is crisp and the juices run clear when the thickest parts of the duckling portions are pricked with a skewer.
3 Meanwhile, to make the sauce, put the orange and lemon juices in a small saucepan, add the shreds of orange and lemon rind, cover and simmer gently for 5 minutes.
4 Add the redcurrant jelly to the citrus juices and let it melt slowly over a gentle heat. Mix the cornflour with the port, then stir into the sauce and bring to the boil, stirring, until the sauce thickens.
5 When the duckling portions are cooked, put them on a warmed serving dish and keep hot while you finish the sauce. Pour off the fat from the roasting tin, leaving the cooking juices behind. Add the brandy and stir over a gentle heat, scraping up the sediment from the bottom of the tin.
6 Add the sauce to the brandy, stir well and serve with the duckling. Garnish with lemon balm.

DUCK JULIENNE EN CROÛTE

SERVES 4

25 g (1 oz) butter	175 g (6 oz) carrots, peeled
2 garlic cloves, crushed	2 courgettes
30 ml (2 tbsp) chopped fresh parsley or 10 ml (2 tsp) dried	450 g (1 lb) frozen puff pastry, thawed
four 200 g (7 oz) duck breasts, boned and skinned	salt and pepper
	1 egg, beaten

1 Melt the butter in a large frying pan, add the garlic and parsley and fry for 2 minutes. Add the duck breasts and fry until browned. Drain and cool.
2 Cut the carrots and courgettes into thin 5 cm (2 inch) strips. Blanch in boiling water for 1–2 minutes, then drain and rinse under cold running water.
3 Roll out one third of the pastry to a 40.5 x 15 cm (16 x 6 inch) rectangle. Divide into four 10 x 15 cm (4 x 6 inch) bases and place on a lightly greased baking sheet. Roll the remaining two thirds to a 51 x 15 cm (20 x 6 inch) rectangle. Divide into four 12.5 x 15 cm (5 x 6 inch) lids.
4 Divide the vegetables between the bases, leaving 0.5 cm (¼ inch) border. Place the duck breasts on the vegetables and season well. Brush the border with egg. Add the lids and seal.
5 Brush with beaten egg and bake in a preheated oven at 200°C (400°F) mark 6 for 45–55 minutes.

─────── **TO MICROWAVE** ───────

Complete step 1. Cut the carrots and courgettes into thin 5 cm (2 inch) strips. Place in a medium bowl and cover with boiling water. Cook on HIGH for 1–1½ minutes, drain and rinse under cold running water. Complete steps 3–5.

DUCK WITH MANGO

SERVES 4

1 ripe, but still firm mango	2.5 ml (½ tsp) ground allspice
four 275 g (10 oz) duck portions	45 ml (3 tbsp) plum jam
60 ml (4 tbsp) peanut oil	20 ml (4 tsp) wine vinegar
	salt and pepper

1 Skin and thickly slice the mango on either side of the large central stone.

2 Remove any excess fat from the duck portions. Divide each portion into three and place in a saucepan. Cover with cold water and bring to the boil. Lower the heat and simmer gently for 15–20 minutes. Drain well and pat dry with absorbent kitchen paper. Trim the bones.

3 Heat the oil in a wok or large frying pan until hot and smoking. Add the duck pieces and allspice and cook until well browned on all sides.

4 Stir in the jam and vinegar. Cook for a further 2–3 minutes, stirring constantly, until well glazed. Stir in the mango slices and season to taste. Heat through, then turn into a warmed serving dish and serve immediately.

VARIATION

Tropical Duck

Other tropical fruits could be used instead of the mango in the above recipe. Try guava, papaya or lychees.

SWEET AND SOUR DUCK JOINTS

SERVES 4

4 duck portions	30 ml (2 tbsp) dry sherry
salt and pepper	juice of 1 orange
60 ml (4 tbsp) soy sauce	2.5 ml (½ tsp) ground ginger
45 ml (3 tbsp) soft brown sugar	a few orange slices and watercress sprigs, to garnish
45 ml (3 tbsp) honey	
45 ml (3 tbsp) wine or cider vinegar	

1 Prick the duck portions all over with a fork, then sprinkle the skin liberally with salt and pepper.

2 Place on a rack in a roasting tin and roast in a preheated oven at 190°C (375°F) mark 5 for 45–60 minutes or until the skin is crisp and the juices run clear when the thickest part of each joint is pierced with a skewer.

3 Meanwhile, to make the sauce, mix together all the remaining ingredients in a saucepan, add 150 ml (¼ pint) water and bring to the boil. Simmer, stirring constantly, for about 5 minutes to allow the flavours to blend and the sauce to thicken slightly. Add salt and pepper to taste.

4 Trim the duck joints neatly by cutting off any knuckles or wing joints. Arrange the duck on a warmed serving platter and coat with some of the sauce. Garnish with orange and watercress.

RABBIT CASSEROLE WITH SAGE DUMPLINGS

SERVES 4

100 g (4 oz) bacon	600 ml (1 pint) chicken stock
4 rabbit portions	salt and pepper
4 celery sticks, chopped	75 g (3 oz) self-raising flour
2 leeks, sliced	40 g (1½ oz) shredded beef suet
1 bay leaf	
225 g (8 oz) carrots, sliced	5 ml (1 tsp) chopped fresh sage or 2.5 ml (½ tsp) dried
30 ml (2 tbsp) plain flour	

1 Using a sharp pair of kitchen scissors, snip the bacon into a flameproof casserole. Fry for 5 minutes or until the fat runs. Add the rabbit and fry gently, then add the celery, leeks, bay leaf and carrots.

2 Sprinkle over the plain flour and stir well, then gradually add the stock and bring to the boil, stirring. Season to taste.

3 Cover the casserole and cook in a preheated oven at 170°C (325°F) mark 3 for about 1½ hours or until the rabbit is tender.

4 To make the dumplings, combine the self-raising flour, shredded suet, sage and salt and pepper in a bowl. Stir in just enough water to mix to a soft dough.

5 Divide the dough into four portions, then shape evenly into balls and place on top of casserole. Re-cover and cook for 20–25 minutes or until the dumplings are well risen and cooked through.

RABBIT CASSEROLE WITH CIDER AND MUSTARD

SERVES 4

50 g (2oz) butter or margarine	25 g (1 oz) plain flour
100 g (4 oz) streaky bacon, diced	1 rabbit, jointed
12–18 small button onions, skinned	10 ml (2 tsp) French mustard
salt and pepper	300 ml (½ pint) dry cider
	450 ml (¾ pint) chicken stock

1 Melt the butter or margarine in a frying pan, add the bacon and onions and fry for 5 minutes or until lightly browned. Remove to a casserole with a slotted spoon.

2 Season the flour with salt and pepper, add the rabbit portions and turn until coated. Shake off and reserve any excess flour. Add the rabbit to the fat remaining in the pan and fry for about 8 minutes or until golden brown. Arrange in the casserole.

3 Stir the remaining flour and the French mustard into the pan. Gradually add the cider and stock, season to taste, then bring to the boil and pour over the rabbit.

4 Cover and cook in a preheated oven at 170°C (325°F) mark 3 for about 2 hours or until the rabbit is tender. Adjust the seasoning before serving.

─── **COOK'S TIP** ───

Small button onions can be very fiddly to skin. Soak them in boiling water for 1–2 minutes first, then the skins should slip off easily. Leave the root ends intact so the onions stay whole during cooking.

GAME PIE

SERVES 4–6

450 g (1 lb) boned game (pigeon, venison, partridge, hare or pheasant)	45 ml (3 tbsp) vegetable oil
30 ml (2 tbsp) plain flour	300 ml (½ pint) red wine
10 ml (2 tsp) dried thyme	6 juniper berries, lightly crushed
2.5 ml (½ tsp) ground cinnamon	350 g (12 oz) pork sausagemeat
salt and pepper	225 g (8 oz) packet frozen puff pastry, thawed
	1 egg, beaten, to glaze

1 Cut the meat into even-sized cubes. Mix the flour with the thyme, cinnamon and seasoning, add the meat and toss until coated.

2 Heat the oil in a flameproof casserole, add the meat and fry over a moderate heat for 5 minutes or until browned on all sides. Pour in the wine, add the juniper berries, then cover and simmer gently for 1–1½ hours or until tender. Leave until cold, preferably overnight.

3 Put half the sausagemeat in the bottom of an ovenproof pie dish. Put the game mixture on top, then cover with the remaining sausagemeat and level the surface.

4 Roll out the pastry on a lightly floured surface to 5 cm, (2 inches) wider than the pie dish. Cut a 2.5 cm (1 inch) strip from the outer edge and use to line the dampened rim of the dish.

5 Moisten the strip of dough, then place the pastry lid on top and press to seal. Knock up and flute the edge. Use pastry trimmings to decorate.

6 Brush the pastry with beaten egg, then bake in a preheated oven at 200°C (400°F) mark 6 for 30 minutes or until the pastry is golden brown and crisp. Leave to stand for 15 minutes before serving, or serve cold.

ROAST PHEASANT WITH HERBY FORCEMEAT BALLS

SERVES 4

2 young oven-ready pheasants	finely grated rind of ½ lemon
150 g (5 oz) butter	25 g (1 oz) shredded beef suet
10 ml (2 tsp) dried thyme	15 ml (1 tbsp) chopped fresh parsley
salt and pepper	15 ml (1 tbsp) chopped fresh lemon thyme or 10 ml (2 tsp) dried
4 rashers of smoked streaky bacon	
450 ml (¾ pint) giblet or chicken stock	15 ml (1 tbsp) chopped sage
225 g (8 oz) pork sausagemeat	1 onion, finely chopped
50 g (2 oz) fresh white breadcrumbs	1 egg, beaten

1 Wash the insides of the pheasants, then dry. Put 15 g (½ oz) butter and 5 ml (1 tsp) thyme inside each bird. Season the birds inside, then truss.

2 Spread the breast of each bird with 25 g (1 oz) softened butter and sprinkle with salt and pepper. Use two bacon rashers to cover each pheasant breast. Stand the pheasants on a rack in a roasting tin, then pour in the stock. Roast at 200°C (400°F) mark 6 for 25 minutes.

3 Mix the sausagemeat, breadcrumbs, lemon rind, suet and herbs together.

4 Melt 50 g (2 oz) butter in a small pan, add the onion and fry gently for 5 minutes or until soft. Mix into the sausagemeat, season, then bind with beaten egg. Form into small balls.

5 Remove the bacon rashers, roll them up and pierce them on to small metal skewers. Arrange on the rack around the pheasants, together with the forcemeat balls.

6 Return to the oven and roast for a further 20 minutes or until the pheasants are tender. Serve hot.

PHEASANT BREASTS WITH VERMOUTH

SERVES 4

1 brace of pheasants	150 ml (¼ pint) chicken stock
salt and pepper	
30 ml (2 tbsp) plain flour	30 ml (2 tbsp) chopped fresh sage or 5 ml (1 tsp) dried
30 ml (2 tbsp) vegetable oil	
50 g (2 oz) onion, finely chopped	30 ml (2 tbsp) single cream
	175 g (6 oz) green grapes, halved and seeded, if necessary
150 ml (¼ pint) dry vermouth	
	sage leaves, to garnish

1 Using a sharp knife, cut all the breast flesh off the bone of each pheasant, keeping each fillet in one piece. You will have four breast fillets, two from each bird. (Use the legs and carcass for a casserole.) Ease off the skin of the fillets, and trim away any fat.

2 Season the flour with salt and pepper, add the breast fillets and turn until coated. Shake off and reserve any excess flour. Heat the oil in a medium sauté pan, add the pheasant and fry until well browned. Remove from the pan with a slotted spoon.

3 Add the onion and any remaining flour to the fat remaining in the pan and cook, stirring, for 1–2 minutes. Blend in the vermouth, stock, sage and seasoning. Bring to the boil, stirring, then return the pheasant to the pan.

4 Cover tightly and simmer for about 30 minutes, turning once. Lift the pheasant out of the juices and place on a warmed serving dish. Cover and keep warm.

5 Stir the cream and grapes into the juices and simmer for 1 minute. Adjust the seasoning. Spoon over the pheasant and garnish with sage leaves.

PHEASANT WITH CHESTNUTS

SERVES 4

25 g (1 oz) butter	450 ml (¾ pint) chicken stock
15 ml (1 tbsp) vegetable oil	
2 oven-ready pheasants, jointed	150 ml (¼ pint) dry red wine
	salt and pepper
2 medium onions, sliced	
225 g (8 oz) peeled chestnuts	juice and grated rind of ½ orange
	10 ml (2 tsp) redcurrant jelly
45 ml (3 tbsp) plain wholemeal flour	
	bouquet garni

1 Heat the butter and oil in a large frying pan, add the pheasant joints and fry for about 5 minutes or until browned. Remove from the pan and put into an ovenproof casserole.

2 Add the onions and chestnuts to the oil and butter remaining in the pan and fry for a few minutes or until brown, then add to the pheasant.

3 Stir the flour into the fat remaining in the pan and cook, stirring, for 2–3 minutes. Remove from the heat and gradually stir in the stock and wine. Bring to the boil, stirring continuously, until thickened and smooth. Season to taste and pour over the pheasant in the casserole. Add the orange juice and rind, redcurrant jelly and bouquet garni.

4 Cover the casserole and cook in a preheated oven at 180°C (350°F) mark 4 for about 1 hour or until the pheasant is tender. Remove the bouquet garni.

PHEASANT AU PORTO

SERVES 6

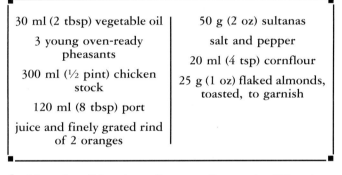

30 ml (2 tbsp) vegetable oil	50 g (2 oz) sultanas
3 young oven-ready pheasants	salt and pepper
300 ml (½ pint) chicken stock	20 ml (4 tsp) cornflour
120 ml (8 tbsp) port	25 g (1 oz) flaked almonds, toasted, to garnish
juice and finely grated rind of 2 oranges	

1 Heat the oil in a large flameproof casserole. When hot, add the pheasants and cook, turning, until brown all over.
2 Pour the stock and port over the birds. Add the orange juice and rind with the sultanas and season well. Bring to the boil. Cover tightly and cook in a preheated oven at 170°C (325°F) mark 3 for 1–1½ hours.
3 Remove the pheasants from the casserole, then joint each into two or three pieces, depending on size, and arrange on a warmed serving dish. Keep warm.
4 Mix the cornflour to a smooth paste with a little water, stir into the juices in the casserole and bring to the boil, stirring. Adjust the seasoning and spoon over the pheasant. Garnish with toasted flaked almonds.

ROAST GOOSE WITH APPLES AND PRUNES

SERVES 8

4–5 kg (9–11 lb) oven-ready goose, with separate giblets	15 ml (1 tbsp) chopped fresh sage or 5 ml (1 tsp) dried
salt and pepper	100 g (4 oz) fresh wholemeal breadcrumbs
15 g (½ oz) butter	6 Cox's Orange Pippin apples
1 large onion, chopped	
450 g (1 lb) no-soak prunes	300 ml (½ pint) dry white wine
60 ml (4 tbsp) port	

1 Prick the skin of the goose all over with a sharp skewer. Pull the inside fat out and reserve. Rub salt over the skin.
2 To make the stuffing, melt the butter in a large frying pan, add the onion and cook for 5–6 minutes or until softened. Separate the goose liver from the giblets and chop, then add to the onion and cook for 2–3 minutes.
3 Remove the stones from half of the prunes and discard. Chop the prunes roughly and stir into the onion with the port. Cover and simmer gently for 5 minutes. Add the sage and breadcrumbs and mix thoroughly together. Season.
4 Spoon the stuffing into the neck end of the goose, then truss with strong cotton or fine string. Weigh the bird.
5 Put the goose on a wire rack in a roasting tin. Cover the breast with the reserved fat and then with foil. Roast in a preheated oven at 200°C (400°F) mark 6 for 15 minutes per 450 g (1 lb) plus 15 minutes, basting frequently.
6 Thirty minutes before the end of the cooking time, drain the fat from the roasting tin and discard. Core the apples and cut into eighths, then add to the tin with the remaining prunes and wine. Remove the foil and goose fat and cook, uncovered, for the last 30 minutes.
7 Serve with the cooking juices and fruit.

CASSEROLED PIGEONS WITH CIDER AND APPLE

SERVES 4

3 medium carrots	sprig of thyme
3 celery sticks	1 bay leaf
4 small eating apples	pinch of cayenne
salt and pepper	pinch of grated nutmeg
4 oven-ready pigeons	20 ml (4 tsp) redcurrant jelly
45 ml (3 tbsp) vegetable oil	Worcestershire sauce (optional)
40 g (1½ oz) butter	watercress sprigs, to garnish
1 medium onion, chopped	
450 ml (¾ pint) dry cider	
150 ml (¼ pint) chicken stock	

1 Roughly chop one carrot and one celery stick. Peel, core and chop two apples. Season the pigeons and brown in 30 ml (2 tbsp) oil and 25 g (1 oz) butter.
2 Fry the chopped onion, carrot, celery and apples. Transfer to a casserole and add the pigeons. Pour the cider and stock into a pan and bring to the boil. Add to the casserole with the herbs and spices. Cover and cook at 150°C (300°F) mark 2 for 1½–2 hours or until tender.
3 Meanwhile, cut the remaining apples in half crossways and scoop out the centres. Place a little redcurrant jelly in the centre of each and place on a greased baking tray. Bake the apples for about 20 minutes or until tender.
4 Cut the remaining carrots and celery into julienne strips and fry in the remaining oil and butter until soft.
5 When the pigeons are cooked, remove them from the casserole and keep warm. Strain the juices into a saucepan and cook until syrupy. Season to taste and add a dash of Worcestershire sauce if the sauce is too sweet.
6 Serve the pigeons on a pool of the sauce and garnish.

VENISON ESCALOPES WITH RED WINE

SERVES 6

six 175 g (6 oz) escalopes of venison cut from the haunch (leg)	300 ml (½ pint) dry red wine
1 small onion, finely chopped	15 g (½ oz) butter
1 bay leaf	15 ml (1 tbsp) vegetable oil
2 parsley sprigs	30 ml (2 tbsp) redcurrant jelly
8 juniper berries	salt and pepper

1 Put the escalopes in a large shallow dish and sprinkle with the onion, bay leaf, parsley and juniper berries. Pour on the wine, cover and marinate in the refrigerator for 3–4 hours or overnight, turning the escalopes occasionally.
2 Remove the escalopes from the marinade, reserving the marinade. Heat the butter and oil in a large frying pan, add the escalopes and fry for 3–4 minutes on each side. Transfer to a warmed serving dish and keep warm while making the sauce.
3 Strain the reserved marinade into the frying pan and stir to loosen any sediment. Increase the heat and boil rapidly for 3–4 minutes or until reduced. Stir in the redcurrant jelly and season to taste. Cook for 1–2 minutes, stirring, then pour over the escalopes. Serve immediately.

COOK'S TIP

You can buy venison from any butcher with a game licence. Young venison is usually tender enough not to need hanging, but older, tougher animals will benefit from it. Your butcher can advise on this.

FISH AND SHELLFISH

Fish is both nutritious and flavoursome and can be cooked in a wonderful variety of ways. Shellfish always adds a touch of luxury, whether cooked on its own or used to add variety to a Gratin of Seafood or a champagne sauce to serve with pasta.

COD WITH CORIANDER IN CREAM

SERVES 4

450 g (1 lb) thick-cut cod fillet	15–30 ml (1–2 tbsp) lemon juice
30 ml (2 tbsp) plain flour	15 ml (1 tbsp) capers
10 ml (2 tsp) ground coriander	1 egg yolk
salt and pepper	90 ml (6 tbsp) single cream
50 g (2 oz) butter	

1 Skin the fish and divide into four portions. Mix the flour, coriander and seasoning and use to coat the fish.
2 Heat the butter in a medium sauté pan, add the fish pieces and sauté gently until golden, turning only once.
3 Add 15 ml (1 tbsp) lemon juice to the pan with the capers, cover tightly and continue cooking for a further 4–5 minutes. Place the fish on a warmed serving dish.
4 Mix the egg yolk and cream together, stir into the pan juices and heat gently, without boiling, until the sauce thickens. Adjust the seasoning and spoon over the fish.

TANDOORI COD

SERVES 4

four 200 g (7 oz) cod fillets	15 ml (1 tbsp) chopped fresh coriander or 5 ml (1 tsp) ground coriander
60 ml (4 tbsp) natural yogurt	
30 ml (2 tbsp) lemon juice	15 ml (1 tbsp) vegetable oil
15 ml (1 tbsp) tandoori paste	coriander sprigs, to garnish

1 Place the fish fillets in a shallow dish. Mix all the remaining ingredients, except the garnish.
2 Spread the yogurt mixture evenly over the fish, turning the fillets to ensure they are evenly coated. Cover and refrigerate for 8 hours or overnight.
3 Cover the grill pan with foil and add the fillets, leaving any excess marinade in the dish.
4 Cook the fillets under a preheated grill for 5–7 minutes, basting them with the remaining marinade. Turn over and grill for a further 5 minutes or until the fish is firm and flakes easily, basting frequently. Transfer the fillets to a warmed serving dish and garnish with coriander sprigs.

COD IN CREAM AND CELERY SAUCE

SERVES 4

HADDOCK AU GRATIN

SERVES 6

4 cod steaks or cutlets	75 ml (2½ fl oz) double cream
15 ml (1 tbsp) lemon juice	
salt and pepper	2.5 ml (½ tsp) dried thyme
25 g (1 oz) butter	50 g (2 oz) Lancashire cheese, crumbled
3 celery sticks, chopped	
25 g (1 oz) plain flour	2 tomatoes, sliced
225 ml (8 fl oz) milk	parsley, to garnish

1 Sprinkle the fish with lemon juice and season to taste. Cook under a preheated grill or bake in a preheated oven at 200°C (400°F) mark 6 for 20 minutes. Place in a warmed, shallow, heatproof serving dish and keep warm.

2 Melt the butter in a saucepan, add the celery and fry for about 10 minutes or until tender. Stir in the flour and cook gently for 1 minute, stirring. Remove the pan from the heat and gradually stir in the milk and cream. Bring slowly to the boil and simmer gently, stirring constantly, until the sauce thickens.

3 Season the sauce to taste, then add the thyme and 25 g (1 oz) cheese. Pour the sauce over the fish and sprinkle with the remaining cheese.

4 Arrange the tomatoes on the dish and place under the grill to brown. Serve hot, garnished with parsley.

─────────── VARIATION ───────────

Haddock in Cream and Leek Sauce
Substitute haddock for the cod in the above recipe and use 1 large leek instead of the celery. Any other white fish would also be suitable.

175 g (6 oz) fresh haddock fillet	50 g (2 oz) butter
175 g (6 oz) smoked haddock fillet	100 g (4 oz) button mushrooms, sliced
60 ml (4 tbsp) dry white wine	30 ml (2 tbsp) plain flour
	pepper
6 peppercorns	50 g (2 oz) Red Leicester cheese, grated
1 bay leaf	
1 small onion, sliced	25 g (1 oz) fresh breadcrumbs

1 Place the fresh and smoked fish in a saucepan with 300 ml (½ pint) water and the wine. Add the peppercorns, bay leaf and onion and bring to the boil. Cover and poach gently for about 15 minutes.

2 Strain off the liquid and reserve. Flake the fish, discarding skin and bones. Discard the flavouring ingredients.

3 Melt the butter in a saucepan, add the mushrooms and sauté for 2 minutes. Stir in the flour and cook gently for 1 minute, stirring. Remove the pan from the heat and gradually stir in the strained cooking liquid. Bring to the boil and continue to cook, stirring, until the sauce thickens. Add the fish, half the grated cheese and season to taste with pepper.

4 Spoon the mixture into six individual soufflé dishes. Top with the remaining cheese and the breadcrumbs.

5 Bake in a preheated oven at 220°C (425°F) mark 7 for about 15 minutes or until golden brown. Serve hot.

HADDOCK AND CARAWAY CHEESE SOUFFLÉ

SERVES 4

450 g (1 lb) floury potatoes	25 g (1 oz) plain flour
450 g (1 lb) fresh haddock fillets	2.5 ml (½ tsp) caraway seeds
100 g (4 oz) button mushrooms, thinly sliced	100 g (4 oz) mature Cheddar cheese, grated
300 ml (½ pint) milk	2 eggs, separated
1 bay leaf	salt and pepper
25 g (1 oz) butter	

1 Scrub the potatoes, then cook in boiling salted water for about 15 minutes or until tender. Drain and peel, then mash three-quarters of the potatoes. Grate the remaining quarter into a bowl and set aside.

2 Meanwhile, place the haddock, mushrooms, milk and bay leaf in a small saucepan. Cover and poach for 15–20 minutes or until tender. Drain, reserving the milk and mushrooms. Flake the fish, discarding the skin and bay leaf.

3 To make the sauce, melt the butter in a saucepan, stir in the flour and cook gently for 1 minute, stirring. Remove from the heat, add the caraway seeds and gradually stir in the milk. Bring to the boil, stirring, and simmer for 2–3 minutes or until thickened and smooth.

4 Stir the mashed potato into the sauce with 75 g (3 oz) cheese, the egg yolks, fish and mushrooms. Season well.

5 Stiffly whisk the egg whites and fold into the fish. Turn into a buttered 1.6 litre (2¾ pint) soufflé dish.

6 Sprinkle over the reserved grated potato and remaining grated cheese. Bake in a preheated oven at 190°C (375°F) mark 5 for about 1 hour or until just set and golden brown.

CREAMY COD BAKE

SERVES 4

454 g (1 lb) packet frozen leaf spinach	FOR THE CHEESE SAUCE
50 g (2 oz) butter or margarine	25 g (1 oz) butter or margarine
4 frozen cod steaks	25 g (1 oz) plain flour
2.5 ml (½ tsp) grated nutmeg	450 ml (¾ pint) milk
salt and pepper	100 g (4 oz) grated Cheddar cheese
100 g (4 oz) Cheddar cheese, grated	5 ml (1 tsp) mustard powder
two 25 g (0.88 oz) packets cheese and onion crisps, finely crushed	salt and pepper

1 To make the cheese sauce, melt the butter in a saucepan, add the flour and cook gently, stirring, for 2 minutes. Remove from the heat and blend in the milk. Bring to the boil and cook, stirring, until thick.

2 Simmer the sauce gently for 2–3 minutes, then add the cheese and stir until melted. Add the mustard and season.

3 Put the frozen spinach in a heavy-based saucepan and heat gently until thawed, adding a few spoonfuls of water if necessary to prevent the spinach sticking. Meanwhile, melt half the butter in a frying pan and fry the cod until golden.

4 Transfer the spinach to the base of an ovenproof dish and mix in the remaining butter or margarine with half the nutmeg and seasoning to taste. Arrange the steaks on top of the spinach and pour over any cooking juices.

5 Stir the remaining nutmeg into the cheese sauce, then pour the sauce evenly over the fish to cover it completely. Mix the grated cheese with the crisps and sprinkle over.

6 Bake in a preheated oven at 190°C (375°F) mark 5 for 30 minutes until golden brown and bubbling. Serve hot.

SPANISH COD WITH PEPPERS, TOMATOES AND GARLIC

SERVES 4

700 g (1½ lb) cod fillets	450 g (1 lb) tomatoes, skinned and chopped
1 litre (1¾ pints) mussels (about 450 g/1 lb)	300 ml (½ pint) white wine
30 ml (2 tbsp) vegetable oil	2.5 ml (½ tsp) Tabasco sauce
2 onions, sliced	1 bay leaf
1 red pepper, sliced	salt and pepper
1 green pepper, sliced	
1–2 garlic cloves, crushed	

1 Using a sharp knife, skin the cod and cut it into chunks.

2 Scrub the mussels, discarding any which are open. Place in a pan, cover and cook over a high heat for about 8 minutes or until the mussels have opened. Discard any that do not open.

3 Shell all but four of the mussels. Heat the oil in a frying pan and cook the onions, peppers and garlic for about 5 minutes or until starting to soften. Add the tomatoes and wine, bring to the boil and simmer for 5 minutes, then add the Tabasco.

4 Using a slotted spoon, remove the vegetables from the wine sauce and layer them with the fish chunks in a casserole. Add the bay leaf and seasoning and pour over the sauce. Push the four unshelled mussels into the top layer. Cover and cook in a preheated oven at 180°C (350°F) mark 4 for 1 hour.

COD IN A SPICY YOGURT CRUST

SERVES 4

30 ml (2 tbsp) chopped mint	10 ml (2 tsp) ground cumin
1 medium onion or 2 large spring onions, roughly chopped	10 ml (2 tsp) dried dill
	150 ml (5 fl oz) natural yogurt
2 garlic cloves, crushed	salt and pepper
5 ml (1 tsp) paprika	four 225 g (8 oz) thick cod steaks or fillets
30 ml (2 tbsp) coriander seeds	

1 First make the marinade mixture. Put the mint, onion, garlic, paprika, coriander, cumin, dill and yogurt in a blender or food processor and process until a thick paste is formed. Season the mixture to taste with salt and pepper.

2 Place the fish in a single layer in a shallow heatproof dish. Spread the paste all over the top of the fish and leave in a cool place to marinate for 2–3 hours.

3 Cook under a preheated hot grill, basting occasionally, until the fish is cooked and the yogurt mixture has formed a crust. Serve immediately.

─── **VARIATION** ───

Haddock in a Spicy Yogurt Crust
Substitute haddock for cod in the above recipe. Steaks or fillets are equally suitable.

HALIBUT CREOLE

SERVES 4

SOLE BONNE FEMME

SERVES 4

30 ml (2 tbsp) vegetable oil	1.25 ml (¼ tsp) Tabasco sauce
1 onion, chopped	
2 garlic cloves, crushed	30 ml (2 tbsp) chopped fresh parsley or 10 ml (2 tsp) dried
1 celery stick, chopped	
1 green pepper, chopped	salt and pepper
397 g (14 oz) can chopped tomatoes	butter, for greasing
	four 275–350 g (10–12 oz) halibut steaks
5 ml (1 tsp) brown sugar	

1 Heat the oil in a medium saucepan, add the onion and garlic and fry for 3 minutes. Add the celery and pepper and cook for 5 minutes or until softened.

2 Add the tomatoes, sugar, Tabasco and parsley and season to taste. Cook for 15–20 minutes or until the vegetables have softened and the sauce has thickened.

3 Butter a large shallow dish and lay the halibut steaks in it. Pour the creole sauce over the fish and cover with foil. Bake in a preheated oven at 200°C (400°F) mark 6 for 25–30 minutes or until the fish is firm and flakes easily.

4 Transfer the fish to a warmed serving platter and spoon the remaining sauce over the top.

TO MICROWAVE

Place the oil, onion and garlic in a medium bowl. Cover and cook on HIGH for 3 minutes. Add the celery, green pepper, tomatoes, sugar, Tabasco, parsley and seasoning. Cook, uncovered, on HIGH for 9–10 minutes. Arrange the fish in a buttered shallow dish and pour over the sauce. Cover and microwave on HIGH for 12–14 minutes or until the fish is firm and flakes easily. Complete step 4.

2 sole fillets	salt and pepper
2 shallots, or 2–3 slices of onion, finely chopped	1 bay leaf
	40 g (1½ oz) butter
100 g (4 oz) button mushrooms	30 ml (2 tbsp) plain flour
	about 150 ml (¼ pint) milk
45 ml (3 tbsp) dry white wine	45 ml (3 tbsp) single cream

1 Trim off the fins, wash and wipe the fillets and fold each into three. Put the shallots or onion in the bottom of an ovenproof dish with the stalks from the mushrooms, (finely chopped). Cover with the fish, pour round the wine and 15 ml (1 tbsp) water, season to taste and add the bay leaf.

2 Cover with foil or a lid and bake in a preheated oven at 180°C (350°F) mark 4 for about 15 minutes or until tender. Strain off the cooking liquid and keep the fish warm.

3 Melt half the butter in a frying pan, add the mushrooms and fry gently until just beginning to soften, then drain well.

4 Melt the remaining butter in a saucepan, stir in the flour and cook gently for 1 minute, stirring. Remove from the heat and gradually stir in the cooking liquid from the fish, made up to 300 ml (½ pint) with milk.

5 Bring to the boil and continue to cook, stirring, until the sauce thickens, then remove from the heat and stir in the cream. Pour the sauce over the fish and serve garnished with the mushroom caps.

SOLE 'STEWED' IN CREAM

SERVES 4

4 sole fillets, skinned and cut in half lengthways	FOR THE GARNISH
25 g (1 oz) butter	lobster coral or salmon eggs (optional)
15 ml (1 tbsp) finely chopped shallots	cooked crayfish or prawns (optional)
300 ml (½ pint) fish stock	puff pastry fleurons or bread croûtes
blade of mace	parsley sprigs
225 ml (8 fl oz) double cream	lemon twists
salt and white pepper	

1 Tie each strip of sole into a loose knot in the centre.

2 Melt half the butter in a large frying pan, add the shallot, cover and cook for about 5 minutes or until softened, shaking the pan occasionally. Stir in the stock and mace and boil rapidly until reduced to 50 ml (2 fl oz). Remove the mace.

3 Stir half the cream into the shallots and bring to the boil. Lower the heat, season lightly and gently lower the fish into the pan. Spoon cream over the fish. Cover with buttered greaseproof paper and poach gently for about 3 minutes, or until the fish just flakes.

4 Carefully transfer the fish to a warmed plate using a fish slice, cover and keep warm. Boil the cooking liquid until slightly thickened. Stir in the remaining butter and adjust the seasoning, if necessary.

5 Spoon the sauce over four warmed serving plates. Arrange the fish on top and garnish attractively.

MOUSSELINES OF SOLE WITH PRAWNS

SERVES 6

450 g (1 lb) sole fillets, skinned and chopped	3 egg yolks, beaten
50 g (2 oz) peeled prawns	75 g (3 oz) butter, softened
1 egg white	10 ml (2 tsp) lemon juice
1.25 ml (¼ tsp) salt	5 ml (1 tsp) tomato purée
1.25 ml (¼ tsp) white pepper	fresh dill sprigs and whole prawns in their shells, to garnish
450 ml (¾ pint) double cream	

1 Combine the chopped fish with the prawns and egg white and season to taste. Put the mixture in a blender or food processor with 300 ml (½ pint) cream and blend until smooth.

2 Butter six 150 ml (¼ pint) ovenproof ramekin dishes and press the mixture well down into the dishes. Cover and chill for 3 hours.

3 Place the ramekins in a roasting tin and pour in enough boiling water to come halfway up the dishes. Cook in a preheated oven at 150°C (300°F) mark 2 for 30–40 minutes. Turn out on to a wire rack to drain. Keep warm.

4 Put the egg yolks, a knob of butter and the lemon juice in the top of a double boiler or in a heatproof bowl over a pan of simmering water. Heat gently, stirring, until of a coating consistency.

5 Remove from the heat and slowly beat in the remaining butter and the tomato purée. Whip the remaining cream until softly stiff and fold into the sauce. Return to the heat to thicken without boiling.

6 Place the moulds in a warmed serving dish and coat with the sauce. Garnish with dill and whole prawns and serve hot.

MUSHROOM-STUFFED PLAICE

SERVES 4

50 g (2 oz) butter	4 large plaice fillets, skinned
1 small onion, finely chopped	25 g (1 oz) plain flour
225 g (8 oz) flat mushrooms, finely chopped	150 ml (¼ pint) milk
grated nutmeg	a few drops of lemon juice
salt and pepper	15 ml (1 tbsp) double cream
30 ml (2 tbsp) finely chopped parsley	chopped parsley, to garnish

1 Melt half the butter in a frying pan, add the onion and fry gently for 5–10 minutes or until soft and golden. Add the mushrooms and cook for about 20 minutes or until all the juices have evaporated.

2 Remove from the heat, season with nutmeg, salt and pepper, then transfer all but 30 ml (2 tbsp) of the mixture to a bowl and mix with 15 ml (1 tbsp) of the parsley.

3 Cut the fish fillets in half lengthways and spread an equal quantity of the mushroom mixture on the skinned side of each piece of fish. Roll up the fillets from the head to tail and place close together in a baking dish.

4 Pour in 150 ml (¼ pint) water and place a piece of buttered foil on top of the fish. Bake in a preheated oven at 180°C (350°F) mark 4 for 20–25 minutes or until tender. Strain off the cooking liquid and transfer the fish to a warmed serving dish. Keep warm.

5 Melt the remaining butter in a saucepan, stir in the flour and cook for 2 minutes, stirring continuously. Remove from the heat and gradually stir in the cooking liquid and milk. Bring to the boil, stirring all the time. Add the remaining mushroom mixture, season with salt, pepper and lemon juice and stir in the cream. Pour over the fish.

STUFFED PLAICE WITH LEMON SAUCE

SERVES 4

4 small whole plaice, cleaned	1.25 ml (¼ tsp) mustard powder
65 g (2½ oz) butter	salt and pepper
100 g (4 oz) button mushrooms, finely chopped	1 egg, beaten
100 g (4 oz) white breadcrumbs	150 ml (¼ pint) dry white wine
90 ml (6 tbsp) chopped parsley	25 g (1 oz) plain flour
45 ml (3 tbsp) green peppercorns, crushed	60 ml (4 tbsp) single cream
juice and finely grated rind of 2 lemons	lemon slices and parsley sprigs, to garnish

1 With the white skin uppermost, cut down the back-bone of each of the four plaice. Carefully make a pocket on each side of the backbone by easing up the white flesh.

2 To make the stuffing, beat 15 g (½ oz) butter until softened, then add the mushrooms, breadcrumbs, parsley, 30 ml (2 tbsp) peppercorns, lemon rind and mustard. Season to taste. Moisten with egg and a little lemon juice.

3 Spoon the stuffing into the pockets in the fish. Place in a buttered ovenproof dish, pour in the wine, cover with foil and cook at 190°C (375°F) mark 5 for 30 minutes.

4 Remove the fish and place on a serving dish. Cover and keep warm. Strain and reserve the cooking liquid.

5 To make the sauce, melt the remaining butter in a saucepan, add the flour and cook for 1–2 minutes. Gradually stir in the fish cooking juices, 150 ml (¼ pint) water and the remaining lemon juice. Bring to the boil, stirring, then stir in the remaining peppercorns sand the cream. Season.

6 Garnish the fish and serve with the sauce.

TROUT IN CREAM
SERVES 4

4 trout	150 ml (5 fl oz) single cream
juice of 1 lemon	30 ml (2 tbsp) fresh breadcrumbs
15 ml (1 tbsp) chopped chives	
15 ml (1 tbsp) chopped parsley	a little butter, melted

1 Clean the fish, leaving the heads on if wished. Wash and wipe the fish and lay them in a buttered shallow flameproof dish.

2 Sprinkle over the lemon juice, herbs and about 15 ml (1 tbsp) water. Cover with foil.

3 Cook in a preheated oven at 180°C (350°F) mark 4 for 10–15 minutes or until tender.

4 Heat the cream gently and pour over the fish. Sprinkle with breadcrumbs and melted butter and brown under a hot grill. Serve immediately.

BAKED TROUT WITH HAZELNUTS AND DILL
SERVES 4

four 275 g (10 oz) trout, cleaned	1 shallot, finely chopped
40 ml (8 tsp) lemon juice	75 g (3 oz) hazelnuts
salt and pepper	50 g (2 oz) butter
4 dill sprigs	lemon slices and dill, to garnish
100 ml (4 fl oz) dry white wine	

1 Cut the fins from the fish, then sprinkle 30 ml (6 tsp) of the lemon juice over the skin and the cavities. Season to taste inside and out and put a sprig of dill in each cavity.

2 Place the trout in a baking dish large enough to hold them tightly in one layer. Pour over the wine and add the shallot. Cover the dish with greased greaseproof paper, then bake in a preheated oven at 180°C (350°F) mark 4 for 20–25 minutes or until the flesh flakes easily.

3 Meanwhile, place the hazelnuts under a moderately hot grill for about 5 minutes or until the skins dry out and flake. Rub off the skins and chop the nuts. Melt the butter in a saucepan, add the hazelnuts and cook over a moderately high heat, stirring frequently, until golden brown. Add the remaining lemon juice and season to taste.

4 Carefully transfer the trout to four warmed serving plates. Boil the cooking juices rapidly until reduced to about 45 ml (3 tbsp). Spoon the juices, hazelnuts and butter over the fish. Garnish and serve at once.

BAKED TROUT WITH CUCUMBER SAUCE

SERVES 4

four 275 g (10 oz) trout, cleaned	300 ml (10 fl oz) soured cream
salt and pepper	5 ml (1 tsp) tarragon vinegar
300 ml (½ pint) fish or vegetable stock	5 ml (1 tsp) chopped tarragon
½ small cucumber	tarragon, to garnish

1 Arrange the trout in a single layer in a shallow ovenproof dish. Season to taste and pour over the stock.
2 Cover and bake in a preheated oven at 180°C (350°F) mark 4 for about 25 minutes or until the trout are tender.
3 Remove the fish from the cooking liquor and carefully peel off the skin, leaving the head and tail intact. Leave to cool.
4 Just before serving, make the sauce. Coarsely grate the cucumber into a bowl, then add the cream, vinegar and chopped tarragon. Season to taste.
5 Coat the trout in some of the sauce, leaving the head and tail exposed. Garnish with tarragon. Serve the remaining sauce separately in a bowl.

TO MICROWAVE

Cook two trout at a time. Arrange in a shallow dish, cover and cook on HIGH for 5–7 minutes or until tender. Repeat with the remaining two trout. Complete the recipe as above.

TROUT STUFFED WITH SPINACH AND WALNUTS

SERVES 4

4 small trout, cleaned, boned and heads removed	juice of 1 lemon
75 g (3 oz) butter	30 ml (2 tbsp) chopped fresh parsley or 10 ml (2 tsp) dried
1 onion, finely chopped	5 ml (1 tsp) grated nutmeg
350 g (12 oz) frozen chopped spinach, thawed	salt and pepper
50 g (2 oz) fresh breadcrumbs	parsley sprigs and lemon and lime slices, to garnish
50 g (2 oz) walnuts, chopped	

1 Butter a large, shallow ovenproof dish and lay the trout in it.
2 Melt 50 g (2 oz) of the butter in a deep frying pan, add the onion and cook for 4–5 minutes or until soft. Stir in the spinach and cook for 5 minutes, stirring frequently.
3 Add the breadcrumbs, walnuts, lemon juice, parsley and nutmeg. Stir well to combine and continue to cook over a gentle heat for 10 minutes, stirring frequently. Remove from the heat and leave to cool.
4 Spoon the stuffing into the cavity of each fish. Lay the fish on their sides and dot with the remaining butter. Season and cover with buttered foil.
5 Cook in a preheated oven at 180°C (350°F) mark 4 for 40–60 minutes or until the fish is firm and flakes easily. Skin the fish, transfer to a warmed serving dish, garnish and serve.

GREY MULLET COOKED IN LEMON AND RED WINE

SERVES 4

15 g (½ oz) butter	salt and pepper
450 g (1 lb) eating apples, peeled, cored and sliced	four 275 g (10 oz) grey mullet, cleaned
6 spring onions, sliced	2 lemons, sliced
juice and finely grated rind of 1 lemon	300 ml (½ pint) dry red wine
1–2 garlic cloves, crushed	60 ml (4 tbsp) double cream

1 To make the stuffing, melt the butter in a medium saucepan and add the apples, spring onions, lemon rind, 30 ml (2 tbsp) of the lemon juice and the garlic. Fry lightly, then season to taste.

2 Make three slashes across both sides of each grey mullet and insert the lemon slices. Sprinkle the cavity of each fish with the remaining lemon juice and fill with the stuffing. Put into a large ovenproof dish.

3 Pour over the red wine and bake in a preheated oven at 180°C (350°F) mark 4 for 20–30 minutes or until tender. Remove the fish and place on a serving dish. Keep hot.

4 Pour the cooking liquid into a small saucepan, stir in the cream and reheat gently. Pour over the fish and serve.

TO MICROWAVE

Melt the butter in a medium bowl on HIGH for 30 seconds. Add the apples, spring onions, lemon rind, 30 ml (2 tbsp) of the lemon juice and the garlic. Cook on HIGH for 8 minutes. Complete step 2. Put the fish into a shallow dish and pour over the red wine. Cook on HIGH for 10 minutes or until tender, rearranging once. Complete step 4. Stir the cream into the cooking liquid and cook on HIGH for 1 minute. Serve poured over the fish.

STEAMED MULLET WITH CHILLI SAUCE

SERVES 2

one 550 g (1¼ lb) grey mullet, cleaned	1 small red pepper, cut into matchsticks
75 ml (5 tbsp) tomato ketchup	1 small green pepper, cut into matchsticks
15 ml (1 tbsp) soy sauce	5 ml (1 tsp) cornflour
pinch of chilli powder	15 ml (1 tbsp) chopped parsley
75 ml (5 tbsp) white wine	salt and pepper

1 Place the mullet in a shallow dish.

2 Whisk together the tomato ketchup, soy sauce, chilli powder and wine. Make three deep slashes in the side of each fish. Pour over the marinade, cover and leave for 2 hours.

3 Drain off the marinade and reserve. Place the fish on a rack over a roasting tin half full of water and cover tightly with foil. Steam the fish over a medium heat for 20–25 minutes or until the fish is cooked. (When cooked, the eyes should be white.)

4 To make the chilli sauce, place the marinade and peppers in a saucepan. Mix the cornflour to a smooth paste with 15 ml (1 tbsp) water and stir into the sauce. Bring to the boil and simmer for 4–5 minutes, stirring. Stir in the parsley and season to taste.

5 Carefully lift the steamed mullet on to a warmed serving plate. Spoon over the sauce and serve.

SKATE WITH CAPERS

SERVES 4

MONKFISH WITH LIME AND PRAWNS

SERVES 4

two 550 g (1¼ lb) skate wings, halved	45 ml (3 tbsp) drained capers
salt	30 ml (2 tbsp) vinegar from the capers
50 g (2 oz) butter	

1 Put the skate in a roasting tin and cover with salted water. Bring to the boil, then simmer for 10–15 minutes or until tender.
2 Meanwhile, melt the butter in a small saucepan and cook until it turns golden brown. Add the capers and vinegar and cook until bubbling.
3 Drain the fish and place on warmed serving plates. Pour over the sauce and serve at once.

───────────── **COOK'S TIP** ─────────────
The 'wings' are the only edible part of the skate. They may look bony but in fact the bones are soft and gelatinous, and the flesh is easily picked off them when the fish is cooked.

550 g (1¼ lb) monkfish	150 ml (¼ pint) dry white wine
salt and pepper	juice and finely grated rind of 1 lime
15 ml (1 tbsp) plain flour	
30 ml (2 tbsp) vegetable oil	pinch of sugar
1 small onion, chopped	100 g (4 oz) peeled prawns
1 garlic clove, chopped	lime slices, to garnish
225 g (8 oz) tomatoes, skinned and chopped	

1 Using a sharp knife, skin the fish, if necessary, then cut the flesh into 2.5 cm (1 inch) chunks. Season the flour with salt and pepper, add the fish and toss until coated.
2 Heat the oil in a flameproof casserole, add the onion and garlic and fry gently for 5 minutes. Add the fish and fry until golden.
3 Stir in the tomatoes, wine, lime rind and juice, sugar and seasoning. Bring to the boil.
4 Cover and cook in a preheated oven at 180°C (350°F) mark 4 for 15 minutes. Add the prawns and continue to cook for a further 15 minutes or until the monkfish is tender. Garnish with lime slices.

FRICASSÉE OF MONKFISH WITH CORIANDER

SERVES 6

700 g (1½ lb) monkfish fillets	40 g (1½ oz) butter
450 g (1 lb) halibut cutlets	45 ml (3 tbsp) plain flour
150 ml (¼ pint) dry vermouth	30 ml (2 tbsp) chopped coriander
1 small onion, sliced	60 ml (4 tbsp) single cream
salt and pepper	coriander sprigs, to garnish
100 g (4 oz) small button mushrooms	

1 Cut the monkfish and halibut into large, fork-sized pieces, discarding skin and bone.
2 Place the fish in a medium saucepan, cover with cold water and bring slowly to the boil. Strain the fish in a colander and rinse off any scum.
3 Return the fish to the clean pan and pour over the vermouth and 300 ml (½ pint) water. Add the onion, season to taste and bring to the boil. Cover the pan, reduce the heat and simmer gently for 8–10 minutes or until the fish is just tender and beginning to flake, adding the mushrooms after 6 minutes' cooking.
4 Strain off the cooking liquor and reserve.
5 Melt the butter in a separate saucepan, stir in the flour and cook for 1–2 minutes. Gradually add the cooking liquor. Bring slowly to the boil, stirring all the time, and bubble for 2 minutes or until thickened and smooth.
6 Stir in the chopped coriander, cream, mushrooms, onion and fish and adjust the seasoning. Warm through gently, being careful not to break up the fish. Serve hot, garnished with sprigs of coriander.

MONKFISH AND MUSSEL SKEWERS

SERVES 6

12 streaky bacon rashers, halved	juice and finely grated rind of 1 large lemon
900 g (2 lb) monkfish, skinned, boned and cut into 2.5 cm (1 inch) cubes	4 garlic cloves, crushed
	salt and pepper
36 frozen cooked mussels, thawed	shredded lettuce, to serve
25 g (1 oz) butter	lemon slices, to garnish
60 ml (4 tbsp) chopped parsley	

1 Roll the bacon rashers up neatly. Thread the cubed fish, mussels and bacon alternately on to 12 oiled skewers.
2 Melt the butter in a saucepan, remove from the heat, then add the parsley, lemon juice and rind and garlic. Season to taste. (Take care when adding salt as both the mussels and the bacon are naturally salty.)
3 Place the skewers on an oiled grill rack. Brush with the butter mixture, then cook under a preheated moderate grill for 15 minutes. Turn the skewers frequently during cooking and brush with the butter mixture with each turn.
4 Arrange the hot skewers on a serving platter lined with shredded lettuce. Garnish with lemon slices and serve at once with any remaining flavoured butter.

―――――――――――― **COOK'S TIP** ――――――――――――
Keep the skewers well brushed with butter while grilling to prevent the fish from drying out.

SALMON WITH HERB SAUCE

SERVES 4

900 g (2 lb) salmon, cleaned	45 ml (3 tbsp) chopped parsley
45 ml (3 tbsp) lemon juice	30 ml (2 tbsp) chopped chervil
50 g (2 oz) butter	5 ml (1 tsp) chopped dill
salt and pepper	150 ml (¼ pint) mayonnaise
1 bunch of watercress, roughly chopped	fresh herbs and lemon rind shapes, to garnish (optional)
100 g (4 oz) fresh spinach leaves, roughly chopped	

1 Place the fish in the centre of a large piece of foil. Add 30 ml (2 tbsp) of the lemon juice, then dot with 25 g (1 oz) of the butter. Season to taste.

2 Seal the foil, weight the fish and place on a baking sheet. Calculate the cooking time at 10 minutes per 450 g (1 lb). Bake in a preheated oven at 180°C (350°F) mark 4 until tender.

3 Remove the fish from the foil, reserving the cooking liquor, then carefully remove the skin while still warm. Place the fish on a serving dish and leave to cool.

4 To make the sauce, put the cooking liquor and the remaining 25 g (1 oz) butter in a saucepan and heat gently. Add the watercress, spinach, parsley, chervil and dill, then cook for 2–3 minutes or until softened.

5 Put the sauce in a blender or food processor and blend until smooth. Transfer to a bowl, add the remaining lemon juice and season to taste. Leave to cool, then fold in the mayonnaise. Turn into a small serving jug and refrigerate until required.

6 Garnish the fish decoratively with herbs and lemon rind shapes, and serve with the herb sauce.

SUMMER POACHED SALMON

SERVES 15

1.8 kg (4 lb) salmon, tail and fins trimmed and eyes removed	salt and pepper
150 ml (¼ pint) dry white wine	300 ml (½ pint) liquid aspic jelly
1 onion, sliced	whole prawns, cucumber slices, endive and chicory, to garnish
1 bay leaf	mayonnaise, to serve

1 Place the salmon in a fish kettle. Pour over the wine and enough water just to cover the fish. Add the onion and bay leaf and season to taste. Bring slowly to the boil, cover and simmer for 25 minutes.

2 Lift the salmon out of the cooking liquid and leave to cool for 2–3 hours. Ease off the skin and place the fish on a serving platter.

3 As the aspic begins to set, brush some over the fish. Leave to set in a cool place for 1–1½ hours. Coat with several layers of aspic.

4 Garnish the salmon with prawns and cucumber slices and brush more aspic on top. Arrange endive, chicory, sliced cucumber and lemon on the side of the dish and serve with mayonnaise.

─────────────── **COOK'S TIP** ───────────────

This is an ideal dish to serve for a summer buffet. Pay particular attention to the garnishing and allow yourself a little extra time for those important finishing touches. The result can look spectacular.

SALMON WITH FENNEL SAUCE

SERVES 4

four 175 g (6 oz) salmon steaks	2 egg yolks
2 shallots, chopped	100 g (4 oz) butter, softened
1 small fennel bulb, finely chopped	salt and pepper
1 bay leaf	lemon juice, to taste
2 parsley stalks, crushed	fennel sprigs, to garnish
150 ml (¼ pint) dry white wine	

1 Place the salmon steaks in a shallow ovenproof dish. Scatter the shallots, fennel, bay leaf and parsley over the top. Pour in the wine, cover tightly and bake in a preheated oven at 180°C (350°F) mark 4 for 15 minutes or until the fish is tender.
2 Strain off 100 ml (4 fl oz) of the cooking liquor into a saucepan. Reserve 10 ml (2 tsp) of the chopped fennel. Turn off the oven, re-cover the salmon and keep warm.
3 Boil the strained liquor until reduced to 15 ml (1 tbsp). Beat the egg yolks together in a medium heat-proof bowl, then stir in the reduced liquor and work in half the butter.
4 Place the bowl over a saucepan of hot water and whisk with a balloon whisk until the butter has melted. Gradually whisk in the remaining butter, whisking well after each addition, to make a thick, fluffy sauce. Remove the bowl from the heat.
5 Add the reserved cooked fennel to the sauce and season to taste, adding a little lemon juice, if necessary.
6 Transfer the salmon to a warmed serving plate. Spoon the sauce over and garnish with fennel sprigs.

SOURED CREAM SALMON PIE

SERVES 8

450 g (1 lb) salmon	150 ml (5 fl oz) soured cream
60 ml (4 tbsp) dry white wine	30 ml (2 tbsp) chopped parsley
salt and pepper	450 g (1 lb) self-raising flour
190 g (6½ oz) butter	50 g (2 oz) lard
40 g (1½ oz) plain flour	milk, to bind
225 g (8 oz) Cheddar cheese, grated	beaten egg, to glaze
3 eggs, hard-boiled and chopped	

1 Place the salmon in a large saucepan and just cover with cold water. Add the wine, season to taste and simmer for about 20 minutes. Remove the fish from the stock and flake, discarding bones and skin. Reserve the stock.
2 Melt 40 g (1½ oz) butter in a saucepan and stir in the plain flour. Remove the pan from the heat and gradually stir in 300 ml (½ pint) reserved fish stock. Bring to the boil and continue to cook, stirring, for 2 minutes. Remove from the heat and stir in 200 g (7 oz) grated cheese, the chopped eggs, soured cream and parsley. Season and cool.
3 To make the pastry, mix the self-raising flour and remaining cheese in a bowl, add the remaining butter and the lard and rub in until the mixture resembles fine breadcrumbs. Add a little milk to bind the mixture.
4 Roll out one third of the pastry on a lightly floured surface to a 30.5 x 10 cm (12 x 4 inch) oblong and place on a baking sheet. Top with some of the sauce mixture, the salmon, then more sauce.
5 Roll out the remaining pastry and use to cover the pie, sealing the edges well. Brush with beaten egg and bake at 190°C (375°F) mark 5 for about 40 minutes. Serve warm.

FISH WELLINGTON

SERVES 6–8

25 g (1 oz) butter	salt and pepper
100 g (4 oz) mushrooms, chopped	368 g (13 oz) packet frozen puff pastry, thawed
50 g (2 oz) onion, finely chopped	2 large cod or haddock fillets, (about 900 g/2 lb), skinned
175 g (6 oz) smooth liver pâté or liver sausage	beaten egg, to glaze
60 ml (4 tbsp) double cream	

1 Melt the butter in a frying pan, add the mushrooms and onion and fry for about 5 minutes or until soft.

2 Mash the liver pâté or sausage in a bowl and stir in the cream, onion and mushrooms. Season to taste.

3 Roll out the pastry on a lightly floured surface to a 35 x 30.5 cm (14 x 12 inch) rectangle. Place one fish fillet in the centre of the pastry, spread the filling mixture over the fillet, then top with the other fillet. Trim the pastry, allowing a good 10 cm (4 inch) border. Reserve the trimmed pastry.

4 Brush round the edges of the pastry with beaten egg, then carefully fold it over the fish and neatly wrap it up like a parcel.

5 Place the parcelled fish on a baking sheet with the sealed edges underneath. Brush with beaten egg. Roll and cut the pastry trimmings into decorative fish shapes and place on top of the pastry parcel.

6 Bake in a preheated oven at 220°C (425°F) mark 7 for about 25 minutes or until the pastry is golden brown and the fish is cooked through.

INDONESIAN FISH CURRY

SERVES 4

1 small onion, chopped	salt
1 garlic clove, chopped	700 g (1½ lb) haddock fillets, skinned and cut into bite-sized pieces
2.5 cm (1 inch) piece of fresh root ginger, chopped	225 g (8 oz) peeled prawns
5 ml (1 tsp) ground turmeric	300 ml (½ pint) coconut milk
2.5 ml (½ tsp) laos powder	juice of 1 lime
1.25 ml (¼ tsp) chilli powder	shredded coconut and lime wedges, to garnish
30 ml (2 tbsp) vegetable oil	

1 Put the first seven ingredients in an electric blender or food processor with 2.5 ml (½ tsp) salt and blend to a paste.

2 Transfer the mixture to a flameproof casserole and fry gently, stirring, for 5 minutes. Add the haddock pieces and prawns and fry for a few minutes more, tossing the fish to coat with the spice mixture.

3 Pour in the coconut milk, shake the pan and turn the fish gently in the liquid. (Take care not to break up the pieces of fish.) Bring slowly to the boil, then lower the heat, cover and simmer for 10 minutes or until tender.

4 Add the lime juice, taste and adjust the seasoning, then transfer to a warmed serving dish and sprinkle with coconut. Serve hot, garnished with lime wedges.

--- COOK'S TIP ---

Loas powder is used extensively in the cooking of South-East Asia. It comes from a root rather like ginger and has a peppery hot taste.

To make 300 ml (½ pint) coconut milk, break 100 g (4 oz) block creamed coconut into a jug and pour in 300 ml (½ pint) boiling water. Stir, then strain.

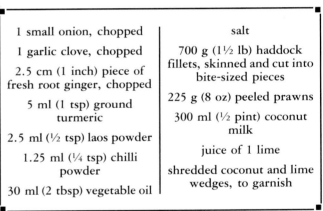

FISH IN SPICY SAUCE WITH TOMATOES

SERVES 4

700 g (1½ lb) white fish (cod, halibut or haddock), skinned and filleted	5 ml (1 tsp) ground turmeric
60 ml (4 tbsp) ghee or vegetable oil	1.25 ml (¼ tsp) chilli powder
7.5 ml (1½ tsp) coriander seeds	5 ml (1 tsp) salt
5 ml (1 tsp) black peppercorns	4 tomatoes, skinned and roughly chopped
1 garlic clove, crushed	2.5 ml (½ tsp) garam masala
	chopped coriander, to garnish

1 Wash the fish under cold running water and pat dry with absorbent kitchen paper. Cut into 2.5 cm (1 inch) cubes.

2 Heat the ghee or oil in a heavy-based frying pan. Add the fish, a few pieces at a time, and fry gently for 2–3 minutes. Remove the fish carefully from the pan with a slotted spoon and set aside on a plate.

3 Put the coriander seeds, peppercorns and garlic in a small electric mill or pestle and mortar and grind to a smooth paste.

4 Add the spice paste to the frying pan with the turmeric, chilli powder and salt, and fry gently for 2 minutes.

5 Stir in the tomatoes and 300 ml (½ pint) water. Bring to the boil, then lower the heat and cook over a medium heat for 5 minutes. Add the fish and simmer, shaking the pan occasionally, for a further 10 minutes or until the fish is tender. *Do not stir.* Remove from the heat.

6 Sprinkle the garam masala over the fish, cover the pan and let the fish stand for 2 minutes, then turn into a warmed serving dish. Garnish with chopped coriander and serve immediately.

ITALIAN FISH STEW

SERVES 4

a good pinch of saffron strands	450 g (1 lb) tomatoes, skinned, seeded and chopped
about 900 g (2 lb) mixed fish fillets (red mullet, bream, bass, brill, monkfish, plaice or cod)	2 canned anchovy fillets, drained
10–12 unpeeled cooked prawns	150 ml (¼ pint) dry white wine
60 ml (4 tbsp) olive oil	2 bay leaves
1 large onion, finely chopped	45 ml (3 tbsp) chopped basil
3 garlic cloves, crushed	salt and pepper
2 slices of canned pimiento, drained and sliced	10–12 mussels, in their shells
	4 slices of hot toast, to serve

1 To prepare the saffron water, soak the saffron strands in a little boiling water for 30 minutes. Meanwhile, skin the fish and cut into bite-sized pieces. Peel the prawns.

2 Heat the oil in a large heavy-based pan, add the onion, garlic and pimiento and fry for 5 minutes or until soft.

3 Add the tomatoes and anchovies and stir with a wooden spoon to break them up. Pour in the wine and 150 ml (¼ pint) water and bring to the boil, then lower the heat and add the bay leaves and half the basil. Simmer, uncovered, for 20 minutes, stirring occasionally.

4 Add the firm fish to the tomato mixture, then strain in the saffron water and season to taste. Cook for 10 minutes, then add the delicate fish and cook for a further 5 minutes.

5 Add the prawns and mussels, cover and cook for 5 minutes or until the mussels open. Discard the bay leaves and any mussels that do not open.

6 To serve, put one slice of toast in each of four individual bowls. Spoon over the stew and sprinkle with basil.

MEDITERRANEAN FISH STEW WITH AÏOLI

SERVES 4

10 garlic cloves	1 small onion, thinly sliced
1 egg yolk	1 leek, thinly sliced
300 ml (½ pint) olive oil	1–2 parsley sprigs
juice of 1 lemon	1 bay leaf
salt and pepper	1 thin strip of orange rind
900 g (2 lb) firm white fish fillets (bass, turbot, whiting, monkfish or halibut), skinned	1 small baguette (French loaf), sliced, to serve
	chopped parsley, to garnish
1.1 litres (2 pints) fish stock	

1 First make the aïoli. Roughly chop eight of the garlic cloves and put in a mortar with the egg yolk. Crush with a pestle. Add the oil a drop at a time and work until the ingredients emulsify and thicken. Continue adding the oil in a thin, stready stream, beating vigorously until the mayonnaise is very thick and smooth.

2 Beat in the lemon juice and 5 ml (1 tsp) lukewarm water. Season to taste and set aside in a cool place.

3 Cut the fish into thick chunks and place in a large saucepan. Pour in the stock, then add the next five ingredients, with the remaining garlic, halved. Season to taste, cover and simmer for 15 minutes or until tender.

4 Transfer the fish and vegetables to a warmed serving dish with a slotted spoon. Keep warm.

5 Strain the cooking liquid into a jug and blend a few spoonfuls into the aïoli. Toast the baguette and keep warm.

6 Put the aïoli in a heavy-based saucepan, then gradually whisk in the remaining cooking liquid. Heat through gently, stirring constantly. Adjust the seasoning. Pour over the fish and sprinkle with parsley. Serve with the toast.

SPECIAL PARSLEY FISH PIE

SERVES 4

450 g (1 lb) whiting fillet	2 eggs, hard-boiled and chopped
300 ml (½ pint) plus 90 ml (6 tbsp) milk	150 ml (¼ pint) single cream
1 bay leaf	30 ml (2 tbsp) chopped parsley
6 peppercorns	
1 onion, sliced	100 g (4 oz) peeled prawns
salt and pepper	900 g (2 lb) potatoes, peeled
65 g (2½ oz) butter	
45 ml (3 tbsp) plain flour	1 egg, beaten, to glaze

1 Place the whiting in a saucepan and pour over the 300 ml (½ pint) milk. Add the bay leaf, peppercorns, onion and a pinch of salt. Simmer for 10 minutes. Lift the fish from the pan, flake the flesh and remove the skin and bones. Strain the cooking liquid and reserve.

2 To make the sauce, melt 40 g (1½ oz) of the butter in the saucepan, add the flour and cook gently, stirring, for 1–2 minutes. Remove from the heat and gradually blend in the reserved cooking liquid. Bring to the boil, stirring constantly, then simmer until thickened and season.

3 Add the eggs to the sauce with the cream, fish, parsley and prawns. Taste and adjust the seasoning, then spoon the mixture into a 29.5 cm (11 inch) oval baking dish.

4 Meanwhile, boil the potatoes, drain and mash without any liquid. Heat the 90 ml (6 tbsp) milk and remaining butter and beat into the potatoes. Season to taste. Pipe or spoon over the fish mixture.

5 Bake in the oven at 200°C (400°F) mark 6 for 10–15 minutes or until the potato is set. Brush the beaten egg over the pie. Return to the oven for a further 15 minutes or until the potato is golden brown.

FISHERMAN'S HOT POT

SERVES 4

450 g (1 lb) cod fillet, skinned	1 medium onion, thinly sliced
40 g (1½ oz) plain flour	225 g (8 oz) mushrooms, sliced
700 g (1½ lb) potatoes, peeled	15 g (½ oz) butter
15–30 ml (1–2 tbsp) lemon juice	150 ml (¼ pint) milk
salt and pepper	100 g (4 oz) Cheddar cheese, grated

1 Cut the cod into 2 cm (¾ inch) squares and toss in 25 g (1 oz) flour.

2 Cook the potatoes in boiling salted water for about 15 minutes or until tender, but not soft, then slice them thinly. Arrange one third in the bottom of a buttered ovenproof casserole. Cover with half the cod, sprinkle with half the lemon juice and season well.

3 Combine the onion and mushrooms and arrange half the mixture over the fish. Cover with the remaining cod, lemon juice, one third of the potatoes and the remaining onions and mushrooms.

4 Melt the butter in a saucepan, stir in the remaining 15 g (½ oz) flour and cook gently for 1 minute, stirring. Remove the pan from the heat and gradually stir in the milk. Bring to the boil and continue to cook, stirring, until the sauce thickens, then add half the cheese and season to taste.

5 Pour the sauce over the ingredients in the casserole, put the remaining potato slices on top, and sprinkle with the remaining cheese.

6 Bake, uncovered, in a preheated oven at 200°C (400°F) mark 6 for about 40 minutes or until golden.

TOMATO FISH BAKE

SERVES 4

50 g (2 oz) fresh breadcrumbs	25 g (1 oz) butter
50 g (2 oz) Cheddar cheese, grated	50 g (2 oz) mushrooms, sliced
1 small onion, finely chopped	25 g (1 oz) plain flour
2.5 ml (½ tsp) dried mixed herbs	30 ml (2 tbsp) tomato purée
300 ml (½ pint) milk, plus 30–45 ml (2–3 tbsp)	5 ml (1 tsp) lemon juice
salt and pepper	pinch of sugar
450 g (1 lb) white fish	450 g (1 lb) potatoes, peeled
	chopped parsley or watercress, to garnish

1 To make the stuffing, mix the breadcrumbs, grated cheese, onion and herbs with the 30–45 ml (2–3 tbsp) milk. Season to taste.

2 Wash and skin the fish. Place half on the base of a buttered shallow flameproof dish. Spread the stuffing over the fish and top with the remaining fish.

3 Melt the butter in a saucepan and fry the mushrooms for about 5 minutes or until soft. Add the flour, the remaining 300 ml (½ pint) milk, the tomato purée, lemon juice, sugar and seasoning. Heat, whisking continuously, until the sauce thickens. Pour over the fish. Bake in a preheated oven at 190°C (375°F) mark 5 for 20 minutes.

4 Meanwhile, cook the potatoes in boiling salted water for about 20 minutes or until tender. Drain and mash. Remove the fish from the oven and pipe a border of mashed potato around the dish. Return to the oven or place under a preheated hot grill to brown. Garnish with chopped parsley or watercress.

HOT FISH TERRINE WITH GRUYÈRE SAUCE

SERVES 6

75 g (3 oz) butter	3 eggs
1 garlic clove, crushed	1 egg yolk
60 ml (4 tbsp) plain flour	salt and pepper
750 ml (1¼ pints) milk	30 ml (2 tbsp) chopped parsley
550 g (1¼ lb) hake fillets, skinned and chopped	100 g (4 oz) peeled cooked prawns, chopped
150 ml (¼ pint) double cream	100 g (4 oz) Gruyère cheese, grated
10 ml (2 tsp) anchovy essence	

1 Lightly butter and base-line a 1.6 litre (2¾ pint) shallow loaf tin or terrine.

2 Melt 40 g (1½ oz) butter and add the garlic. Stir in 45 ml (3 tbsp) flour and cook, stirring, for 1–2 minutes. Off the heat, blend in 450 ml (¾ pint) milk. Bring to the boil, stirring, then simmer for 2 minutes or until thick.

3 Turn the sauce into a blender or food processor. Add the hake, cream, anchovy essence, eggs and egg yolk and blend to a purée. Season lightly.

4 Spoon half the fish mixture into the tin. Sprinkle with parsley and half the prawns, then spoon in the rest of the fish mixture. Cover with buttered greaseproof paper. Place in a roasting tin and pour in hot water to come halfway up the sides. Cook at 150°C (300°F) mark 2 for 1¾ hours.

5 Just before the terrine is cooked, make the sauce. Melt 25 g (1 oz) butter, add the remaining flour and cook, stirring, for 1–2 minutes. Off the heat, blend in the remaining milk. Cook, stirring, for 2 minutes until thick. Stir in the cheese and remaining prawns. Season to taste.

6 Invert the terrine on to a warmed serving dish and drain off the juices. Spoon over a little sauce before serving.

FISH MOUSSES WITH CORIANDER AND TOMATO SAUCE

SERVES 4

225 g (8 oz) haddock or cod fillets, skinned	pinch of cayenne
	FOR THE SAUCE
100 g (4 oz) peeled prawns	25 g (1 oz) butter
1 egg	3 spring onions, chopped
150 ml (¼ pint) double cream	400 g (14 oz) can chopped tomatoes
150 ml (¼ pint) natural yogurt	15 ml (1 tbsp) tomato purée
30 ml (2 tbsp) chopped fresh coriander or 10 ml (2 tsp) ground coriander	5 ml (1 tsp) sugar
	15 ml (1 tbsp) chopped fresh coriander or 5 ml (1 tsp) ground coriander
10 ml (2 tsp) lemon juice	
salt and pepper	coriander sprigs, to garnish

1 Put the fish and prawns in a blender or food processor and blend to a purée. Blend in the egg, cream, yogurt, coriander and lemon juice and season to taste with salt, pepper and cayenne.

2 Butter four 175 ml (6 fl oz) ovenproof ramekin dishes and divide the fish mixture between them. Cover loosely with foil, place in a roasting tin and pour in enough hot water to come halfway up the sides. Cook in a preheated oven at 180°C (350°F) mark 4 for 20–30 minutes or until firm.

3 For the sauce, melt the butter in a small saucepan, add the spring onions and cook for 3 minutes. Put the tomatoes in a food processor or blender and purée until smooth. Add the tomatoes to the onions and stir in the tomato purée and sugar. Cook for 5–6 minutes. Sieve the sauce and stir in the chopped coriander. Unmould the mousses and serve with the sauce. Garnish with coriander sprigs.

FISH MEDALLIONS WITH DILL SAUCE

SERVES 4

HERRINGS IN OATMEAL

SERVES 2

225 g (8 oz) salmon fillets, skinned	FOR THE SAUCE
	25 g (1 oz) butter
350 g (12 oz) plaice fillets, skinned	1 small onion, very finely chopped
150 ml (¼ pint) dry white wine	15 ml (1 tbsp) plain flour
	300 ml (½ pint) single cream
30 ml (2 tbsp) lemon juice	
pepper	1 bay leaf
a few dill sprigs	30 ml (2 tbsp) chopped fresh dill or 10 ml (2 tsp) dried
	salt and pepper

1 Cut the fish fillets lengthways into 0.5 cm (¼ inch) thick strips. Using two of one colour and one of the other, lay alternate colours alongside each other and coil round to form a spiral, securing with a wooden cocktail stick. Continue to make eight medallions.

2 Place the wine and lemon juice in a frying pan. Add the medallions, season with pepper and scatter over the dill sprigs. Poach gently for 5–7 minutes or until the fish is firm and moist. Remove the dill sprigs and cocktail sticks. Transfer the medallions to a warmed serving dish and cover with foil to keep warm.

3 For the sauce, melt the butter in a saucepan and cook the onion for 2–3 minutes or until softened. Stir in the flour and cook, stirring continuously, for a further minute. Remove from the heat and gradually stir in the cream. Add the bay leaf. Heat gently, without boiling, for 3–5 minutes or until the sauce is thickened, stirring continuously. Remove the bay leaf and stir in the dill. Season to taste.

4 Serve the fish medallions with the dill sauce.

2 medium herrings, cleaned, heads and tails removed	15 ml (1 tbsp) vegetable oil
	15 g (½ oz) butter
salt and pepper	lemon wedges, to serve
50 g (2 oz) medium oatmeal	

1 To remove the backbone of the fish, open out on a board, cut side down, and press lightly with the fingers along the middle of the back. Turn the fish over and ease the backbone up with your fingers. Fold the fish in half. Season well and coat with the oatmeal.

2 Heat the oil and butter in a large frying pan and fry the herrings for about 5 minutes on each side. Drain well before serving hot with lemon wedges.

─────── **TO MICROWAVE** ───────

Complete step 1. Heat a large browning dish on HIGH for 5–8 minutes or according to the manufacturer's instructions. Put the oil and butter into the browning dish, then quickly add the herrings. Cook on HIGH for 1 minute, then turn over and cook on HIGH for 1–2 minutes or until tender. Serve hot with lemon wedges.

STUFFED HERRINGS

SERVES 4

65 g (2½ oz) butter	juice and finely grated rind of 1 lemon
1 medium onion, finely chopped	45 ml (3 tbsp) chopped fresh mixed herbs (chives, parsley, rosemary, thyme)
50 g (2 oz) fresh wholemeal breadcrumbs	
50 g (2 oz) walnut pieces, roughly chopped	salt and pepper
	four 275 g (10 oz) herrings, cleaned, boned and heads and tails, removed
15 ml (1 tbsp) prepared English mustard	

1 Melt 15 g (½ oz) of the butter in a saucepan, add the onion and fry gently for about 5 minutes or until softened, stirring occasionally.

2 Meanwhile, mix together the breadcrumbs, walnuts, mustard, lemon rind, 15 ml (1 tbsp) lemon juice and the mixed herbs. Season to taste. Add the onion and mix together well.

3 Open the herring fillets and lay skin side down. Press the stuffing mixture evenly over each fillet. Fold the herring fillets back in half and slash the skin several times.

4 Melt the remaining butter in a large frying pan, add the fish and fry for about 10 minutes or until they are tender and browned on each side, turning the fish once.

VARIATION
Stuffed Mackerel

Substitute four mackerel for the herrings in the above recipe if preferred.

MACKEREL PARCELS

SERVES 4

four 175 g (6 oz) fresh mackerel	30 ml (2 tbsp) chopped mint
about 25 g (1 oz) margarine	5 ml (1 tsp) sugar
½ large cucumber, sliced	salt and pepper
60 ml (4 tbsp) white wine vinegar	natural yogurt and mint leaves, to serve

1 With the back of a knife and working from the tail towards the head, scrape off the scales from the skin of the mackerel. Cut off the heads just below the gills with a sharp knife. Cut off the fins and tails with kitchen scissors.

2 Slit the underside of the fish open from head to tail end with a sharp knife or scissors. With the flat of the knife blade, scrape out the entrails of the fish, together with any membranes and blood. Wash the fish thoroughly.

3 Lay the fish flat on a board or work surface with the skin uppermost. Press firmly along the backbone with your knuckles to flatten the fish and loosen the backbone.

4 Turn the fish over and lift out the backbone. Cut each fish lengthways into two fillets. Dry thoroughly.

5 Grease eight squares of kitchen foil with a little margarine. Put a mackerel fillet in the centre of each square, skin side down.

6 Arrange cucumber slices down one half of the length of each fillet, then sprinkle with vinegar, mint and sugar. Season. Dot with the remaining margarine.

7 Fold the mackerel fillets over lengthways to enclose the cucumber filling, then wrap in the foil. Place the foil parcels in a single layer in an ovenproof dish. Cook at 200°C (400°F) mark 6 for 30 minutes or until tender.

8 To serve, unwrap the foil parcels and carefully place the mackerel fillets in a circle on a warmed platter. Spoon the yogurt in the centre and garnish with mint.

GRILLED MACKEREL WITH SAGE SAUCE

SERVES 4

SMOKED MACKEREL SOUFFLÉ

SERVES 4

4 mackerel, cleaned	75 ml (3 fl oz) dry white wine
salt and pepper	
150 ml (¼ pint) olive oil	75 ml (3 fl oz) dry vermouth
30 ml (2 tbsp) lemon juice	5 ml (1 tsp) very finely chopped sage

200 ml (7 fl oz) milk	25 g (1 oz) butter
a few onion and carrot slices	salt and pepper
1 bay leaf	4 eggs, separated
6 black peppercorns	75 g (3 oz) cooked smoked mackerel, skinned, boned and finely flaked
30 ml (2 tbsp) plain flour	

1 Cut the fins from the mackerel and cut three diagonal slits in the skin across both sides of each fish. Season the fish inside and out, then place in a dish large enough to hold them in a single layer.

2 Mix the oil, lemon juice and wine together and pour over the fish. Cover and leave to marinate in a cool place for 1½ hours, turning the fish occasionally.

3 Remove the mackerel from the marinade. Cook under a preheated hot grill for 5–8 minutes on each side, depending on the thickness of the fish, until the flesh flakes easily. Transfer to a warmed serving dish, cover and keep hot.

4 Carefully remove the oil from the top of the marinade and pour the marinade into a saucepan with the cooking juices from the grill pan. Add the vermouth and sage leaves and simmer for 2–3 minutes. Season to taste and pour over the mackerel.

1 Grease a 1.3 litre (2¼ pint) soufflé dish.

2 Put the milk in a medium saucepan with the onion and carrot slices, bay leaf and peppercorns. Bring slowly to the boil, remove from the heat, cover and leave to infuse for 30 minutes. Strain and reserve the milk.

3 Put the flour, butter and reserved milk in a medium saucepan. Heat, whisking continuously, until the sauce thickens, boils and is smooth. Simmer for 1–2 minutes. Season to taste, then leave to cool slightly.

4 Beat the egg yolks into the cooled sauce, one at a time. Sprinkle the fish over the sauce and stir in until evenly blended. Whisk all the egg whites until stiff.

5 Mix one large spoonful of egg white into the sauce to lighten its texture. Gently pour the sauce over the remaining egg whites and fold the ingredients lightly together.

6 Pour the soufflé mixture gently into the prepared dish and smooth the surface.

7 Place the soufflé on a baking sheet and bake in a preheated oven at 180°C (350°F) mark 4 for about 30 minutes or until golden brown on top, well risen and just firm to the touch. Serve immediately.

CHEESY SMOKED SALMON ROULADE

SERVES 4–6

FOR THE ROULADE	FOR THE FILLING
100 g (4 oz) butter	225 g (8 oz) smoked salmon, finely shredded
100 g (4 oz) plain flour	75 ml (5 tbsp) double cream
300 ml (½ pint) milk	5 ml (1 tsp) lemon juice
100 g (4 oz) Gruyère cheese, grated	15 ml (1 tbsp) chopped fresh dill or 5 ml (1 tsp) dried
4 eggs, separated	
30 ml (2 tbsp) freshly grated Parmesan cheese	dill sprigs and lemon slices, to garnish

1 Grease and line a 23 x 33 cm (9 x 13 inch) Swiss roll tin. Grease the paper.

2 To make the roulade, melt the butter in a saucepan, stir in the flour and cook for 1 minute. Remove from the heat and gradually stir in the milk. Gently bring to the boil, stirring continuously. Beat in the Gruyère and egg yolks.

3 Whisk the egg whites until stiff. Fold into the cheese mixture and pour into the prepared tin. Bake in a preheated oven at 190°C (375°F) mark 5 for 25–30 minutes or until firm to the touch and golden.

4 Lay a sheet of greaseproof paper on a work surface and sprinkle with the Parmesan cheese. Turn the roulade on to the paper and remove the lining paper. Cover with a damp cloth.

5 To make the filling, place the smoked salmon in a small saucepan and stir in the cream, lemon juice and chopped dill. Heat very gently for 1–2 minutes. Spread the filling over the roulade and roll up, using the greaseproof paper to assist. Serve immediately cut into slices and garnished with dill sprigs and lemon slices.

ITALIAN SQUID STEW

SERVES 4

1 kg (2¼ lb) small squid	2 garlic cloves, crushed
75 ml (5 tbsp) olive oil	juice of ½ lemon
salt and pepper	15 ml (1 tbsp) chopped parsley
75 ml (3 fl oz) dry white wine	

1 Wash the squid in plenty of cold water. Grip the head and tentacles firmly and pull them away from the body. The entrails will follow. Discard these and pull out the transparent quill.

2 With your hands, carefully peel the skin from the body and fins of the squid.

3 Cut the tentacles from the head and remove the skin. Reserve two ink sacs, being careful not to pierce them. Discard the rest of the head.

4 Cut the squid bodies into 0.5 cm (¼ inch) rings. Place in a bowl with the tentacles and spoon over 45 ml (3 tbsp) of the oil. Season well and leave for 3 hours.

5 Pour the squid and marinade into a large frying pan and cook the squid for 5 minutes, turning frequently. Add the wine and garlic and cook for a further 5 minutes. Add the ink sacs, breaking them up with a spoon.

6 Cover and cook over a low heat for about 40 minutes or until the squid is tender.

7 Add the remaining oil, the lemon juice and parsley. Stir for 3 minutes over a high heat, taste and adjust the seasoning and serve.

SCALLOPS IN CREAMY BASIL SAUCE

SERVES 4

900 g (2 lb) shelled scallops, thawed if frozen	150 ml (¼ pint) dry white wine
30 ml (2 tbsp) vegetable oil	20 ml (4 tsp) chopped basil
15 g (½ oz) butter	salt and pepper
1 small onion, finely chopped	150 ml (5 fl oz) double cream
2 garlic cloves, crushed	a few fresh basil sprigs, to garnish

1 Cut the scallops (including the coral) into fairly thick slices. Pat dry with absorbent kitchen paper and set aside.
2 Heat the oil and butter in a large frying pan, add the onion and garlic, and fry gently for 5 minutes or until soft and lightly coloured.
3 Add the scallops to the pan and toss to coat in the oil and butter. Stir in the wine and basil and season to taste.
4 Fry the scallops over a moderate heat for 10 minutes or until they are tender, turning them constantly so that they cook evenly on all sides. Do not overcook or they will become tough and rubbery.
5 Remove the scallops from the liquid with a slotted spoon and set aside on a plate. Boil the liquid until reduced by about half, then stir in the cream, a little at a time, and simmer until the sauce is thick.
6 Return the scallops to the pan and heat gently. Taste and adjust the seasoning and serve garnished with basil.

MUSSEL AND ONION STEW

SERVES 4

2 kg (4½ lb) fresh mussels, scrubbed and 'beards' removed	25 g (1 oz) plain wholemeal flour
150 ml (¼ pint) dry white wine	300 ml (½ pint) milk
25 g (1 oz) butter	30 ml (2 tbsp) chopped parsley
2 large onions, chopped	30 ml (2 tbsp) single cream

1 Discard any mussels that are cracked or do not close when tapped sharply with a knife.
2 Put the wine in a large saucepan and bring to the boil. Add the mussels, cover and cook over a high heat for 3–4 minutes or until the mussels open, shaking the pan occasionally. Discard any mussels that have not opened.
3 Drain the mussels, reserving the juice. Remove the mussels from the shells.
4 Melt the butter in a saucepan, add the onions and fry lightly for about 5 minutes or until soft but not coloured. Stir in the flour and cook for 1 minute.
5 Gradually add the milk and the mussel cooking liquid, stirring, until the sauce thickens, boils and is smooth. Simmer for 1–2 minutes.
6 Return the mussels to the pan with the parsley and cream. Reheat gently and serve at once.

MUSSELS AND CLAMS WITH TOMATOES

SERVES 2–3

900 g (2 lb) fresh mussels, scrubbed and 'beards' removed	150 ml (¼ pint) dry white wine
450 g (1 lb) small clams, such as venus clams	225 g (8 oz) ripe tomatoes, chopped
25 g (1 oz) butter	finely grated rind of 1 lemon
1–2 large garlic cloves, crushed	30 ml (2 tbsp) chopped parsley
1 small onion, finely chopped	salt and pepper

1 Discard any cracked mussels, or any that do not close when tapped sharply with a knife. Scrub the clams thoroughly and discard any that are cracked or open.
2 Melt the butter in a saucepan and cook the garlic and onion until soft. Add the wine, tomatoes, lemon rind and half the parsley. Bring to the boil.
3 Add the mussels and clams to the pan, cover and cook over a high heat for 3–4 minutes or until the mussels and clams are open, shaking the pan occasionally. Discard any mussels or clams that have not opened.
4 Season to taste. Transfer to two or three large bowls or soup plates and sprinkle with the remaining parsley.

TAGLIATELLE WITH SEAFOOD AND CHAMPAGNE SAUCE

SERVES 4

16 fresh mussels, scrubbed and 'beards' removed	225 g (8 oz) fresh tagliatelle
175 g (6 oz) fresh clams, scrubbed	75 g (3 oz) butter
150 ml (¼ pint) fish stock	salt and pepper
one 300 g (11 oz) red mullet, filleted	50 g (2 oz) leek, cut into fine julienne strips
175 g (6 oz) salmon fillets, skinned	150 ml (¼ pint) champagne or sparkling dry white wine
4 large uncooked Pacific prawns, peeled and deveined	300 ml (½ pint) double cream
4 fresh scallops, shelled	pinch of cayenne
	12 fresh basil leaves

1 Discard any open mussels or clams which do not close when tapped. Place in a pan with the stock, cover and cook until the shells open. Discard any closed shells. Leave to cool, then remove the mussels and clams from their shells. Strain the stock and reserve.
2 Cut the fish into 1 cm (½ inch) strips. Cut each prawn in half. Separate the coral from each scallop and cut the scallops in half crossways.
3 Cook the tagliatelle in boiling salted water for 2–3 minutes. Drain and toss in half the butter. Season.
4 Melt the remaining butter in a saucepan and fry the leeks, prawns and scallop coral for 30 seconds. Add the fish fillets, champagne and reserved stock and simmer for 1 minute. Remove the fish from the pan and keep warm.
5 Boil the cooking liquid rapidly until reduced by half. Add the cream and boil until thick. Season and add the cayenne. Return the fish to the sauce with the seafood and basil. Warm and serve with the tagliatelle.

BUTTER BEAN AND TUNA GRATIN

SERVES 4

225 g (8 oz) dried butter beans	450 g (1 lb) fresh or frozen broccoli
450 ml (¾ pint) milk	198 g (7 oz) can tuna, drained
a small piece of onion	salt and pepper
a small piece of carrot	40 g (1½ oz) butter
1 bay leaf	60 ml (4 tbsp) plain flour
6 peppercorns	50 g (2 oz) Cheddar cheese, grated
a blade of mace	

1 Soak the beans overnight in cold water.
2 Put the milk, vegetables, bay leaf and spices in a saucepan and bring slowly to the boil. Remove from the heat, cover and leave to infuse for 30 minutes, then strain and reserve.
3 Drain the beans and cook in a pan of gently boiling water for 1¼ hours or until tender. Drain well.
4 Meanwhile, break the broccoli into florets and cook in a little boiling salted water for about 5 minutes or until just tender. Drain and arrange in a buttered shallow ovenproof dish.
5 Flake the tuna and combine with the cooked beans. Season to taste and pile in the centre of the dish.
6 To make the sauce, melt the butter in a saucepan, stir in the flour and cook gently for 1 minute, stirring. Remove the pan from the heat and gradually stir in the strained milk. Bring to the boil and continue to cook, stirring, until the sauce thickens, then season to taste. Pour over the tuna and broccoli mixture.
7 Sprinkle with the cheese and bake in a preheated oven at 200°C (400°F) mark 6 for 15–20 minutes or until golden.

FISHERMAN'S PIE

SERVES 4

65 g (2½ oz) butter or margarine	100 g (4 oz) button mushrooms, halved
100 g (4 oz) red pepper, thinly sliced	450 ml (¾ pint) tomato juice
100 g (4 oz) green pepper, thinly sliced	550 g (1¼ lb) cod fillet, skinned
50 g (2 oz) onion, sliced	450 g (1 lb) potatoes, peeled and thinly sliced
salt and pepper	50 g (2 oz) Edam cheese, grated

1 Melt 25 g (1 oz) of the butter or margarine in a frying pan, add the peppers and onion and fry gently for 10 minutes or until soft but not coloured. Transfer to a 2.3 litre (4 pint) ovenproof dish. Season well.
2 Cook the mushrooms in the fat remaining in the frying pan, stirring frequently, for 3–4 minutes or until evenly coloured.
3 Pour the tomato juice evenly over the pepper and onion mixture in the dish.
4 Cut the fish into large cubes. Arrange the cubes on top of the tomato juice, pressing them down gently into the juice. Top with the mushrooms. Season again with salt and pepper.
5 Arrange the sliced potatoes on top of the mushrooms. Melt the remaining butter or margarine and brush over the potatoes. Bake in the oven at 190°C (375°F) mark 5 for 25 minutes.
6 Sprinkle the grated cheese over the pie, return to the oven and bake for a further 15 minutes or until melted and bubbling. Serve hot, straight from the dish.

SEAFOOD STIR-FRY

SERVES 4

2 celery sticks, trimmed	1 garlic clove, crushed
1 medium carrot	100 g (4 oz) peeled prawns
350 g (12 oz) coley, haddock or cod fillets, skinned	425 g (15 oz) can whole baby sweetcorn, drained
350 g (12 oz) Iceberg or Cos lettuce	5 ml (1 tsp) anchovy essence
about 45 ml (3 tbsp) peanut oil	salt and pepper

1 Slice the celery and carrot into thin matchsticks, 5 cm (2 inches) long. Cut the fish into 2.5 cm (1 inch) chunks.
2 Shred the lettuce finely with a sharp knife, discarding the core and any thick stalks.
3 Heat 15 ml (1 tbsp) of the oil in a wok or large frying pan until smoking. Add the lettuce and fry for about 30 seconds or until lightly cooked. Transfer to a warmed serving dish with a slotted spoon and keep warm.
4 Heat another 30 ml (2 tbsp) oil in the pan until smoking. Add the celery, carrot, white fish and garlic and stir-fry over a high heat for 2–3 minutes, adding more oil if necessary.
5 Lower the heat and add the prawns, baby sweetcorn and anchovy essence. Toss well together for 2–3 minutes to heat through and coat all the ingredients in the sauce (the fish will flake apart).
6 Season to taste, spoon on top of the lettuce and serve immediately.

CURRIED PRAWN CRÊPES

SERVES 4

	FOR THE FILLING
100 g (4 oz) plain flour	25 g (1 oz) butter
salt	15 ml (1 tbsp) curry powder
1 egg, beaten	25 g (1 oz) plain flour
300 ml (½ pint) milk	300 ml (½ pint) milk
vegetable oil, for frying	225 g (8 oz) peeled prawns
100 g (4 oz) mature Cheddar cheese, grated	30 ml (2 tbsp) chopped fresh parsley or 10 ml (2 tsp) dried
parsley sprigs and lemon wedges, to garnish	salt and pepper

1 To make the crêpes, sift the flour and salt into a bowl. Add the egg and 150 ml (¼ pint) of the milk and beat well. Gradually beat in the remaining milk.
2 Heat a small frying pan or crêpe pan and brush with oil. Add about 45 ml (3 tbsp) of the batter and swirl to coat the pan. Cook for 1–2 minutes or until the underside is golden, then flip over and cook the other side until golden. Turn on to a plate and repeat the process, making eight to ten crêpes.
3 To make the filling, melt the butter in a saucepan, stir in the curry powder and flour and cook for 1 minute. Remove from the heat and gradually stir in the milk. Return to the heat and slowly bring to the boil, stirring continuously. Add the prawns and parsley and season.
4 Divide the filling between the crêpes, placing it towards one edge. Roll up the crêpes and arrange, side by side, in an ovenproof dish. Sprinkle over the cheese.
5 Bake in a preheated oven at 180°C (350°F) mark 4 for 15–20 minutes. Garnish with parsley and lemon.

VEGETARIAN DISHES

Full of goodness and flavour, vegetarian dishes can be both satisfying and simple for family meals, yet special enough for entertaining. Carefully selected combinations of vegetables, herbs, nuts and seeds are delicious served in a wide range of wholesome dishes.

GRANDMA'S CHEESE PUDDING

SERVES 8

1.1 litres (2 pints) milk	8 eggs
100 g (4 oz) fresh breadcrumbs	5 ml (1 tsp) French mustard
450 g (1 lb) Cheddar cheese, grated	salt and pepper

1 Put the milk in a saucepan and bring to the boil. Place the breadcrumbs in a bowl and pour the hot milk over. Stir in the cheese.
2 Lightly beat the eggs with the mustard and the milk and breadcrumb mixture. Season to taste.
3 Butter a shallow 2.8 litre (5 pint) ovenproof dish and pour in the cheese pudding mixture. Bake in a preheated oven at 180°C (350°F) mark 4 for about 45 minutes or until lightly set and golden. Serve at once.

STUFFED AUBERGINES

SERVES 4

2 aubergines	1 shallot, chopped
25 g (1 oz) butter or margarine	1 onion, chopped
4 small tomatoes, skinned and chopped	50 g (2 oz) brown breadcrumbs
10 ml (2 tsp) chopped fresh marjoram or 5 ml (1 tsp) dried	salt and pepper
	50 g (2 oz) cheese, grated
	parsley sprigs, to garnish

1 Steam or boil the aubergines for 30 minutes or until tender. Cut in half lengthways, scoop out the flesh and chop finely. Reserve the shells.
2 Melt the butter in a saucepan, add the tomatoes, marjoram, shallot and onion and cook for 10 minutes. Stir in the aubergine and a few breadcrumbs, then season.
3 Stuff the aubergine shells with this mixture, then sprinkle with the remaining breadcrumbs and the grated cheese. Grill until golden brown. Garnish and serve.

CHEESE SOUFFLÉ
SERVES 4

40 g (1½ oz) butter	10 ml (2 tsp) French mustard
200 ml (7 fl oz) milk	salt and pepper
1 onion, sliced	4 eggs, separated, plus 1 egg white
1 carrot, sliced	
1 bay leaf	150 g (5 oz) Double Gloucester cheese, grated
6 peppercorns	
30 ml (2 tbsp) plain flour	

1 Grease the inside of a 1.4 litre (2½ pint) soufflé dish with 15 g (½ oz) butter.

2 Place the milk, onion, carrot, bay leaf and peppercorns in a saucepan, bring slowly to the boil, then remove from the heat. Leave to infuse for 15 minutes, then strain and reserve the milk.

3 Melt the remaining butter in a saucepan, stir in the flour and cook gently for 1 minute, stirring. Remove from the heat and gradually stir in the reserved milk. Bring to the boil and continue to cook, stirring, until the sauce thickens, then add the mustard and season to taste. Leave to cool slightly.

4 Beat the egg yolks into the sauce, one at a time. Add the cheese, reserving 15 ml (1 tbsp), and stir until well blended.

5 Whisk the egg whites until stiff. Mix in one spoonful of sauce, then pour the remaining sauce over the egg whites and fold the ingredients lightly together.

6 Turn the mixture gently into the prepared dish. Smooth the top and sprinkle over the remaining cheese. Place on a baking sheet and bake in the centre of the oven at 180°C (350°F) mark 4 for 30 minutes. Serve at once.

COURGETTE, PARMESAN AND TOMATO BAKE
SERVES 4

700 g (1½ lb) courgettes	30 ml (2 tbsp) tomato purée
salt and pepper	
about 150 ml (¼ pint) vegetable oil	15 ml (1 tbsp) chopped fresh marjoram or 5 ml (1 tsp) dried
1 medium onion, finely chopped	two 170 g (6 oz) packets Mozzarella cheese, thinly sliced
450 g (1 lb) tomatoes, skinned and chopped	75 g (3 oz) freshly grated Parmesan cheese
1 large garlic clove, crushed	

1 Cut the courgettes into 0.5 cm (¼ inch) thick slices. Put in a colander, sprinkling each layer generously with salt, and leave for at least 20 minutes.

2 Heat 30 ml (2 tbsp) of the oil in a saucepan, add the onion and fry for about 5 minutes or until just beginning to brown.

3 Stir in the tomatoes, garlic and tomato purée and season to taste. Simmer for about 10 minutes, stirring to break down the tomatoes. Stir in the marjoram and remove from the heat.

4 Rinse the courgettes and pat dry with absorbent kitchen paper. Heat half the remaining oil in a frying pan, add half the courgettes and fry until golden brown. Drain well on absorbent kitchen paper while frying the remaining courgettes in the remaining oil.

5 Layer the courgettes, tomato sauce and Mozzarella cheese in a shallow ovenproof dish, finishing with a layer of Mozzarella. Sprinkle with the Parmesan cheese.

6 Bake in a preheated oven at 180°C (350°F) mark 4 for about 40 minutes or until brown and bubbling. Serve hot, straight from the dish.

ITALIAN STUFFED TOMATOES

SERVES 4–6

15 ml (1 tbsp) olive oil	45 ml (3 tbsp) pine nuts
4 spring onions, finely chopped	397 g (14 oz) can flageolet beans, drained
2 garlic cloves, crushed	salt and pepper
15 ml (1 tbsp) tomato purée	4 large beefsteak tomatoes or 6 medium tomatoes
12 pimiento-stuffed green olives, sliced	basil sprigs, to garnish
30 ml (2 tbsp) chopped fresh basil or 15 ml (1 tbsp) dried	

1 Heat the oil in a large saucepan and cook the spring onions and garlic for 2–3 minutes or until soft.
2 Add the tomato purée, olives, basil and nuts and cook for 2 minutes. Stir in the beans. Season.
3 Slice the tops off the tomatoes, reserving them for the lids, and scoop out the seeds and flesh to make them hollow. Chop the flesh and add to the filling mixture. Arrange the tomato shells in a buttered ovenproof dish and divide the filling between them. Add the lids and cover with foil.
4 Bake in a preheated oven at 180°C (350°F) mark 4 for 15–20 minutes. Garnish and serve.

JERUSALEM ARTICHOKE GRATIN

SERVES 4

900 g (2 lb) Jerusalem artichokes	3 medium leeks, thickly sliced
salt and pepper	225 g (8 oz) fresh or frozen peas
75 g (3 oz) butter or margarine	150 ml (¼ pint) double cream
15 ml (1 tbsp) olive oil	75 g (3 oz) Gruyère cheese, grated
225 g (8 oz) button onions, skinned	75 g (3 oz) Cheddar cheese, grated
2 garlic cloves, crushed	50 g (2 oz) dried wholemeal breadcrumbs
150 ml (¼ pint) dry white wine or vegetable stock	
1.25 ml (¼ tsp) grated nutmeg	

1 Parboil the artichokes in salted water for 10 minutes. Remove with a slotted spoon and leave to cool.
2 Peel the artichokes and slice thickly. Set aside.
3 Heat 50 g (2 oz) butter with the oil in a saucepan, add the onions and garlic and toss until well coated.
4 Pour in the wine or stock and 150 ml (¼ pint) water and bring to the boil. Add the nutmeg, cover and simmer for 10 minutes. Add the artichokes, leeks and peas and continue simmering for 5 minutes or until tender. Transfer the vegetables to a flameproof gratin dish.
5 Boil the cooking liquid rapidly until reduced by about half, then lower the heat and stir in the cream.
6 Mix the two cheeses together. Stir half into the sauce, season and stir until melted.
7 Pour the cheese sauce over the vegetables. Mix the remaining cheese and breadcrumbs, then sprinkle on top.
8 Dot the remaining butter over the gratin, then bake at 220°C (425°F) mark 7 for 10 minutes or until golden.

122

CYPRUS STUFFED PEPPERS

SERVES 4

8 peppers	5 ml (1 tsp) sugar
75 ml (5 tbsp) olive oil	salt and pepper
2 onions, chopped	45 ml (3 tbsp) chopped coriander
4 garlic cloves, crushed	225 g (8 oz) Italian risotto rice
350 g (12 oz) tomatoes, skinned, seeded and chopped	2.5 ml (½ tsp) ground cinnamon
15 ml (1 tbsp) tomato purée	

1 Cut the stalk end off each pepper and reserve. Remove the cores and seeds and discard. Wash and pat dry.
2 Heat 60 ml (4 tbsp) oil in a frying pan, add the peppers and fry for 10 minutes, turning frequently. Remove from the pan with a slotted spoon and drain.
3 To make the stuffing, drain off all but 30 ml (2 tbsp) oil from the pan, then add the onions and garlic and fry very gently for about 15 minutes. Add the tomatoes and fry gently to soften, stirring constantly. Increase the heat and cook rapidly until thick and pulpy.
4 Lower the heat and add the tomato purée and sugar. Season to taste and simmer gently for 5 minutes. Remove from the heat and stir in the coriander and rice. Spoon into the peppers, dividing it equally between them.
5 Stand the peppers close together in a large heavy-based pan or flameproof casserole. Sprinkle with the cinnamon, then the remaining oil. Put the reserved 'lids' on top.
6 Pour 150 ml (¼ pint) water into the base of the pan, then bring to the boil. Lower the heat, cover with a plate which just fits inside the pan, then place weights on top.
7 Simmer gently for 1 hour, then remove from the heat and leave to cool. Chill in the refrigerator overnight, still with the weights on top. Serve the peppers chilled.

CABBAGE AND HAZELNUT ROLLS

MAKES 16

450 g (1 lb) potatoes, peeled	50 g (2 oz) hazelnuts, toasted and chopped
salt and pepper	2 eggs, beaten
900 g (2 lb) green cabbage, roughly chopped	100 g (4 oz) dry breadcrumbs
45 ml (3 tbsp) milk, if necessary	vegetable oil, for deep frying
50 g (2 oz) butter	lemon twists, to garnish
50 g (2 oz) plain flour	

1 Cook the potatoes in boiling salted water for 20 minutes or until tender. Drain and mash without adding liquid.
2 Cook the cabbage in boiling salted water for 5–10 minutes or until just tender. Drain well, then put in a blender or food processor and blend to a purée, adding the milk if necessary – you should have 450 ml (¾ pint) purée.
3 Melt the butter in a saucepan, add the flour and cook gently, stirring, for 1–2 minutes. Gradually blend in the cabbage purée, bring to the boil and simmer for 5 minutes.
4 Stir the mashed potatoes and hazelnuts into the sauce, season to taste and mix well. Transfer to a bowl, cool, cover and chill for at least 1½ hours or until firm.
5 With dampened hands, shape the mixture into 16 rolls. Place on a greased baking sheet and chill again for at least 20 minutes.
6 Coat the rolls in beaten egg, then roll in the breadcrumbs. Heat the oil to 180°C (350°F) in a deep-fat fryer. Deep-fry the rolls in batches for about 4 minutes or until crisp and golden. Remove with a slotted spoon and drain on absorbent kitchen paper while frying the remainder. Serve hot, garnished with lemon twists.

BAKED POTATOES WITH CHICK-PEAS

SERVES 4

CAULIFLOWER AND COURGETTE BAKE

SERVES 4

four 275 g (10 oz) baking potatoes	2.5 ml (½ tsp) ground cumin
45 ml (3 tbsp) vegetable oil	400 g (14 oz) can chick-peas, drained
salt and pepper	60 ml (4 tbsp) chopped parsley
1 medium onion, roughly chopped	150 ml (¼ pint) natural yogurt
2.5 ml (½ tsp) ground coriander	chopped parsley, to garnish

1 Scrub the potatoes and pat dry. Brush them with 15 ml (1 tbsp) of the vegetable oil and sprinkle lightly with salt.
2 Run thin skewers through the potatoes to help conduct the heat through them. Place them directly on the oven shelves and bake in a preheated oven at 200°C (400°F) mark 6 for 1¼ hours or until tender.
3 Meanwhile, heat the remaining oil in a large saucepan, add the onion, coriander and cumin and fry for 4 minutes, stirring occasionally. Add the chick-peas and cook for a further 1–2 minutes, stirring all the time.
4 Halve the potatoes and scoop out the flesh, keeping the skin intact. Add the potato flesh to the chick-pea mixture with the parsley and yogurt. Mash until smooth, then season to taste.
5 Place the potato skins on a baking sheet and fill with the potato and chick-pea mixture. Return to the oven and bake for a further 10–15 minutes. Serve hot, sprinkled with chopped parsley.

700 g (1½ lb) cauliflower	45 ml (3 tbsp) wholemeal flour
salt and pepper	150 ml (¼ pint) milk
50 g (2 oz) butter or margarine	3 eggs, separated
225 g (8 oz) courgettes, thinly sliced	15 ml (1 tbsp) grated Parmesan cheese

1 Divide the cauliflower into small florets, trimming off thick stalks and leaves. Cook in boiling salted water for 10–12 minutes or until tender.
2 Meanwhile, in a separate pan, melt 25 g (1 oz) of the butter or margarine, add the courgettes and cook until beginning to soften. Remove from the pan with a slotted spoon and drain on absorbent kitchen paper.
3 Melt the remaining butter or margarine in the pan, stir in the flour and cook, stirring, for 1–2 minutes. Remove from the heat and add the milk, a little at a time, whisking constantly after each addition. Return to the heat and bring to the boil, stirring. Simmer until thickened.
4 Drain the cauliflower well and place in a blender or food processor with the warm sauce, egg yolks and plenty of seasoning. Blend together until evenly mixed, then turn into a large bowl.
5 Whisk the egg whites until stiff and carefully fold into the cauliflower mixture.
6 Spoon half the mixture into a 1.6 litre (2¾ pint) soufflé dish. Arrange the courgettes on top, reserving a few for garnish, then cover with the remaining cauliflower mixture. Top with the reserved courgettes.
7 Sprinkle over the Parmesan cheese and bake in a preheated oven at 190°C (375°F) mark 5 for 35–40 minutes or until golden. Serve immediately.

LEEK AND MACARONI GRATIN

SERVES 4

100 g (4 oz) short-cut macaroni	175 g (6 oz) Double Gloucester cheese with chives, grated
50 g (2 oz) butter	salt and pepper
275 g (10 oz) leeks, roughly chopped	25 g (1 oz) breadcrumbs
25 g (1 oz) plain flour	30 ml (2 tbsp) chopped chives
568 ml (1 pint) milk	

1 Cook the macaroni in boiling salted water for 8–10 minutes or until tender, but not soft. Drain well.
2 Melt the butter in a frying pan, add the leeks and sauté for 2 minutes. Stir in the flour and cook gently for 1 minute, stirring. Remove the pan from the heat and gradually stir in the milk. Bring to the boil and continue to cook, stirring for 2 minutes. Remove from the heat and stir in the macaroni and all but 30 ml (2 tbsp) cheese. Season to taste.
3 Spoon the mixture into a buttered 1.1 litre (2 pint) shallow ovenproof dish. Mix together the breadcrumbs, chives and remaining cheese and sprinkle evenly in lines across the dish.
4 Bake in a preheated oven at 190°C (375°F) mark 5 for 30–35 minutes or until golden. Serve immediately.

PASTA AND MUSHROOMS BAKED WITH TWO CHEESES

SERVES 2–3

225 g (8 oz) ribbon noodles	60 ml (4 tbsp) double cream
25 g (1 oz) butter	salt and pepper
1 garlic clove, crushed	1 egg, lightly beaten
225 g (8 oz) mushrooms, thinly sliced	100 g (4 oz) Mozzarella cheese
50 g (2 oz) Stilton cheese	

1 Cook the noodles in boiling salted water for about 7 minutes or until just tender.
2 Meanwhile, melt the butter in a large frying pan, add the garlic and mushrooms and fry for about 5 minutes or until just softened, stirring frequently. Crumble in the Stilton cheese and cook for 1–2 minutes, stirring continuously. Stir in the cream and season to taste.
3 Drain the pasta and season with lots of pepper. Mix into the mushroom sauce. Stir in the egg and mix thoroughly.
4 Turn the mixture into a buttered ovenproof dish and grate the Mozzarella on top. Cover with foil and bake in a preheated oven at 180°C (350°F) mark 4 for 10 minutes, then remove the foil and bake at 220°C (425°F) mark 7 for a further 10–15 minutes or until brown and crusty on top.

_____ **TO MICROWAVE** _____

Complete step 1. Meanwhile, put the butter, garlic and mushrooms in a large bowl, cover and cook on HIGH for 3–4 minutes or until the mushrooms are softened, stirring occasionally. Stir in the Stilton cheese and the cream and cook on HIGH for 2 minutes, stirring once. Complete step 3. Turn the mixture into a buttered flameproof dish and grate the Mozzarella on top. Cook on HIGH for 3–4 minutes or until heated through. Brown the top under a hot grill.

VEGETABLE LASAGNE

SERVES 4

225 g (8 oz) carrots, thinly sliced	1 chicken stock cube
225 g (8 oz) courgettes, thinly sliced	25 g (1 oz) butter
	30 ml (2 tbsp) plain flour
1 onion, thinly sliced	300 ml (½ pint) milk
100 g (4 oz) green pepper, thinly sliced	salt and pepper
	175 g (6 oz) lasagne
100 g (4 oz) celery, thinly sliced	175 g (6 oz) Cheddar cheese, grated

1 Place the vegetables in a saucepan with the stock cube and pour over 150 ml (¼ pint) boiling water. Bring to the boil, cover and simmer for 10 minutes.

2 Melt the butter in a pan, stir in the flour and cook gently for 1 minute, stirring. Remove from the heat and gradually stir in the milk. Bring to the boil and continue to cook, stirring, until the sauce thickens, then season to taste. If the sauce is too thick, add a little stock from the vegetables.

3 Meanwhile, cook the lasagne in fast boiling salted water until tender, but not soft, or according to packet instructions. Drain, being careful not to break up the lasagne sheets.

4 Make alternate layers of lasagne, vegetables and cheese (use 100 g/4 oz) in a 1.7 litre (3 pint) shallow ovenproof dish, finishing with a layer of lasagne. Top with the sauce, then sprinkle over the remaining cheese.

5 Bake in a preheated oven at 190°C (375°F) mark 5 for about 30 minutes.

SPAGHETTI WITH RATATOUILLE SAUCE

SERVES 4

1 aubergine	3 medium courgettes, cut into thin strips
salt and pepper	
1 onion, finely chopped	350 g (12 oz) tomatoes, skinned and finely chopped
1 garlic clove, crushed	10 ml (2 tsp) chopped basil
1 green pepper, cut into thin strips	400 g (14 oz) wholewheat spaghetti
1 red pepper, cut into thin strips	freshly grated Parmesan cheese, to serve

1 Dice the aubergine, then spread out on a plate and sprinkle with salt. Leave for 30 minutes or until the juices flow.

2 Tip the diced aubergine into a sieve and rinse under cold running water. Put into a large, heavy-based saucepan with the prepared vegetables and basil. Season to taste, cover and cook over a moderate heat for 30 minutes. Shake the pan and stir the vegetables frequently during this time, to encourage the juices to flow.

3 Meanwhile, plunge the spaghetti into a large saucepan of boiling salted water. Simmer, uncovered, for 12 minutes or according to packet instructions, until *al dente* (tender but firm to the bite).

4 Drain the spaghetti thoroughly and turn into a warmed serving dish. Taste and adjust the seasoning of the ratatouille sauce, then pour over the spaghetti. Serve immediately, with the Parmesan cheese.

FRESH TAGLIATELLE WITH LEEK AND ROQUEFORT SAUCE

SERVES 4

75 g (3 oz) butter	5 ml (1 tsp) olive oil
1 garlic clove, crushed	pepper
450 g (1 lb) leeks, sliced	150 ml (¼ pint) whipping cream
150 g (5 oz) Roquefort cheese, roughly chopped	15–30 ml (1–2 tbsp) grated Parmesan cheese
30 ml (2 tbsp) chopped fresh chervil or 10 ml (2 tsp) dried	chervil sprigs, to garnish
700 g (1½ lb) fresh tagliatelle	

1 Melt 50 g (2 oz) of the butter in a medium saucepan, add the garlic and leeks and fry for 2–3 minutes or until softened.
2 Stir in the Roquefort cheese and chervil. Cook for 2–3 minutes or until the cheese has melted, stirring constantly.
3 Meanwhile, add the tagliatelle to a large saucepan of boiling water, with the olive oil added, and cook for 3–4 minutes. Drain and return to the clean pan. Add the remaining butter, toss well and season with pepper.
4 Pour the cream into the sauce, whisking vigorously. Cook, stirring, for a few minutes or until thick.
5 Serve the tagliatelle on warmed individual serving plates with the sauce poured over. Sprinkle with Parmesan cheese and garnish with chervil sprigs.

——— TO MICROWAVE ———

Dice the butter into a medium bowl. Cover and cook on HIGH for 1 minute. Add the garlic and leeks. Cover and cook on HIGH for 2–3 minutes. Add the cheese and chervil and cook for 1–1½ minutes. Whisk in the cream and cook on HIGH for 1–1½ minutes. Complete steps 3 and 5 as above.

TAGLIATELLE WITH CHEESE AND NUT SAUCE

SERVES 4

400 g (14 oz) wholewheat or green (spinach) tagliatelle	5 ml (1 tsp) chopped fresh sage or 2.5 ml (½ tsp) dried
salt and pepper	75 ml (5 tbsp) olive oil
100 g (4 oz) Gorgonzola cheese	15 ml (1 tbsp) chopped parsley, to garnish
100 g (4 oz) walnuts, chopped	

1 Plunge the tagliatelle into a large saucepan of boiling salted water. Simmer, uncovered, for 10 minutes, or according to packet instructions, until *al dente* (tender but firm to the bite).
2 Meanwhile, crumble the cheese into a blender or food processor. Add two thirds of the walnuts and the sage and blend to combine.
3 Add the oil gradually through the funnel (as when making mayonnaise) and blend until the sauce is evenly incorporated.
4 Drain the tagliatelle well and return to the pan. Add the nut sauce and fold in gently to mix. Season to taste.
5 Transfer the pasta and sauce to a warmed serving bowl and sprinkle with the remaining walnuts. Serve immediately, garnished with chopped parsley.

RATATOUILLE PASTA BAKE

SERVES 4–6

30 ml (2 tbsp) olive oil	30 ml (2 tbsp) chopped fresh basil or 5 ml (1 tsp) dried
1 large onion, thinly sliced	
1 red pepper, cut into 5 cm (2 inch) strips	pinch of sugar
1 yellow pepper, cut into 5 cm (2 inch) strips	salt and pepper
	450 ml (¾ pint) vegetable stock
225 g (8 oz) courgettes, cut into 5 cm (2 inch) strips	350 g (12 oz) mixed coloured pasta twists
450 g (1 lb) ripe tomatoes, skinned and chopped	50 g (2 oz) butter
2 garlic cloves, crushed	175 g (6 oz) mature Cheddar cheese, grated
30 ml (2 tbsp) tomato purée	

1 Heat the oil in a large pan, add the onion and peppers, and cook for 5 minutes or until softened, stirring. Add the courgettes and cook for 5 minutes.
2 Stir in the tomatoes, garlic, tomato purée, basil and sugar. Season to taste and simmer for 25–30 minutes, stirring occasionally and gradually adding the stock.
3 Meanwhile, bring a large saucepan of salted water to the boil and add the pasta twists. Cook for 15–20 minutes, stirring occasionally. Drain, then return to the pan, add the butter, toss well and season to taste. Transfer to a deep flameproof dish.
4 Pour the ratatouille sauce over the pasta and sprinkle over the cheese. Grill until golden.

WHOLEWHEAT MACARONI BAKE

SERVES 4–6

175 g (6 oz) wholewheat macaroni	5 ml (1 tsp) dried oregano
salt and pepper	30 ml (2 tbsp) plain wholemeal flour
1 onion, chopped	300 ml (½ pint) milk
30 ml (2 tbsp) vegetable oil	100 g (4 oz) low-fat soft cheese
225 g (8 oz) button mushrooms	1 egg, beaten
350 g (12 oz) tomatoes, skinned and roughly chopped	5 ml (1 tsp) English mustard powder
300 ml (½ pint) vegetable stock	30 ml (2 tbsp) wholemeal breadcrumbs
15 ml (1 tbsp) tomato purée	30 ml (2 tbsp) grated Parmesan cheese
5 ml (1 tsp) dried mixed herbs	

1 Cook the macaroni in boiling salted water for 10 minutes. Drain. Fry the onion in the oil for 5 minutes.
2 Cut the small mushrooms in half and slice the larger ones. Add to the pan and toss with the onion for 1–2 minutes.
3 Add the tomatoes and stock and bring to the boil, stirring constantly. Lower the heat, add the tomato purée and herbs and season to taste. Simmer for 10 minutes.
4 Put the flour and milk in a blender and blend for 1 minute. Transfer to a pan and simmer, stirring constantly, for 5 minutes or until thick. Remove from the heat and beat in the cheese, egg and mustard. Season.
5 Mix the macaroni with the mushroom and tomato sauce, then pour into a baking dish. Pour over the cheese sauce and sprinkle with breadcrumbs and Parmesan.
6 Bake in a preheated oven at 190°C (375°F) mark 5 for 20 minutes or until golden brown and bubbling. Serve hot.

SPINACH AND LENTIL ROULADE

SERVES 4

175 g (6 oz) red lentils	salt and pepper
1 small onion, finely chopped	450 g (1 lb) spinach
	50 g (2 oz) plain flour
30 ml (2 tbsp) tomato ketchup	300 ml (½ pint) milk
15 ml (1 tbsp) horseradish sauce	2 eggs, separated
	dry breadcrumbs
100 g (4 oz) butter	

1 Butter and line a 28 cm (11 inch) Swiss roll tin.
2 Cook the lentils with the onion in a large saucepan of boiling salted water until tender. Drain well, then return to the pan and heat to evaporate excess moisture. Add the tomato ketchup, horseradish and 50 g (2 oz) butter. Rub through a sieve, season to taste and set aside.
3 Trim and wash the spinach but do not dry. Pack into a large saucepan, sprinkle with salt, cover tightly and cook gently for 3–4 minutes.
4 To make the sauce, melt the remaining butter in a saucepan, stir in the flour and cook gently for 1 minute, stirring. Remove from the heat and gradually stir in the milk. Bring to the boil and continue to cook, stirring, until the sauce thickens. Remove from the heat. Stir in the spinach and egg yolks. Season to taste.
5 Whisk the egg whites until stiff and gently fold into the spinach mixture. Spoon into the prepared tin and level the surface. Bake in a preheated oven at 200°C (400°F) mark 6 for 20 minutes or until well risen and golden.
6 Turn out on to a sheet of greaseproof paper sprinkled with the breadcrumbs. Peel off the lining paper. Spread the lentil purée over the surface and roll up Swiss-roll style. Return to the oven to heat through before serving.

SPINACH AND STILTON CRÊPES

SERVES 8

900 g (2 lb) fresh spinach	150 ml (5 fl oz) single cream
salt and pepper	
50 g (2 oz) butter	8 crêpes (see page 119)
50 g (2 oz) salted peanuts, chopped	300 ml (½ pint) milk
2.5 ml (½ tsp) paprika	50 g (2 oz) Blue Stilton cheese, grated
40 ml (8 tsp) plain flour	

1 Tear the stalks off the spinach and wash, but do not dry. Place in a large saucepan, sprinkle with salt, cover tightly and cook for 10 minutes. Drain well and chop.
2 Heat 25 g (1 oz) butter in a small saucepan, add the peanuts and paprika and fry gently for 1 minute. Stir in the spinach, 20 ml (4 tsp) flour and the cream. Season to taste. Bring to the boil and cook for 2–3 minutes, stirring. Divide the filling between the crêpes, roll up and place, side by side, in a buttered ovenproof dish.
3 Melt the remaining butter in a saucepan, stir in the remaining flour and cook for 1 minute, stirring. Remove from the heat and gradually stir in the milk. Bring to the boil, stirring all the time, until the sauce thickens. Stir in the cheese and season to taste. Pour over the crêpes, cover lightly with foil and bake in a preheated oven at 180°C (350°F) mark 4 for 25–30 minutes.

VARIATION

Spinach and Ricotta Crêpes
Ricotta is a fragrant Italian cheese made from the whey left over when producing other cheeses. It has a delicate, smooth flavour and is often mixed with spinach in stuffings for ravioli or cannelloni. It would make an ideal substitute for Stilton in the above recipe.

VEGETARIAN MEDLEY

SERVES 4

VEGETABLE CURRY

SERVES 4

25 g (1 oz) butter	100 g (4 oz) lentils, cooked
2 carrots, sliced	15 ml (1 tbsp) raisins
1 large onion, chopped	30 ml (2 tbsp) unsalted peanuts
1 green pepper, sliced	
2 tomatoes, chopped	salt and pepper
1 large cooking apple, peeled, cored and chopped	300 ml (10 fl oz) natural yogurt
1 garlic clove, crushed	25 g (1 oz) cream cheese
15 ml (1 tbsp) chopped fresh sage or 5 ml (1 tsp) dried	

I Melt the butter in a large frying pan, add the carrots, onion, green pepper, tomatoes, apple, garlic and sage and fry lightly for 15 minutes or until softened
2 Add the lentils, raisins and peanuts. Season to taste. Stir the yogurt into the cream cheese and mix well to blend. Stir into the mixture. Reheat gently for 5 minutes.

―――――――― **TO MICROWAVE** ――――――――

Melt the butter in a large bowl on HIGH for 45 seconds. Add the carrots, onion, green pepper, tomatoes, apple, garlic and sage and cook on HIGH for 7 minutes, stirring occasionally. Add the remaining ingredients, as in step 2, and cook on HIGH for 2 minutes. Serve at once.

30 ml (2 tbsp) vegetable oil	2 potatoes, peeled and roughly chopped
10 ml (2 tsp) ground coriander	2 carrots, sliced
5 ml (1 tsp) ground cumin	1 green pepper, chopped
2.5–5 ml (½–1 tsp) chilli powder	225 g (8 oz) tomatoes, roughly chopped
2.5 ml (½ tsp) ground turmeric	150 ml (5 fl oz) natural yogurt
2 garlic cloves, crushed	salt and pepper
1 medium onion, chopped	
1 small cauliflower, cut into small florets	

I Heat the oil in a large saucepan, add the coriander, cumin, chilli, turmeric, garlic and onion and fry for 2–3 minutes, stirring continuously.
2 Add the cauliflower, potatoes, carrots and green pepper and stir to coat in the spices. Stir in the tomatoes and 150 ml (¼ pint) water. Bring to the boil, cover and simmer gently for 25–30 minutes or until the vegetables are tender.
3 Remove from the heat, stir in the yogurt and season.

―――――――― **TO MICROWAVE** ――――――――

Put the oil, coriander, cumin, chilli, turmeric, garlic and onion in a large bowl and cook on HIGH for 2 minutes, stirring once. Add the cauliflower, potatoes, carrots and green pepper and stir to coat in the spices. Stir in the tomatoes and 150 ml (¼ pint) water. Cover and cook on HIGH for 20 minutes or until the vegetables are tender, stirring occasionally. Complete step 3.

MOONG DAL AND SPINACH

SERVES 6

225 g (8 oz) moong dal (split, washed moong beans)	1 garlic clove, crushed
	10 ml (2 tsp) ground coriander
900 g (2 lb) fresh spinach, washed and trimmed, or 450 g (1 lb) frozen chopped spinach	5 ml (1 tsp) ground turmeric
	2.5 ml (½ tsp) chilli powder
75 g (3 oz) ghee or clarified butter	1.25 ml (¼ tsp) asafoetida (optional)
100 g (4 oz) onion, finely chopped	salt and pepper
15 g (½ oz) fresh root ginger, finely chopped	lemon wedges, to garnish

1 Rinse the dal under cold running water. Place in a bowl, cover with cold water and leave to soak for about 2 hours, then drain.

2 Place the fresh spinach in a saucepan with only the water that clings to the leaves. Cover and cook gently for about 5 minutes or until tender. Drain well and chop roughly. If using frozen spinach, place in a saucepan and cook for 7–10 minutes to thaw and to remove as much liquid as possible.

3 Heat the ghee or butter in a large sauté pan, add the onion, ginger and garlic and fry for 2–3 minutes.

4 Stir in the coriander, turmeric, chilli powder, asafoetida (if using) and the dal. Fry, stirring, for 2–3 minutes.

5 Pour in 300 ml (½ pint) water, season to taste and bring to the boil. Cover and simmer for about 15 minutes or until the dal is almost tender. Add a little more water if necessary, but the mixture should be almost dry.

6 Stir in the spinach and cook, stirring for 2–3 minutes or until heated through. Taste and adjust the seasoning before serving, garnished with lemon wedges.

VEGETABLE BIRYANI

SERVES 4

350 g (12 oz) Basmati rice	2.5 ml (½ tsp) chilli powder
salt and pepper	
50 g (2 oz) ghee or clarified butter	3 medium carrots, thinly sliced
1 large onion, chopped	225 g (8 oz) fresh or frozen green beans, cut in two lengthways
2.5 cm (1 inch) piece of fresh root ginger, grated	
1–2 garlic cloves, crushed	225 g (8 oz) cauliflower florets, divided into small sprigs
5 ml (1 tsp) ground coriander	5 ml (1 tsp) garam masala
10 ml (2 tsp) ground cumin	juice of 1 lemon
5 ml (1 tsp) ground turmeric	hard-boiled egg slices and coriander sprigs, to garnish

1 Rinse the rice and put in a saucepan with 600 ml (1 pint) water and 5 ml (1 tsp) salt. Bring to the boil, then simmer for 10 minutes or until only just tender.

2 Meanwhile, heat the ghee or butter in a large heavy-based saucepan, add the onion, ginger and garlic and fry gently for 5 minutes or until soft but not coloured. Add the coriander, cumin, turmeric and chilli powder and fry for 2 minutes more, stirring constantly.

3 Remove the rice from the heat and drain. Add 900 ml (1½ pints) water to the onion and spice mixture and season to taste. Stir well and bring to the boil. Add the carrots and beans and simmer for 15 minutes, then add the cauliflower and simmer for a further 10 minutes. Lastly, add the rice. Fold gently to mix and simmer until reheated.

4 Stir the garam masala and lemon juice into the biryani and simmer for a few minutes more to reheat and allow the flavours to develop. Season, garnish and serve.

VEGETABLE HOT POT
SERVES 4

450 g (1 lb) carrots, thinly sliced	bouquet garni
2 large onions, thinly sliced	salt and pepper
3 celery sticks, thinly sliced	425 g (15 oz) can butter beans, drained
450 g (1 lb) potatoes, peeled and sliced	100 g (4 oz) frozen peas
100 g (4 oz) swede, thinly sliced	175 g (6 oz) fresh breadcrumbs
450 ml (¾ pint) vegetable stock	175 g (6 oz) hard cheese, grated

1 Layer the carrots, onions, celery, potato and swede in a 2.3 litre (4 pint) casserole.
2 Pour the vegetable stock into the casserole and add the bouquet garni. Season to taste.
3 Cover the casserole, and cook in a preheated oven at 180°C (350°F) mark 4 for 1 hour.
4 Remove the bouquet garni. Add the beans and peas to the casserole. Mix the breadcrumbs and cheese together and spoon over the hot pot. Return to the oven and cook, uncovered, for about 20 minutes.

─────────────── VARIATION ───────────────

The vegetables used in this satisfying dish can be varied according to the season. Other root vegetables, such as parsnips or turnips could replace the swede, and any canned beans could be used instead of butter beans. When available, replace the frozen peas with fresh.

BUCKWHEAT AND LENTIL CASSEROLE
SERVES 4

salt and pepper	3 bay leaves
150 g (5 oz) buckwheat	30 ml (2 tbsp) lemon juice
30 ml (2 tbsp) vegetable oil	1 garlic clove, crushed
1 red or green pepper, cut into strips	2 rosemary sprigs
1 onion, finely chopped	5 ml (1 tsp) cumin seeds
350 g (12 oz) courgettes, sliced	600 ml (1 pint) vegetable stock
175 g (6 oz) mushrooms, sliced	25 g (1 oz) butter
225 g (8 oz) red lentils	chopped parsley, to garnish

1 Put 450 ml (¾ pint) water in a saucepan, add a pinch of salt, then bring to the boil. Sprinkle in the buckwheat and return to the boil. Boil rapidly for 1 minute, reduce the heat, cover and cook gently for 12 minutes or until the water has been absorbed. Do not stir. Transfer to a buttered casserole.
2 Heat the oil in a flameproof casserole, add the pepper and onion and fry for 5 minutes. Add the courgettes and mushrooms and fry for a further 5 minutes. Stir in the lentils, bay leaves, lemon juice, garlic, rosemary, cumin and stock. Add to the buckwheat and stir well.
3 Simmer for about 45 minutes or until the lentils are cooked, stirring occasionally. Add the butter, adjust the seasoning and sprinkle with parsley. Serve hot.

COUSCOUS

SERVES 6

450 g (1 lb) couscous	salt and pepper
4 courgettes, cut into 1 cm (½ inch) slices	225 g (8 oz) chick-peas, soaked overnight, then drained
1 red pepper, diced	
1 green pepper, diced	25 g (1 oz) blanched almonds
2 onions, diced	5 ml (1 tsp) ground turmeric
2 carrots, diced	
225 g (8 oz) turnips, diced	10 ml (2 tsp) paprika
1 small cauliflower, cut into small florets	2.5 ml (½ tsp) ground coriander
4 large tomatoes, skinned and chopped	75 g (3 oz) butter, melted
2 garlic cloves, crushed	100 g (4 oz) dried apricots, soaked overnight
1.1 litres (2 pints) vegetable stock	

1 Place the couscous in a large bowl with 450 ml (¾ pint) tepid water and leave to soak for 1 hour.
2 Place the prepared vegetables in a large saucepan with the garlic, stock, pepper to taste, chick-peas, almonds and spices. Bring to the boil, cover and simmer for 30 minutes.
3 Drain the couscous and place in a steamer over the vegetables. Cover and cook for a further 40 minutes, then remove the steamer and cover the saucepan.
4 Place the couscous in a large mixing bowl. Beat the butter into the couscous with 50 ml (2 fl oz) salted water.
5 Drain and quarter the apricots, add them to the vegetables and simmer for 15 minutes. Stir the couscous well to remove any lumps, return it to the steamer over the simmering vegetables, cover and cook for 20 minutes.
6 Season the vegetables and serve with the couscous.

VEGETABLE CHILLI

SERVES 4

30 ml (2 tbsp) olive oil	150 ml (¼ pint) dry red wine
1 large onion, chopped	
2 garlic cloves, crushed	30 ml (2 tbsp) chopped fresh oregano or 5 ml (1 tsp) dried
5–10 ml (1–2 tsp) chilli powder	
225 g (8 oz) courgettes, diced	397 g (14 oz) can red kidney beans, drained
100 g (4 oz) carrots, sliced	15 ml (1 tbsp) cornflour
1 red pepper, diced	150 ml (¼ pint) Greek strained yogurt and chopped parsley, to serve
397 g (14 oz) can chopped tomatoes	

1 Heat the oil in a large saucepan, add the onion, garlic and chilli powder and cook for 2–3 minutes or until softened. Add the courgettes and carrots and cook for a further 3–4 minutes.
2 Add the red pepper and chopped tomatoes. Cook for 5 minutes. Stir in the wine, oregano and kidney beans, cover and cook for 25–30 minutes.
3 Mix 45 ml (3 tbsp) water with the cornflour to give a smooth paste. Stir the paste into the chilli and bring to the boil. Simmer for 2–3 minutes, stirring. Serve with yogurt and parsley.

SOUTHERN BAKED BEANS

SERVES 4

275 g (10 oz) dried haricot beans, soaked overnight	30 ml (2 tbsp) treacle
15 ml (1 tbsp) vegetable oil	300 ml (½ pint) tomato juice
2 onions, chopped	45 ml (3 tbsp) tomato purée
225 g (8 oz) carrots, chopped	300 ml (½ pint) beer
15 ml (1 tbsp) mustard powder	salt and pepper

1 Drain the beans, place in a saucepan and cover with fresh water. Bring to the boil and simmer for 25 minutes, then drain.

2 Meanwhile, heat the oil in a flameproof casserole, add the onions and carrots and fry for 5 minutes or until lightly golden.

3 Remove from the heat and add the mustard, treacle, tomato juice, tomato purée, beer and beans. Stir well.

4 Bring to the boil, cover and cook in a preheated oven at 140°C (275°F) mark 1 for about 5 hours or until the beans are tender and the sauce is the consistency of syrup, stirring occasionally. Season well.

——————————— VARIATION ———————————

If haricot beans are not available, cannellini beans can be used instead.

VEGETARIAN ROAST

SERVES 4–6

175 g (6 oz) long grain brown rice	100 g (4 oz) fresh wholemeal breadcrumbs
15 g (½ oz) butter	100 g (4 oz) almonds, finely chopped
1 medium onion, chopped	
1 garlic clove, crushed	100 g (4 oz) mature Cheddar cheese, grated
2 carrots, grated	2 eggs
100 g (4 oz) button mushrooms, finely chopped	salt and pepper

1 Cook the rice in boiling salted water for 30–35 minutes or until tender. Drain well.

2 Meanwhile, heat the butter in a medium frying pan, add the onion, garlic, carrots and mushrooms and fry for 5–10 minutes or until softened, stirring frequently. Stir in the breadcrumbs, almonds, cooked rice, cheese and eggs. Season to taste and mix thoroughly together.

3 Pack the mixture into a greased 1.7 litre (3 pint) loaf tin and bake in a preheated oven at 180°C (350°F) mark 4 for 1–1¼ hours or until firm to the touch and brown on top. Serve sliced, hot or cold.

——————————— VARIATION ———————————

Any type of chopped nuts can be used in the above recipe. Try substituting brazils or unsalted peanuts or cashews for the almonds.

CURRIED EGGS

SERVES 4

MIXED VEGETABLE RING

SERVES 4

30 ml (2 tbsp) vegetable oil	15 ml (1 tbsp) tomato purée
1 onion, chopped	2.5 ml (½ tsp) chilli powder
1 medium cooking apple, peeled, cored and chopped	salt and pepper
10 ml (2 tsp) garam masala	300 ml (½ pint) natural yogurt
300 ml (½ pint) vegetable stock or water	4 eggs, hard-boiled
227 g (8 oz) can tomatoes	

1 Heat the oil in a deep, heavy-based saucepan. Add the onion, apple and garam masala and fry gently for about 5 minutes or until soft, stirring frequently.

2 Pour in the stock or water and tomatoes with their juice and bring to the boil, stirring to break up the tomatoes as much as possible. Stir in the tomato purée with the chilli powder. Season to taste. Lower the heat and simmer, uncovered, for 20 minutes to allow the flavours to develop.

3 Cool the sauce slightly, then pour into a blender or food processor. Add half the yogurt and blend to a purée. Return to the rinsed-out pan.

4 Shell the eggs and cut them in half lengthways. Add them to the sauce, cut side up, then simmer very gently for 10 minutes. Taste the sauce and adjust the seasoning if necessary. Serve hot, with the remaining yogurt drizzled over the top.

100 g (4 oz) butter	salt and pepper
1 large onion, sliced	215 ml (7½ fl oz) milk
50 g (2 oz) mushrooms	100 g (4 oz) plain flour
2 courgettes, sliced	3 eggs, beaten
175 g (6 oz) aubergine, quartered and sliced	40 g (1½ oz) walnut pieces, chopped
1 red pepper, sliced	100 g (4 oz) Double Gloucester cheese with chives, grated
3 tomatoes, skinned and chopped	

1 Melt 25 g (1 oz) of the butter in a large saucepan, add the onion and mushrooms and fry lightly for 5 minutes or until softened.

2 Add the courgettes, aubergine and red pepper and cook for 5 minutes, stirring occasionally. Add the tomatoes and season to taste.

3 Melt the remaining butter in a medium saucepan with the milk, then bring to the boil. Remove the pan from the heat, tip in all the flour and beat thoroughly with a wooden spoon. Allow to cool slightly, then beat in the eggs, a little at a time. Stir in the walnuts. Pipe or spoon the mixture around the edge of a well-greased 900 ml (1½ pint) ovenproof serving dish.

4 Fill the centre with the vegetables and bake in a preheated oven at 200°C (400°F) mark 6 for 35–40 minutes or until the pastry is risen and golden. Sprinkle with the cheese, then return to the oven until the cheese has melted. Serve at once.

VEGETABLE JALOUSIE
SERVES 4

SPICED POTATO AND CAULIFLOWER PASTRIES
SERVES 4

550 g (1¼ lb) fresh broad beans, shelled	45 ml (3 tbsp) grated Parmesan cheese
4 new carrots, thinly sliced	1.25 ml (¼ tsp) ground mace
3 medium leeks, thickly sliced	salt and pepper
25 g (1 oz) butter or margarine	400 g (14 oz) frozen puff pastry, thawed
50 g (2 oz) plain flour	10 ml (2 tsp) chopped fresh summer savory or 5 ml (1 tsp) dried
300 ml (½ pint) milk	
100 g (4 oz) Caerphilly or Wensleydale cheese, grated	a little beaten egg, to glaze

1 Parboil the beans for 4 minutes, the carrots for 2 minutes and the leeks for 1 minute. Remove with a slotted spoon and reserve 30 ml (2 tbsp) of the blanching water.
2 Melt the butter in a clean pan, add the flour and cook, stirring, for 1–2 minutes. Off the heat, blend in the milk. Bring to the boil, stirring, then simmer for 3 minutes or until thick. Add the cheese and mace and season.
3 Remove the cheese sauce from the heat and fold in the vegetables. Cover and leave until cold.
4 Roll out half the pastry thinly to a 30.5×23 cm (12× 9 inch) rectangle. Place on a wetted baking sheet.
5 Stir the reserved blanching water and savory into the cold filling, then spread over the pastry.
6 Roll out the remaining pastry to a slightly larger rectangle than the first. Fold in half lengthways. Cut through the double thickness of the pastry six times at 5 cm (2 inch) intervals along the folded edge. Unfold the pastry and place over the top of the filling. Seal the edges firmly.
7 Brush the pastry with beaten egg, then bake in a preheated oven at 220°C (425°F) mark 7 for 30 minutes.

30 ml (2 tbsp) vegetable oil	(6 oz) tiny cauliflower florets
1 onion, finely chopped	100 g (4 oz) potatoes, peeled and diced
2 garlic cloves, crushed	
5 ml (1 tsp) ground turmeric	75 ml (3 fl oz) vegetable stock
15 ml (1 tbsp) ground coriander	350 g (12 oz) frozen wholemeal puff pastry, thawed
10 ml (2 tsp) ground cumin	
15 ml (1 tbsp) mango chutney	beaten egg, to glaze

1 Heat the oil in a large saucepan, add the onion, garlic and spices and cook for 4–5 minutes or until soft, stirring.
2 Add the mango chutney, cauliflower florets and potatoes, stir in the stock and cook for 15–20 minutes or until the liquid has evaporated. Leave to cool.
3 Roll out the pastry on a lightly floured surface and cut out four 18 cm (7 inch) rounds. Divide the filling between the rounds, placing it on one half of each round. Brush beaten egg around the edges of the rounds and fold the pastry over the filling to encase. Seal the edges, then flute.
4 Place on a greased baking sheet and brush with egg. Bake in a preheated oven at 200°C (400°F) mark 6 for 20–25 minutes or until golden. Serve hot or cold.

─────── **TO MICROWAVE** ───────

Place the oil, onion and garlic in a medium bowl. Cover and cook on HIGH for 3 minutes. Stir in the spices, re-cover and cook on HIGH for a further minute. Add the mango chutney, cauliflower and potatoes with 60 ml (4 tbsp) of the stock. Cook on HIGH for 10–12 minutes or until tender. Cool. Complete steps 3 and 4.

LIGHT MEALS

The recipes in this chapter are ideal for lunches and suppers, when you want something quick and easy yet tasty and satisfying. Soups are included for serving simply with chunks of crusty bread or toast. For cooking in advance, choose from the wide selection of savoury flans and quiches.

COCK-A-LEEKIE SOUP

SERVES 4

15 g (½ oz) butter	1 bouquet garni
275–350 g (10–12 oz) chicken (1 large or 2 small chicken portions)	salt and pepper
	6 prunes, stoned and halved
350 g (12 oz) leeks	
1.1 litres (2 pints) chicken stock	

1 Melt the butter in a large saucepan, add the chicken and fry quickly until golden on all sides.
2 Cut the white parts of the leeks into four lengthways and chop into 2.5 cm (1 inch) pieces. Wash well. Add the white parts to the pan and fry for 5 minutes or until soft.
3 Add the stock and bouquet garni and season to taste. Bring to the boil and simmer for 30 minutes.
4 Shred the green parts of the leeks, then add to the pan with the prunes. Simmer for a further 30 minutes.
5 To serve, remove the chicken from the pan and cut the meat into large pieces, discarding the skin and bones. Put the meat in a warmed soup tureen and pour over the soup.

PEA SOUP

SERVES 6

50 g (2 oz) butter	2 large mint sprigs
1 small onion, finely chopped	salt and pepper
900 g (2 lb) fresh peas, shelled	2 egg yolks, size 2
1.1 litres (2 pints) chicken stock	150 ml (5 fl oz) double cream
2.5 ml (½ tsp) caster sugar	mint sprig, to garnish

1 Melt the butter in a large saucepan, add the onion and cook for 5 minutes or until soft. Add the peas, stock, sugar and mint sprigs. Bring to the boil and cook for about 30 minutes.
2 Pass the soup through a fine sieve or purée in a blender or food processor. Return to the pan and season to taste.
3 Beat together the egg yolks and cream and add to the soup. Heat gently, stirring, but do not boil.
4 Transfer to a warmed soup tureen and garnish with mint before serving.

MUSHROOM SOUP

SERVES 4

25 g (1 oz) butter	100 g (4 oz) mushrooms, finely chopped
25 g (1 oz) plain flour	salt and pepper
300 ml (½ pint) chicken stock	15 ml (1 tbsp) lemon juice
300 ml (½ pint) milk	30 ml (2 tbsp) cream
15 ml (1 tbsp) chopped parsley	

1 Place all the ingredients, except the lemon juice and cream, in a large saucepan. Bring to the boil, whisking continuously. Cover and simmer for 10 minutes.
2 Remove from the heat and add the lemon juice and cream, stirring well.
3 Pour into a tureen or individual dishes, and serve immediately with Melba toast.

HARVEST VEGETABLE SOUP

SERVES 4

25 g (1 oz) butter	salt and pepper
450 g (1 lb) carrots, diced	½ bay leaf
1 medium onion, sliced	40 g (1½ oz) plain flour
2 medium potatoes, peeled and diced	450 ml (¾ pint) milk
1 small green pepper, chopped	100 g (4 oz) Cheddar cheese, grated
50 g (2 oz) lentils	croûtons, to garnish

1 Melt the butter and fry the carrots, onion, potatoes and green pepper until soft.
2 Add 450 ml (¾ pint) water, the lentils, salt and pepper to taste and the bay leaf and simmer for 30 minutes.
3 Mix the flour with a little of the milk and gradually blend in the rest. Stir well into the soup until it thickens. Simmer for 5 minutes, then stir in 75 g (3 oz) cheese.
4 Pour into a serving dish, sprinkle with the remaining cheese and garnish with croûtons. Serve immediately.

———— VARIATION ————
Vegetable and Oatmeal Broth
Substitute 25 g (1 oz) medium oatmeal and 225 g (8 oz) swede for the lentils and potatoes.

QUICK WINTER SOUP

SERVES 4–6

4 medium carrots, roughly chopped	1 slice of wholemeal bread, crusts removed
2 small white turnips, roughly chopped	2.5 ml (½ tsp) salt
2 small potatoes, peeled and roughly chopped	10 ml (2 tsp) sugar
2 leeks or 1 small onion, roughly chopped (optional)	pepper
1 medium cooking apple, peeled, cored and chopped	2 chicken stock cubes, crumbled

1 Put all the prepared vegetables in a blender or food processor with the apple and bread and blend until finely minced.

2 Transfer to a large saucepan and add 1.1 litres (2 pints) water. Bring slowly to the boil, then add the salt, sugar and pepper and the stock cubes. Simmer for 45–60 minutes.

————— VARIATION —————
Curried Winter Soup

Stir in a little curry powder to taste with the seasoning, sugar and stock cubes.

BROAD BEAN AND BACON SOUP

SERVES 2

225 g (8 oz) shelled broad beans	300 ml (½ pint) vegetable stock
225 g (8 oz) shelled peas	salt and pepper
1 large onion, chopped	2 rashers back bacon, grilled and chopped, to garnish
450 ml (¾ pint) milk	

1 Put the beans, peas and onion in a large saucepan and add the milk and stock. Bring to the boil, then simmer for 20 minutes or until the beans are tender.

2 Leave to cool slightly, then purée one third of the soup in a blender or food processor. Add to the remaining soup, then season to taste. Reheat gently. Serve hot, garnished with chopped bacon.

————— TO MICROWAVE —————
Cook the vegetables, milk and stock in a large bowl on HIGH for 20–25 minutes, stirring occasionally. Complete step 2, reheating on HIGH for 2–3 minutes.

————— VARIATION —————
Use frozen vegetables when fresh broad beans and peas are not available.

MULLIGATAWNY SOUP

SERVES 6

CREAM OF ONION SOUP

SERVES 4

50 g (2 oz) butter	15 ml (1 tbsp) tomato purée
1 medium onion, finely chopped	30 ml (2 tbsp) mango chutney
100 g (4 oz) carrot, finely chopped	1.4 litres (2½ pints) beef stock
100 g (4 oz) swede, finely chopped	5 ml (1 tsp) dried mixed herbs
1 small eating apple, peeled, cored and finely chopped	pinch of ground mace
	pinch of ground cloves
50 g (2 oz) streaky bacon, finely chopped	salt and pepper
25 g (1 oz) plain flour	50 g (2 oz) long grain rice
15 ml (1 tbsp) mild curry paste	150 ml (5 fl oz) double cream

1 Melt the butter in a large saucepan, add the onion, carrot, swede, apple and bacon and fry for 5–10 minutes or until lightly browned.

2 Stir in the flour, curry paste, tomato purée and chutney. Cook for 1–2 minutes before adding the stock, herbs and spices. Season to taste.

3 Bring to the boil, skim, cover and simmer for 30–40 minutes. Sieve the soup or purée in a blender or food processor.

4 Return the soup to the pan, bring to the boil, add the rice and boil gently for about 12 minutes or until the rice is tender.

5 Adjust the seasoning. Stir in the cream, reserving a little for garnish. Heat gently, without boiling, then pour into a warmed soup tureen or individual bowls and swirl with cream.

25 g (1 oz) butter	salt and pepper
450 g (1 lb) onions, thinly sliced	20 ml (4 tsp) cornflour
	45 ml (3 tbsp) single cream
568 ml (1 pint) milk	parsley sprigs, to garnish

1 Melt the butter in a saucepan, add the onions, cover and cook gently for about 5 minutes or until softened, shaking the pan occasionally to prevent browning.

2 Add the milk and 300 ml (½ pint) water, season to taste and bring to the boil, stirring. Reduce the heat, cover and simmer for about 25 minutes or until the onion is tender.

3 Blend the cornflour to a smooth paste with 45 ml (3 tbsp) water, stir into the soup and bring to the boil. Cook gently for a few minutes or until slightly thickened, stirring. Add the cream, adjust the seasoning and reheat without boiling. Garnish with parsley sprigs.

CURRIED PARSNIP SOUP

SERVES 6

40 g (1½ oz) butter	1.4 litres (2½ pints) chicken stock
1 medium onion, sliced	salt and pepper
700 g (1½ lb) parsnips, finely diced	150 ml (5 fl oz) single cream
5 ml (1 tsp) curry powder	paprika, to garnish
2.5 ml (½ tsp) ground cumin	

1 Melt the butter in a large saucepan, add the onion and parsnip and fry for about 3 minutes.

2 Stir in the curry powder and cumin and fry for a further 2 minutes.

3 Add the stock, bring to the boil, reduce the heat, cover and simmer for about 45 minutes or until the vegetables are tender.

4 Cool slightly, then transfer the vegetables to a blender or food processor, using a slotted spoon. Add a little stock and blend to a smooth purée.

5 Return the soup to the pan. Season to taste, add the cream and reheat gently, without boiling. Serve sprinkled with paprika.

CULLEN SKINK

SERVES 4

one 350 g (12 oz) Finnan haddock, skinned	700 g (1½ lb) potatoes
1 medium onion, chopped	knob of butter
568 ml (1 pint) milk	salt and pepper
	chopped parsley, to garnish

1 Put the haddock in a medium saucepan, just cover with 900 ml (1½ pints) boiling water and bring to the boil again. Add the onion, cover and simmer for 10–15 minutes or until tender. Drain off the liquid and reserve.

2 Remove the bones from the haddock and flake the flesh, then set aside. Return the bones and strained stock to the pan with the milk. Cover and simmer for a further hour.

3 Meanwhile, peel and roughly chop the potatoes, then cook in boiling salted water for about 20 minutes or until tender. Drain well, then mash.

4 Strain the liquid from the bones and return it to the pan with the flaked fish. Add the mashed potato and butter and stir well to give a creamy consistency. Season and garnish.

TO MICROWAVE

Put the haddock, onion and 600 ml (1 pint) boiling water in a large bowl. Cover and cook on HIGH for 10 minutes or until the haddock is cooked. Drain off the liquid and reserve. Remove the bones from the haddock and flake the flesh, then set aside. Return the bones and strained stock to the bowl with the milk, cover and cook on HIGH for 20 minutes. Meanwhile, complete step 3. Strain the liquid from the bones and return it to the bowl with the flaked fish. Add the mashed potato and butter and stir well to give a creamy consistency. Season, garnish and serve.

HADDOCK AND CORN CHOWDER

SERVES 4–6

DEVONSHIRE CRAB SOUP

SERVES 6

25–50 g (1–2 oz) butter or margarine	salt and pepper
450 g (1 lb) old potatoes, peeled and cut into 1 cm (½ inch) dice	225 g (8 oz) fresh haddock fillets
2 medium onions, thinly sliced	225 g (8 oz) smoked haddock fillets
2.5 ml (½ tsp) chilli powder	298 g (10½ oz) can cream-style sweetcorn
600 ml (1 pint) fish or vegetable stock	100 g (4 oz) cooked peeled prawns
568 ml (1 pint) milk	chopped parsley

25 g (1 oz) butter	300 ml (½ pint) chicken stock
1 small onion, finely chopped	5 ml (1 tsp) anchovy essence
1 celery stick, chopped	salt and pepper
75 g (3 oz) long grain rice	30 ml (2 tbsp) brandy
568 ml (1 pint) milk	150 ml (5 fl oz) double cream
meat of 1 cooked crab, or 225 g (8 oz) frozen or canned crab meat, drained and flaked	chopped parsley, to garnish

1 Melt the butter or margarine in a large saucepan. Add the vegetables and the chilli powder and stir over a moderate heat for 2–3 minutes.

2 Pour in the stock and milk and season to taste. Bring to the boil, cover and simmer for 10 minutes.

3 Meanwhile, skin the fresh and smoked haddock fillets and divide the flesh into bite-sized pieces, discarding all the bones.

4 Add the haddock to the pan with the corn. Bring back to the boil, cover and simmer until the potatoes are tender and the fish begins to flake apart. Skim the surface of the soup.

5 Stir in the prawns with plenty of parsley. Adjust the seasoning and serve.

1 Melt the butter in a large saucepan, add the onion and celery and cook for 10 minutes or until soft. Add the rice and milk, cover and cook for 15 minutes or until the rice is cooked. Cool slightly.

2 Pass the soup through a sieve or purée in a blender or food processor. Return to the pan together with the crab meat. Add the stock and anchovy essence, season to taste and reheat.

3 Add the brandy and cream and heat gently without boiling. Transfer to a warmed soup tureen, sprinkle with chopped parsley and serve very hot.

—————————— COOK'S TIP ——————————

Melba toast makes a good accompaniment to many soups, including the one above. To make it, simply toast bread slices lightly on both sides, cut off the crusts, then, holding the toast flat, slide a knife between the toasted edges to split the bread. Cut each piece into triangles and toast under the grill, untoasted side uppermost, until golden and the edges curl.

SPAGHETTI BOLOGNESE

SERVES 4

25 g (1 oz) butter or margarine	1 garlic clove, finely chopped
45 ml (3 tbsp) olive oil	1 bay leaf
2 rashers unsmoked streaky bacon, finely chopped	15 ml (1 tbsp) tomato purée
225 g (8 oz) lean minced beef	150 ml (¼ pint) dry white wine
1 small onion, finely chopped	150 ml (¼ pint) beef stock
1 small carrot, finely chopped	salt and pepper
1 small celery stick, finely chopped	450–700 g (1–1½ lb) fresh or dried spaghetti

1 Melt the butter or margarine with the oil in a saucepan, add the bacon and cook for 2–3 minutes or until soft.

2 Add the minced beef and cook for a further 5 minutes or until lightly browned.

3 Add the onion, carrot, celery, garlic and bay leaf. Stir and cook for 2 minutes. Add the tomato purée, wine and stock. Season to taste.

4 Bring to the boil, then simmer, uncovered for 1–1½ hours, stirring occasionally.

5 Cook the spaghetti in a large saucepan of boiling salted water for about 10 minutes for dried pasta, 3 minutes for fresh.

6 Drain the spaghetti well and turn into a warmed serving dish. Top with the sauce and serve immediately.

PAN HAGGERTY

SERVES 4

25 g (1 oz) butter	100 g (4 oz) Cheddar or Lancashire cheese, grated
15 ml (1 tbsp) vegetable oil	salt and pepper
450 g (1 lb) potatoes, peeled and thinly sliced	
2 medium onions, thinly sliced	

1 Heat the butter and oil in a large heavy-based frying pan. Remove the pan from the heat and pour in layers of potatoes, onions and grated cheese, seasoning well with salt and pepper between each layer, and ending with a top layer of cheese.

2 Cover and cook the vegetables gently for about 30 minutes or until the potatoes and onions are almost cooked.

3 Uncover and brown the top of the dish under a hot grill. Serve straight from the pan.

─────────── COOK'S TIP ───────────

Choose firm-fleshed potatoes for this dish, such as Desirée, Romano or Maris Piper, as they will keep their shape and not crumble into mash at the end of the cooking time.

RED FLANNEL HASH

SERVES 4

450 g (1 lb) potatoes, scrubbed	5 ml (1 tsp) garlic salt
salt and pepper	225 g (8 oz) cooked beetroot, diced
225 g (8 oz) salt beef or corned beef, chopped	30 ml (2 tbsp) chopped parsley
1 medium onion, finely chopped	50 g (2 oz) butter or margarine

1 Cook the potatoes in their skins in lightly salted boiling water for about 20 minutes or until tender.

2 Drain the potatoes, leave until cool enough to handle, then peel off the skins with your fingers. Dice the flesh.

3 Put the diced potatoes in a large bowl, add the beef, onion, garlic salt, beetroot and parsley and toss to combine. Add pepper to taste.

4 Heat the butter or margarine in a heavy-based frying pan until very hot. Add the hash mixture and spread evenly with a fish slice or spatula.

5 Lower the heat to moderate and cook the hash, uncovered, for 10–15 minutes. Break up and turn frequently with the slice or spatula, so that the hash becomes evenly browned. Serve hot.

SPICY SCOTCH EGGS

SERVES 4

25 g (1 oz) butter or margarine	salt and pepper
1 onion, very finely chopped	4 hard-boiled eggs, shelled
	plain flour, for coating
10 ml (2 tsp) medium-hot curry powder	1 egg, beaten
450 g (1 lb) pork sausagemeat	100–175 g (4–6 oz) dried breadcrumbs
100 g (4 oz) mature Cheddar cheese, finely grated	vegetable oil, for deep frying

1 Heat the butter or margarine in a small saucepan, add the onion and curry powder and fry gently for 5 minutes or until soft.

2 Put the sausagemeat and cheese in a bowl, add the onion and season to taste. Mix with your hands to combine the ingredients well.

3 Divide the mixture into four equal portions and flatten out on a floured board or work surface.

4 Place an egg in the centre of each piece. With floured hands, shape and mould the sausagemeat around the eggs. Coat lightly with more flour.

5 Brush each Scotch egg with beaten egg, then roll in the breadcrumbs until evenly coated. Chill for 30 minutes.

6 Heat the oil in a deep-fat fryer to 170°C (325°F). Carefully lower the Scotch eggs into the oil with a slotted spoon and deep-fry for 10 minutes, turning them occasionally until golden brown on all sides. Drain and cool on absorbent kitchen paper.

COLD BEEF IN SOURED CREAM

SERVES 4

30 ml (2 tbsp) vegetable oil	10 ml (2 tsp) chopped fresh thyme or 2.5 ml (½ tsp) dried
450 g (1 lb) lean rump steak in a thin slice, cut into thin strips	1 green eating apple, cored and thinly sliced
salt and pepper	142 ml (5 fl oz) soured cream
1 medium onion, finely chopped	15 ml (1 tbsp) lemon juice
225 g (8 oz) button mushrooms, thinly sliced	crisp lettuce, to serve
5 ml (1 tsp) French mustard	

1 Heat the oil in a large frying pan. When hot, add the steak in a shallow layer and cook over a high heat until browned, turning occasionally. Do not crowd the pan; the meat should remain pink in the centre.

2 Transfer the beef to a bowl using a slotted spoon. Season to taste.

3 Reheat the fat remaining in the pan, add the onion and fry until golden brown. Add the mushrooms, mustard and thyme and fry over a high heat for 1 minute. Add to the beef, cover and leave to cool.

4 Combine the apple with the soured cream and lemon juice.

5 To serve, line a shallow dish with crisp lettuce. Combine the beef mixture with the soured cream, adjust the seasoning and pile into the centre of the lettuce.

CASHEW STUFFED MUSHROOMS

SERVES 4

8 medium flat mushrooms	15 ml (1 tbsp) chopped fresh oregano or 2.5 ml (½ tsp) dried
15 ml (1 tbsp) olive oil	
2 small onions, finely chopped	10 ml (2 tsp) tomato purée
2 garlic cloves, crushed	30–45 ml (2–3 tbsp) grated Parmesan cheese
50 g (2 oz) unsalted cashew nuts, chopped	

1 Remove the stalks from the mushrooms, chop and set aside. Bring a large saucepan of salted water to the boil, add the mushroom caps and cook for 30–60 seconds. Drain, set aside and keep warm.

2 Heat the oil in a medium saucepan, add the onions and garlic and fry gently for 3–5 minutes or until the onions have softened. Stir in the mushroom stalks, cashew nuts and oregano. Cook for 3–5 minutes or until the nuts begin to brown. Stir in the tomato purée.

3 Arrange the mushroom caps on a lightly oiled baking sheet. Divide the topping mixture between them and sprinkle over the Parmesan cheese.

4 Bake in a preheated oven at 190°C (375°F) mark 5 for 10–15 minutes or until golden.

— **TO MICROWAVE** —

Complete step 1. Place the oil, onion and garlic in a bowl, cover and cook on HIGH for 2½–3 minutes. Add the chopped mushroom stalks, cashew nuts and oregano. Cover and cook on HIGH for 2–3 minutes. Stir in the tomato purée. Arrange four filled mushrooms in a circle on a plate and cook on HIGH for 3–4 minutes, rearranging occasionally. Repeat with the remaining four mushrooms. Grill to brown, if liked.

GARLIC MUSHROOM PARCELS

SERVES 4–6

15 ml (1 tbsp) olive oil	pepper
1 onion, finely chopped	50 g (2 oz) cream cheese
1–2 garlic cloves, crushed	6 sheets of frozen filo pastry, thawed
225 g (8 oz) button mushrooms, chopped	25 g (1 oz) butter, melted
15 ml (1 tbsp) chopped fresh thyme or 5 ml (1 tsp) dried	

1 Heat the oil in a medium saucepan, add the onion and garlic and cook gently for 3–5 minutes or until the onion has softened. Add the mushrooms, thyme and pepper to taste. Cook for 5–6 minutes, stirring.

2 Drain off any excess juices and add the cheese, stirring continuously until the cheese has melted. Cook for a further 2 minutes, then leave to cool.

3 To make the parcels, lay the first sheet of filo pastry lengthways on a work surface. Brush with butter, then lay a second sheet on top. Brush with butter, then cut into eight equal strips.

4 Place 5 ml (1 tsp) of the cooked filling in one corner of a strip of pastry. Fold this corner over to make a triangle, encasing the filling. Continue to fold in the shape of a triangle, brushing with a little extra melted butter just before the final fold. Repeat to make 24 parcels. Place on a greased baking sheet.

5 Bake in a preheated oven at 200°C (400°F) mark 6 for 10–15 minutes or until golden brown and crisp, turning the parcels over halfway through cooking. Serve hot or cold.

TORTILLA

SERVES 4

30 ml (2 tbsp) olive oil	5 eggs, beaten
225 g (8 oz) potatoes, peeled and thinly sliced	salt and pepper
1 Spanish onion, thinly sliced	15 ml (1 tbsp) chopped fresh parsley or 10 ml (2 tsp) dried
1 red pepper, chopped	

1 Heat the oil in a frying pan, add the potatoes, onion and pepper and fry gently for 20–25 minutes or until the potatoes are golden and cooked.

2 Pour the beaten egg into the pan, season to taste and sprinkle over the parsley.

3 Cook the tortilla over a gentle heat for 7–10 minutes or until golden. Carefully invert the tortilla on to a plate, then slide it back into the frying pan to cook the other side for a further 3–5 minutes.

4 Turn the tortilla on to a warmed serving plate.

——————————— **TO MICROWAVE** ———————————

Place the oil, potatoes, onion and pepper in a shallow 20.5 cm (8 inch) dish. Cover and cook on HIGH for 7–10 minutes or until tender, rearranging occasionally. Pour in the beaten eggs, season to taste and sprinkle over the parsley. Cover and cook on HIGH for 3–4 minutes or until almost set. Carefully invert the tortilla on to a plate, then slide back into the dish and cook on HIGH for a further 2–3 minutes or until almost set. Complete step 4 as above.

FARMHOUSE CAULIFLOWER SOUFFLÉS

SERVES 8

225 g (8 oz) small cauliflower florets	15 ml (1 tbsp) whole grain mustard
salt and pepper	100 g (4 oz) farmhouse Cheddar cheese, grated
40 g (1½ oz) butter	4 eggs, separated
45 ml (3 tbsp) plain flour	
200 ml (7 fl oz) milk	

1 Grease eight individual ramekin dishes.
2 Put the cauliflower in a saucepan and just cover with boiling salted water. Cover and simmer until tender, then drain.
3 Meanwhile, prepare a white sauce. Put the butter, flour and milk in a saucepan. Heat, whisking continuously, until the sauce thickens, boils and is smooth. Simmer for 1–2 minutes, then add the mustard and season to taste.
4 Turn the sauce into a blender or food processor. Add the cauliflower and blend to an almost smooth purée.
5 Turn into a large bowl and leave to cool slightly. Stir in the cheese with the egg yolks.
6 Whisk the egg whites until stiff but not dry and fold into the sauce mixture. Spoon into the dishes.
7 Bake in a preheated oven at 180°C (350°F) mark 4 for 25 minutes or until browned and firm. Serve at once.

--- **TO MICROWAVE** ---

The sauce can be prepared in the microwave. Put the butter, flour and milk in a medium bowl. Cook on HIGH for 4–5 minutes or until boiling and thickened, whisking frequently. Add the mustard and season.

OMELETTE ARNOLD BENNETT

SERVES 2

100 g (4 oz) smoked haddock	3 eggs, separated
50 g (2 oz) butter	salt and pepper
150 ml (¼ pint) double cream	50 g (2 oz) Cheddar cheese, grated

1 Put the fish in a saucepan and cover with water. Bring to the boil and simmer gently for 10 minutes. Drain and flake the fish, discarding the skin and bones.
2 Put the fish in a saucepan with half the butter and 30 ml (2 tbsp) cream. Toss over a high heat until the butter melts, then leave to cool.
3 Beat the egg yolks in a bowl with 15 ml (1 tbsp) cream. Season to taste and stir in the fish mixture. Stiffly whisk the egg whites and fold in.
4 Heat the remaining butter in an omelette pan or small frying pan. Pour in the egg mixture and cook gently until beginning to set but still fairly fluid. Do not fold over. Slide the omelette on to a heatproof serving dish.
5 Blend together the cheese and remaining cream and pour over the omelette. Put under a preheated grill until golden and bubbling. Serve immediately.

CHICKEN EGGAH

SERVES 4–6

SMOKED HADDOCK GOUGÈRES

SERVES 4

8 chicken thighs	6 eggs
600 ml (1 pint) chicken stock	50 g (2 oz) butter or margarine
10 ml (2 tsp) ground cumin	1 medium onion, sliced
1.25 ml (¼ tsp) chilli powder	1 garlic clove, crushed
salt and pepper	10 ml (2 tsp) paprika
100 g (4 oz) Chinese egg noodles	

1 Put the chicken thighs in a large saucepan, then add the chicken stock, cumin and chilli powder and season to taste. Simmer for 30 minutes or until the chicken is tender.
2 Remove the chicken from the pan and set aside. Add 1.1 litres (2 pints) water to the pan and bring to the boil. Add the noodles and boil for about 5 minutes, or according to the packet instructions, until tender. Leave to drain thoroughly in a colander or sieve.
3 Remove the chicken flesh from the bones and discard the skin. Cut the meat into small strips.
4 Using kitchen scissors, cut the cooked, drained egg noodles into short lengths.
5 Beat the eggs lightly in a large bowl, then add the noodles and chicken and stir gently to mix. Melt the butter or margarine in a large heavy-based frying pan, add the onion, garlic and paprika and fry gently for about 5 minutes.
6 Pour in the egg mixture and stir lightly with a fork. Cook over a moderate heat for 15 minutes or until set and golden brown underneath.
7 Turn the eggah out on to a plate, then slide back into the pan so that the underside is uppermost. Cook for a further 15 minutes or until golden brown. Serve hot.

90 g (3½ oz) butter	2 tomatoes, skinned, seeded and cut into strips
150 g (5 oz) plain flour	salt and pepper
3 eggs, beaten	lemon juice, to taste
450 g (1 lb) smoked haddock	15 ml (1 tbsp) fresh white breadcrumbs
1 medium onion, chopped	15 g (½ oz) Cheddar cheese, grated
300 ml (½ pint) milk	chopped parsley, to garnish (optional)
10 ml (2 tsp) capers	
2 hard-boiled eggs, shelled and chopped	

1 To make the choux pastry, put 75 g (3 oz) butter and 200 ml (7 fl oz) water in a saucepan and bring to the boil. Add 100 g (4 oz) of the flour, then beat well until the mixture leaves the sides of the pan. Cool for 5 minutes, then gradually beat in the eggs.
2 Using a 1 cm (½ inch) plain nozzle, pipe the mixture in two circles (one on top of the other) inside each of four 200 ml (7 fl oz) ovenproof dishes. Bake at 220°C (425°F) mark 7 for 25 minutes or until risen and golden brown.
3 Meanwhile, poach the haddock for 10 minutes. Drain, flake the flesh and discard the skin and bones.
4 Melt the remaining butter, add the onion and fry for 5 minutes. Add the remaining flour and cook, stirring, for 1–2 minutes. Off the heat, blend in the milk. Bring to the boil, stirring, then simmer for 3 minutes until thick.
5 Stir in the capers, eggs, fish and strips of tomato. Add salt, pepper and lemon juice to taste.
6 Spoon the mixture into the centre of the cooked gougères. Mix together the breadcrumbs and cheese, sprinkle on top and return to the oven for 10 minutes.

HADDOCK AND MUSHROOM PUFFS

SERVES 4

397 g (14 oz) packet puff pastry, thawed if frozen	20 ml (4 tsp) capers, chopped
450 g (1 lb) haddock fillets, skinned	15 ml (1 tbsp) snipped fresh chives or 5 ml (1 tsp) dried
213 g (7½ oz) can creamed mushrooms	salt and pepper
5 ml (1 tsp) lemon juice	1 egg

1 Roll out the pastry on a lightly floured surface into a 40.5 cm (16 inch) square. Using a sharp knife, cut into four squares, trim the edges and reserve the trimmings.
2 Place the squares on dampened baking sheets. Divide the fish into four and place diagonally across the pastry squares.
3 Combine the creamed mushrooms with the lemon juice, capers and chives. Season to taste. Mix well, then spoon over the pieces of haddock fillet.
4 Brush the edges of each square lightly with water. Bring the four points of each square together over the filling and seal the edges to form an envelope-shaped parcel.
5 Decorate with pastry trimmings and make a small hole in the centre of each parcel. Chill in the refrigerator for 30 minutes.
6 Beat the egg with a pinch of salt and use to glaze the pastry. Bake in a preheated oven at 220°C (425°F) mark 7 for about 20 minutes or until the pastry is golden brown and well risen. Serve hot.

―――――――――――― VARIATION ――――――――――――
Monkfish and Mushrooms Puffs
Substitute monkfish (or any other white fish) for the haddock in the above recipe.

MOCK CRAB

SERVES 2

1 hard-boiled egg, shelled	100 g (4 oz) Red Leicester cheese, grated
15 g (½ oz) butter	2 cooked chicken breast fillets, skinned and finely chopped
7.5 ml (1½ tsp) prepared English mustard	
a few drops of anchovy essence	lettuce leaves, sliced tomato and cucumber, to garnish
pepper	

1 Separate the egg yolks from the whites, sieve the yolks and chop the whites. Reserve a little of the egg yolk and mix the remainder with the butter, mustard, anchovy essence and pepper to taste.
2 Mix in the cheese with a fork so that it is evenly blended but as many shreds as possible of the cheese remain separate.
3 Mix in the chicken lightly, then taste and adjust the seasoning. Cover and leave in a cool place for at least 2 hours for the flavours to develop.
4 Serve on a small bed of lettuce, in crab shells if available, garnished with the reserved egg yolk, chopped egg white and a little sliced tomato and cucumber.

―――――――――――― COOK'S TIP ――――――――――――
This was a popular Victorian luncheon dish, cleverly invented to deceive the eye and even the palate. The 'crab' is in fact finely shredded chicken and grated Red Leicester cheese, and the fishy disguise is made all the more convincing with anchovy flavouring.

LEEKS IN CHEESE SAUCE

SERVES 4

8 medium leeks	salt and pepper
50 g (2 oz) butter	8 thin slices of ham or bacon
75 ml (5 tbsp) plain flour	fresh breadcrumbs
568 ml (1 pint) milk	
100 g (4 oz) Cheddar cheese, grated	

1 Put the whole leeks in a saucepan of boiling salted water and boil gently for 20 minutes or until soft. Drain and keep warm.
2 Meanwhile, melt three-quarters of the butter in a pan, stir in the flour and cook gently for 1 minute, stirring. Remove the pan from the heat and gradually stir in the milk. Bring to the boil and continue to cook, stirring, for about 5 minutes, then add 75 g (3 oz) cheese and season to taste.
3 Wrap each leek in a slice of ham or bacon, place in an ovenproof dish and coat with sauce. Top with breadcrumbs and the remaining cheese. Dot with the remaining butter and brown under a preheated grill.

——— VARIATION ———
Asparagus in Cheese Sauce
When in season, asparagus would make an interesting substitute for the leeks in the above recipe.

MACARONI AND BROCCOLI CHEESE

SERVES 2

75 g (3 oz) wholewheat macaroni	75 g (3 oz) Red Leicester cheese, grated
salt and pepper	100 g (4 oz) broccoli florets
25 g (1 oz) butter	15 ml (1 tbsp) fresh wholemeal breadcrumbs
25 g (1 oz) plain flour	
300 ml (½ pint) milk	

1 Cook the macaroni in 1.1 litres (2 pints) boiling salted water for 15 minutes, then drain.
2 Put the butter, flour and milk in a saucepan. Heat, whisking continuously, until the sauce boils, thickens and is smooth. Simmer for 1–2 minutes.
3 Remove the pan from the heat, add most of the cheese and stir until melted. Season to taste.
4 Cook the broccoli in boiling water for 7 minutes or until tender. Drain well.
5 Put the broccoli in the base of a 900 ml (1½ pint) heatproof serving dish. Cover with the macaroni and cheese sauce. Sprinkle with the remaining cheese and the breadcrumbs. Brown under a preheated hot grill.

——— TO MICROWAVE ———
Put the macaroni in a large bowl. Pour over boiling water to cover the pasta by about 2.5 cm (1 inch). Cover and cook on HIGH for 4 minutes. Stand for 3 minutes. Put the butter, flour and milk in a medium bowl and cook on HIGH for about 4 minutes, until boiling and thickened, whisking frequently. Complete step 3. Cook the broccoli in a large bowl in 45 ml (3 tbsp) water on HIGH for 3½ minutes. Drain well. Complete step 5.

COURGETTE QUICHE

SERVES 4

CAULIFLOWER AND STILTON FLAN

SERVES 4–6

175 g (6 oz) plain flour	3 eggs
salt and pepper	150 ml (5 fl oz) double cream
100 g (4 oz) butter or margarine	10 ml (2 tsp) chopped fresh basil
100 g (4 oz) grated Cheddar cheese	finely grated rind of 1 lime (optional)
1 egg yolk, beaten	a little egg white
350 g (12 oz) courgettes	

175 g (6 oz) plus 30 ml (2 tbsp) plain flour	200 ml (7 fl oz) milk
1.25 ml (¼ tsp) salt	pepper
100 g (4 oz) butter	100 g (4 oz) Blue Stilton cheese, crumbled
450 g (1 lb) cauliflower florets	25 g (1 oz) Cheddar cheese, grated
225 g (8 oz) onions, chopped	

1 To make the pastry, sift the flour into a bowl with a pinch of salt. Rub in the butter or margarine.
2 Stir in the cheese, then the egg yolk. Gather the mixture together with your fingers to make a smooth ball of dough. Wrap the dough and chill for 30 minutes.
3 Meanwhile, prepare the filling. Trim the courgettes, then cut into 2 cm (¾ inch) chunks. Plunge into boiling salted water, bring back to the boil, then simmer for 3 minutes. Drain and set aside.
4 Beat the eggs lightly with the cream. Stir in the basil, lime rind (if using) and season to taste. Set aside.
5 Roll out the chilled dough and use to line a 23 cm (9 inch) loose-bottomed flan tin. Chill for 15 minutes.
6 Prick the base of the dough with a fork, then line with foil and baking beans. Stand the tin on a preheated baking sheet and bake blind in a preheated oven at 200°C (400°F) mark 6 for 10 minutes.
7 Remove the foil and beans and brush the pastry case with egg white. Return to the oven for 5 minutes.
8 Stand the courgette chunks upright in the pastry case and slowly pour in the egg and cream mixture. Return to the oven for 20 minutes.

1 Sift 175 g (6 oz) flour and the salt into a bowl. Add 75 g (3 oz) of the butter and rub in until the mixture resembles fine breadcrumbs. Add a little water and bind to a dough. Chill in the refrigerator for about 10 minutes.
2 Roll out the pastry on a lightly floured surface and use to line a 23 cm (9 inch) flan dish or ring placed on a baking sheet. Chill again for 10–15 minutes.
3 Prick the base of the dough with a fork, then line with foil and baking beans and bake blind in a preheated oven at 200°C (400°F) mark 6 for 10–15 minutes or until set. Remove the foil and beans.
4 Cook the cauliflower florets in boiling salted water for 4–5 minutes or until just tender. Drain well and cool.
5 Melt the remaining butter in a pan, add the onions and cook for about 5 minutes or until soft, then stir in the 30 ml (2 tbsp) flour. Cook gently for 2 minutes, stirring. Remove the pan from the heat and gradually stir in the milk. Bring to the boil and continue to cook, stirring, until the sauce thickens, then add pepper to taste.
6 Sprinkle the Stilton evenly over the base of the flan. Arrange the cauliflower on top. Spoon over the onion sauce and sprinkle with the Cheddar cheese.
7 Bake in the oven at 190°C (375°F) mark 5 for 25–30 minutes or until golden and bubbly. Serve hot.

TARTE À L'OIGNON
SERVES 4–6

50 g (2 oz) butter	50 ml (2 fl oz) milk
700 g (1½ lb) onions, thinly sliced	150 ml (5 fl oz) single cream
175 g (6 oz) frozen shortcrust pastry, thawed	salt and pepper
2 eggs	pinch of grated nutmeg

1 Melt the butter in a large frying pan, add the onions, cover and cook gently for 20 minutes.

2 Roll out the pastry on a lightly floured surface and use to line a 20.5 cm (8 inch) flan dish or ring placed on a baking sheet.

3 Beat together the eggs, milk and cream until smooth. Season to taste and add the nutmeg.

4 Pour a little of the egg mixture into the pastry case. Add the onions, then pour in the remaining egg mixture.

5 Bake in a preheated oven at 200°C (400°F) mark 6 for 30 minutes or until golden brown and set.

SPICED PEPPER AND ONION FLAN
SERVES 4

175 g (6 oz) plus 30 ml (2 tbsp) plain flour	5 ml (1 tsp) ground cumin
salt	150 ml (¼ pint) milk
75 g (3 oz) block margarine	150 ml (5 fl oz) natural yogurt
15 ml (1 tbsp) vegetable oil	2 egg yolks
2 onions, thinly sliced	30 ml (2 tbsp) grated Parmesan cheese
1 red pepper, sliced	
25 g (1 oz) butter	

1 To make the pastry, sift 175 g (6 oz) flour and a pinch of salt into a bowl. Add the margarine and rub in until the mixture resembles breadcrumbs. Bind to a manageable dough with cold water. Knead until smooth.

2 Roll out the dough on a lightly floured surface and use to line a 20.5 cm (8 inch) plain flan ring placed on a baking sheet.

3 Chill for 15–20 minutes, then line with foil and baking beans. Bake blind in a preheated oven at 200°C (400°F) mark 6 for 10–15 minutes or until set but not browned. Remove the foil and beans.

4 Heat the oil in a frying pan, add the sliced onions and pepper, reserving a few slices to garnish, and sauté for 4–5 minutes. Put into the flan case.

5 Melt the butter in a saucepan, stir in the 30 ml (2 tbsp) flour and the cumin. Cook for 2 minutes, stirring, then remove from the heat and gradually stir in the milk and yogurt. Bring to the boil, stirring briskly, and simmer for 2–3 minutes. Beat in the egg yolks.

6 Pour the sauce over the onion and pepper and sprinkle with Parmesan. Cook in the oven at 190°C (375°F) mark 5 for 35–40 minutes. Serve hot garnished with pepper slices.

HOT CRAB AND RICOTTA QUICHES

SERVES 6

175 g (6 oz) plain flour	150 ml (¼ pint) milk
salt and pepper	225 g (8 oz) crab meat, flaked
75 g (3 oz) block margarine	175 g (6 oz) Ricotta cheese, crumbled
2 eggs	
150 ml (¼ pint) single cream	30 ml (2 tbsp) grated Parmesan cheese

1 To make the pastry, sift the flour and a pinch of salt into a bowl. Add the margarine and rub in until the mixture resembles fine breadcrumbs. Add enough cold water to bind to a manageable dough and knead until smooth.

2 Roll out the pastry on a lightly floured surface and use to line six 8.5 cm (3½ inch) fluted, loose-bottomed, flan tins. Line with foil and baking beans and bake blind in a preheated oven at 200°C (400°F) mark 6 for 10–15 minutes. Remove the foil and beans.

3 Meanwhile whisk the eggs, cream and milk together in a bowl and add the crab meat, Ricotta, Parmesan and plenty of salt and pepper. Pour into the flan cases.

4 Reduce the oven temperature to 190°C (375°F) mark 5 and bake the quiches for 35 minutes or until golden.

——— VARIATION ———

Make one large quiche instead of six individual ones, if preferred. You will need to use a 20.5 cm (8 inch) flan dish or ring.

SMOKED HADDOCK FLAN

SERVES 4–6

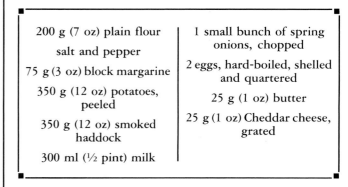

200 g (7 oz) plain flour	1 small bunch of spring onions, chopped
salt and pepper	2 eggs, hard-boiled, shelled and quartered
75 g (3 oz) block margarine	
350 g (12 oz) potatoes, peeled	25 g (1 oz) butter
350 g (12 oz) smoked haddock	25 g (1 oz) Cheddar cheese, grated
300 ml (½ pint) milk	

1 To make the pastry, sift 175 g (6 oz) of the flour into a bowl with a pinch of salt. Rub in the margarine. Add cold water to bind to a dough and knead until smooth.

2 Roll out the pastry and use to line a 20.5 cm (8 inch) flan dish or ring placed on a baking sheet. Bake blind at 200°C (400°F) mark 6 for 10–15 minutes or until set.

3 Cook the potatoes in boiling salted water for about 20 minutes or until tender, then drain and mash. Set aside. Place the fish in a saucepan with the milk, bring to the boil and simmer for 15 minutes.

4 Strain the milk into a bowl. Remove the skin and bones from the fish and flake. Place in the flan case.

5 Plunge the chopped onions into a pan of boiling water, blanch for 1 minute, then drain. Sprinkle the onions over the fish and cover with the eggs.

6 Melt the butter in a saucepan, stir in the remaining flour and cook gently for 1 minute, stirring. Remove from the heat and gradually stir in the reserved milk. Bring to the boil and cook, stirring, until the sauce thickens. Season.

7 Spoon the sauce into the flan case and pipe potato across the top in a lattice design. Sprinkle with cheese and bake in the oven for about 25 minutes or until brown. Serve hot.

SPINACH AND PRAWN QUICHE

SERVES 4–6

200 g (7 oz) plain wholemeal flour	150 ml (¼ pint) milk
salt and pepper	100 g (4 oz) cooked peeled prawns
100 g (4 oz) butter	155 g (5 oz) packet frozen chopped spinach, thawed and drained
1 egg, beaten	

1 Sift the flour into a bowl with a pinch of salt, add the butter and rub in until the mixture resembles fine breadcrumbs. Stir in enough cold water to bind to a manageable dough and knead until smooth.

2 Roll out the pastry on a lightly floured surface and use to line a 20.5 cm (8 inch) flan ring placed on a baking sheet. Line with foil and baking beans and bake blind in a preheated oven at 200°C (400°F) mark 6 for 20 minutes or until set. Remove the foil and beans.

3 Mix the egg, milk, prawns and spinach, season well and pour into the flan case.

4 Bake in the oven at 180°C (350°F) mark 4 for about 40 minutes, until just set. Serve hot.

CURRIED BACON FLAN

SERVES 4–6

175 g (6 oz) plain flour	5 ml (1 tsp) curry powder
salt and pepper	3 eggs, beaten
75 g (3 oz) margarine	150 ml (5 fl oz) natural yogurt
25 g (1 oz) butter	225 g (8 oz) tomatoes, skinned and thinly sliced
100 g (4 oz) celery heart, sliced	
100 g (4 oz) streaky bacon, diced	

1 To make the pastry, sift the flour and a pinch of salt into a bowl. Add the margarine and rub in until the mixture resembles fine breadcrumbs. Add enough cold water to bind to a manageable dough and knead until smooth.

2 Roll out the pastry on a lightly floured surface and use to line a 21.5 cm (8½ inch), loose-bottomed French fluted flan tin. Line with foil and baking beans and bake blind in a preheated oven at 200°C (400°F) mark 6 for 10–15 minutes or until set.

3 Melt the butter in a small frying pan, add the celery and bacon and sauté until golden brown. Stir in the curry powder and cook for 2 minutes.

4 Blend the eggs with the yogurt, add the pan ingredients, season to taste, and turn into the flan case. Top with tomato slices.

5 Bake in the oven at 190°C (375°F) mark 5 for about 25 minutes or until golden brown and set. Serve hot or cold.

FETA CHEESE PUFFS WITH BASIL

MAKES 8

225 g (8 oz) Feta cheese, grated	pepper
150 ml (5 fl oz) natural yogurt	397 g (14 oz) packet frozen puff pastry, thawed
30 ml (2 tbsp) chopped fresh basil or 5 ml (1 tsp) dried	beaten egg
	basil leaves, to garnish

1 Mix the grated cheese with the yogurt, chopped basil and pepper to taste. (Don't add salt as the cheese adds sufficient.)
2 Roll out the pastry thinly on a lightly floured surface and cut out sixteen 10 cm (4½ inch) rounds. Fold and re-roll the pastry as necessary.
3 Place half the rounds on two dampened baking sheets. Spoon some of the cheese mixture into the centre of each one.
4 Brush the pastry edges with egg. Cover with the remaining rounds, knocking up and pressing the pastry edges together to seal. Make a small slit in the top of each pastry puff.
5 Brush with beaten egg. Bake in a preheated oven at 220°C (425°F) mark 7 for about 15 minutes or until well browned and crisp. Serve warm, garnished with basil.

--- COOK'S TIP ---

Feta is a Greek cheese made from goat's or ewe's milk. Vacuum packs, which tend to be rather salty, are available at some large supermarkets, but the best Feta (sold loose in brine) is found in Greek and Middle Eastern stores.

CREAMY HAM AND LEEK PIES

SERVES 4

50 g (2 oz) butter	30 ml (2 tbsp) chopped fresh parsley or 10 ml (2 tsp) dried
450 g (1 lb) leeks, thickly sliced	5 ml (1 tsp) grated nutmeg
225 g (8 oz) carrots, sliced	salt and pepper
50 g (2 oz) plain flour	350 g (12 oz) packet puff pastry
300 ml (½ pint) vegetable stock	beaten egg, to glaze
300 ml (½ pint) milk	
225 g (8 oz) cooked ham, diced	

1 Melt the butter in a large saucepan, add the leeks and carrots and fry for 5 minutes. Stir in the flour and cook, stirring continuously, for 1 minute.
2 Gradually stir in the stock, then add the milk. Cook over a medium heat, stirring, until the mixture comes to the boil and thickens. Stir in the ham, parsley and nutmeg. Season to taste, then leave to cool.
3 Roll out the pastry on a lightly floured surface to 0.5 cm (¼ inch) thick. Use a 350 ml (12 fl oz) individual pie dish as a template to cut out four lids for the pies.
4 Divide the ham and leek filling between four 350 ml (12 fl oz) individual pie dishes. Dampen the edges of the dishes with water. Cut the remaining trimmings of pastry into thin strips and place around the rim of each dish. Moisten the strips and lay a lid over each pie. Press the edges to seal, trim and flute.
5 Make a small cut in the top of each pie and brush with beaten egg to glaze. Bake in a preheated oven at 220°C (425°F) mark 7 for 25–30 minutes or until golden brown.

CORNISH PASTIES
SERVES 6

400 g (14 oz) plain flour	175 g (6 oz) swede, diced
salt and pepper	1 medium onion, chopped
225 g (8 oz) butter or margarine	2.5 ml (½ tsp) dried mixed herbs
450 g (1 lb) stewing steak, cut into small pieces	1 egg, beaten
175 g (6 oz) potatoes, peeled and diced	

1 To make the pastry, sift the flour into a bowl with a pinch of salt. Add 200 g (7 oz) of the butter or margarine and rub in until the mixture resembles fine breadcrumbs. Add enough cold water to bind to a manageable dough and knead until smooth.

2 Put the meat, potato, swede and onion in a bowl. Mix in the herbs and season to taste.

3 Divide the pastry into six equal pieces. Roll out each piece on a lightly floured surface to a 20 cm (8 inch) circle.

4 Spoon some of the filling on to half of each pastry circle and top with a little of the remaining butter.

5 Brush the edges of the pastry with water, then fold over and seal the edges firmly together.

6 Place the pasties on a baking sheet and brush with beaten egg. Bake in a preheated oven at 220°C (425°F) mark 7 for 15 minutes. Reduce the heat to 170°C (325°F) mark 3 and cook for a further 1 hour. Serve warm or cold.

CHICKEN PARCELS
SERVES 4

15 g (½ oz) butter	5 ml (1 tsp) lemon juice
1 small onion, chopped	225 g (8 oz) boneless cooked chicken, chopped
2 medium carrots, diced	salt and pepper
15 ml (1 tbsp) plain wholemeal flour	368 g (13 oz) packet frozen puff pastry, thawed
5 ml (1 tsp) mild curry powder	beaten egg, to glaze
300 ml (½ pint) chicken stock	

1 Melt the butter in a large saucepan, add the onion and carrots, cover and cook for 4–5 minutes or until the onion is transparent. Stir in the flour and curry powder and cook, stirring, for 1 minute. Remove from the heat and gradually stir in the stock. Bring to the boil, stirring continuously, then simmer for 2–3 minutes or until thickened.

2 Reduce the heat, add the lemon juice and chicken and season to taste. Leave to cool.

3 When the chicken mixture is cool, roll out the pastry on a lightly floured surface to a 35.5 cm (14 inch) square. Using a sharp knife, cut into four squares.

4 Place the pastry squares on dampened baking sheets, then spoon the chicken mixture on to the pastry, leaving a border round the edges. Brush the edges of each square lightly with water. Fold each square in half and seal and crimp the edges to make a parcel.

5 Make two small slashes in the top of each parcel. Brush with beaten egg to glaze.

6 Bake in a preheated oven at 220°C (425°F) mark 7 for 15–20 minutes or until the pastry is golden brown. Serve hot or cold.

PISSALADIÈRE
SERVES 6

CHILLI PIZZA FINGERS
SERVES 6

100 g (4 oz) plain flour	225 g (8 oz) tomatoes, skinned and sliced
salt and pepper	30 ml (2 tbsp) tomato purée
50 g (2 oz) butter or margarine	5 ml (1 tsp) chopped herbs (marjoram, thyme or sage)
90 ml (6 tbsp) vegetable oil	
450 g (1 lb) onions, finely sliced	anchovy fillets and black olives, to garnish
2 garlic cloves, crushed	

1 To make the pastry, sift the flour and a pinch of salt into a bowl. Add the butter or margarine and rub in until the mixture resembles fine breadcrumbs. Add about 30 ml (2 tbsp) water and mix until it forms a smooth dough. Wrap and chill in the refrigerator for 15 minutes.

2 Roll out the pastry on a lightly floured surface and use to line a 20.5 cm (8 inch) plain flan ring placed on a baking sheet. Line with foil and baking beans and bake blind in a preheated oven at 200°C (400°F) mark 6 for 20 minutes. Remove the foil and beans.

3 Meanwhile, make the filling. Heat the oil in a large saucepan, add the onions and garlic and fry for 10 minutes or until very soft but not brown.

4 Add the tomatoes to the pan and continue cooking for 10 minutes or until the liquid has evaporated. Stir in the tomato purée and herbs and season to taste.

5 Turn the mixture into the flan case. Brush with a little oil and cook in the oven at 200°C (400°F) mark 6 for 20 minutes.

6 To serve, garnish the pissaladière with a lattice of anchovy fillets and the black olives. Serve either hot or cold.

225 g (8 oz) lean minced beef	225 g (8 oz) plain wholemeal flour
2.5 ml (½ tsp) chilli powder	50 g (2 oz) medium oatmeal
1 garlic clove, crushed	15 ml (1 tbsp) baking powder
1 medium onion, chopped	salt and pepper
1 small green pepper, chopped	50 g (2 oz) butter or margarine
100 g (4 oz) mushrooms, sliced	1 egg, beaten
225 g (8 oz) tomatoes, skinned and chopped	60 ml (4 tbsp) milk
213 g (7.51 oz) can red kidney beans, drained	15 ml (1 tbsp) tomato purée
150 ml (¼ pint) beef stock	175 g (6 oz) Mozzarella cheese, thinly sliced

1 First prepare the topping. Put the minced beef, chilli powder and garlic in a saucepan and fry for 3–4 minutes, stirring occasionally. Add the onion, green pepper and mushrooms and fry for a further 1–2 minutes. Stir in the tomatoes, red kidney beans and beef stock. Bring to the boil and simmer for about 15 minutes or until most of the liquid has evaporated, stirring occasionally.

2 Meanwhile, combine the flour, oatmeal, baking powder and a pinch of salt in a bowl. Rub in the butter or margarine. Bind to a soft dough with the egg and milk, then knead lightly until smooth.

3 Roll out the dough to a 25×18 cm (10×7 inch) rectangle. Lift on to a baking sheet, then spread with tomato purée. Pile chilli mixture on top and cover with cheese.

4 Bake at 200°C (400°F) mark 6 for about 30 minutes or until golden and bubbling. Cut into fingers.

PASTA WITH PEAS AND HAM IN CREAM SAUCE

SERVES 4

275–350 g (10–12 oz) tagliatelle	100 g (4 oz) frozen peas, cooked
100 g (4 oz) butter	60 ml (4 tbsp) single cream
1 large onion, sliced	100 g (4 oz) Cheddar cheese, grated
100 g (4 oz) ham, cut into thin strips	salt and pepper

1 Cook the tagliatelle in boiling salted water for about 10 minutes or until tender, but not soft. Drain well.

2 Meanwhile, melt the butter in a pan, add the onion and cook for about 3 minutes or until soft. Add the ham and peas and cook for a further 5 minutes.

3 Add the drained tagliatelle to the pan, stir well and add the cream and most of the cheese. Toss gently, season to taste and serve at once, sprinkled with the remaining cheese.

VARIATION

Spaghetti with Peas and Ham in Cream Sauce
Substitute spaghetti for the tagliatelle in the above recipe.

BACON CAKES

MAKES 8

7 rashers streaky bacon	50 ml (¼ pint) milk
225 g (8 oz) self-raising flour	15 ml (1 tbsp) tomato ketchup
pinch of salt	a dash of Worcestershire sauce
25 g (1 oz) butter	milk, to glaze
75 g (3 oz) Cheddar cheese, grated	

1 Cook three rashers of the bacon under a preheated grill until crisp, then cut into small pieces.

2 Sift the flour and salt together into a bowl, add the butter and rub in until the mixture resembles fine breadcrumbs. Add all but 15 g (½ oz) of the cheese and the crumbled bacon.

3 Mix the milk, tomato ketchup and Worcestershire sauce together and add to the dry ingredients. Mix to a soft dough, roll out to an 18 cm (7 inch) circle, brush with milk and cut into eight wedges.

4 Arrange the wedges on a buttered, floured baking tray in a circle with edges overlapping. Sprinkle with the remaining cheese.

5 Bake in a preheated oven at 200°C (400°F) mark 6 for 30 minutes. Cut the remaining bacon in half and roll up. Place the rolls on a skewer and grill until crisp. Use to garnish the bacon cakes.

FISH CAKES WITH HERBS

SERVES 4

275 g (10 oz) haddock, skinned and boned	15 ml (1 tbsp) snipped chives
15 ml (1 tbsp) lemon juice	15 ml (1 tbsp) chopped parsley
15 ml (1 tbsp) Worcestershire sauce	350 g (12 oz) potatoes, cooked and mashed
15 ml (1 tbsp) horseradish sauce	50 g (2 oz) fresh wholemeal breadcrumbs
100 ml (4 fl oz) milk	

1 Put the fish in a blender or food processor with the lemon juice, Worcestershire sauce and horseradish and blend to a purée. Transfer to a bowl and stir in the milk, chives, parsley and potatoes.
2 Shape the mixture into four fish cakes and coat with breadcrumbs.
3 Cook under a preheated moderate grill for 5 minutes on each side or until browned. Serve immediately.

―――――――― VARIATION ――――――――
Cod Fish Cakes with Herbs
The above fish cakes are equally good made with cod instead of haddock.

CHICKEN LIVER SKEWERS

SERVES 4

2 small oranges	1 green pepper, roughly chopped
200 ml (7 fl oz) unsweetened orange juice	100 g (4 oz) onion, roughly chopped
5 ml (1 tsp) chopped fresh tarragon or 2.5 ml (½ tsp) dried	275 g (10 oz) beansprouts
450 g (1 lb) whole chicken livers, thawed if frozen	1 small bunch of chives, snipped
2 slices of bread, crumbed	salt and pepper

1 Finely grate the rind of one of the oranges. Place in a saucepan with the orange juice and tarragon and simmer for 2–3 minutes or until reduced by half.
2 Cut the tops and bottoms off both oranges, then remove the peel by working around the oranges in a spiral.
3 Divide the oranges into segments by cutting through the membranes on either side of each segment.
4 Cut the chicken livers in half and toss lightly in the breadcrumbs. Place in a lightly greased grill pan and cook under a preheated grill for 2 minutes on each side.
5 Thread the pepper and onion on to four oiled kebab skewers alternately with the livers.
6 Place the skewers in the grill pan and spoon over a little of the reduced orange juice. Grill for 2–3 minutes on each side, turning and basting occasionally.
7 Meanwhile, steam the beansprouts for 2–3 minutes. Warm the orange segments in a separate pan with the remaining reduced orange juice.
8 Mix the beansprouts with the chives and season to taste. Arrange on a warmed serving dish. Top with the skewers and spoon over the orange segments and juices.

JANSSON'S TEMPTATION
SERVES 6

4 medium baking potatoes	salt and pepper
two 50 g (2 oz) cans anchovy fillets, soaked in milk for 20 minutes and drained	1 large onion, finely chopped
25 g (1 oz) butter or margarine	450 ml (¾ pint) single cream
	30 ml (2 tbsp) chopped parsley, to garnish

1 Peel the potatoes and cut into very thin matchstick strips. Cut the anchovies into thin strips.
2 Arrange half of the potato strips in a layer in the bottom of a well-buttered ovenproof dish. Sprinkle with a little salt and plenty of pepper.
3 Arrange the strips of anchovy and chopped onion over the potato layer, then top with the remaining potato. Sprinkle with salt and pepper as before.
4 Pour half the cream slowly into the dish, then dot with the remaining butter. Bake in a preheated oven at 180°C (350°F) mark 4 for 30 minutes. Add the remaining cream and bake for a further 1 hour or until the potatoes feel tender when pierced with a skewer. Cover the dish with foil if the potatoes show signs of over-browning during cooking. Serve hot, sprinkled with the parsley.

--- **COOK'S TIP** ---

In Sweden, this dish is usually served as a starter, but it is easily substantial enough to serve as a main course. To refresh the palate, follow with a crisp green salad tossed in a sharp oil and vinegar dressing.

SALMON KEDGEREE
SERVES 6

350 g (12 oz) salmon	salt and pepper
150 ml (¼ pint) dry white wine	350 g (12 oz) long grain rice
2 small onions, chopped	50 g (2 oz) butter
1 carrot, sliced	7.5 ml (1½ tsp) English mustard powder
1 celery stick, chopped	3 eggs, hard-boiled, shelled and quartered
15 ml (1 tbsp) lemon juice	cayenne, to finish
6 peppercorns	celery leaves or parsley sprigs, to garnish
1 bouquet garni	

1 Put the salmon in a saucepan and pour in the wine and enough water to cover the fish. Add half of the chopped onions, the carrot, celery, lemon juice, peppercorns, bouquet garni and 5 ml (1 tsp) salt. Bring slowly to the boil, then remove from the heat. Cover tightly and cool.
2 Cook the rice in boiling salted water until tender.
3 Meanwhile, remove the salmon from the liquid and flake the flesh, discarding the skin and any bones. Strain the cooking liquid and reserve.
4 Melt half the butter in a large frying pan, add the remaining onion and fry gently for about 5 minutes or until soft. Drain the rice thoroughly, then add to the onion with the remaining butter. Toss to coat and stir in the mustard.
5 Add the flaked salmon and the hard-boiled eggs and a few spoonfuls of the strained cooking liquid to moisten. Heat through. Shake the pan and toss the ingredients gently so that the salmon and eggs do not break up.
6 Transfer to a warmed serving dish and sprinkle with cayenne to taste. Garnish and serve immediately.

PRAWN RISOTTO

SERVES 4

QUICK CHICKEN AND MUSSEL PAELLA

SERVES 4–6

75 g (3 oz) onion, thinly sliced	½ sachet saffron strands
1 garlic clove, crushed	salt and pepper
1 litre (1¾ pints) chicken stock	225 g (8 oz) peeled prawns
225 g (8 oz) long grain brown rice	50 g (2 oz) frozen petits pois
50 g (2 oz) small button mushrooms	12 cooked whole prawns, to garnish

1 Place the onion, garlic, stock, rice, mushrooms and saffron in a large saucepan or flameproof casserole. Season to taste. Bring to the boil and simmer, uncovered, for 35 minutes, stirring occasionally.
2 Stir in the prawns and petits pois. Cook over a high heat for about 5 minutes or until most of the liquid has been absorbed, stirring occasionally.
3 Taste and adjust the seasoning, then turn into a warmed serving dish. Garnish with the whole prawns and serve immediately.

60 ml (4 tbsp) olive oil	1.2 litres (2¼ pints) boiling chicken stock
about 450 g (1 lb) boneless chicken meat, skinned and cut into bite-sized cubes	5 ml (1 tsp) paprika
1 onion, chopped	2.5 ml (½ tsp) saffron powder
2 garlic cloves, crushed	salt and pepper
1 large red pepper, sliced into thin strips	two 150 g (5 oz) jars mussels, drained
3 tomatoes, skinned and chopped	lemon wedges, cooked peeled prawns and fresh mussels (optional), to garnish
400 g (14 oz) Valencia or risotto rice	

1 Heat the oil in a large, deep frying pan, add the cubes of chicken and fry over a moderate heat until golden brown on all sides. Remove from the pan and set aside.
2 Add the onion, garlic and red pepper to the oil remaining in the pan and fry gently for 5 minutes or until softened. Add the tomatoes and fry for a few more minutes or until the juices run, then add the rice and stir to combine.
3 Pour in 1 litre (1¾ pints) of the boiling stock (it will bubble furiously), then add half the paprika and the saffron powder. Season to taste. Stir well and add the chicken.
4 Simmer, uncovered, for 30 minutes or until the chicken is cooked through, stirring frequently during this time to prevent the rice from sticking. When the mixture becomes dry, stir in a few more tablespoons of boiling stock. Repeat as often as necessary to keep the paella moist.
5 To serve, fold in the mussels and heat through. Taste and adjust the seasoning, then garnish with lemon wedges, prawns, mussels and a sprinkling of paprika.

SPAGHETTI ALLA CARBONARA

SERVES 4

4 eggs	350 g (12 oz) spaghetti
150 ml (5 fl oz) single cream	175 g (6 oz) Cheddar cheese, grated
25 g (1 oz) butter	salt and pepper
225 g (8 oz) streaky bacon, chopped	30 ml (2 tbsp) chopped parsley

1 Beat together the eggs and cream. Heat the butter in a frying pan, add the bacon and fry until crisp.
2 Meanwhile, cook the spaghetti in boiling salted water for about 8 minutes or until tender, but not soft. Drain and add it to the bacon in the frying pan.
3 Cook for 1 minute, stirring all the time. Remove from the heat and add the egg mixture. Mix well. (The heat of the spaghetti will be enough to cook the eggs).
4 Stir in 100 g (4 oz) cheese and season to taste. Transfer to a warmed serving dish and serve immediately, sprinkled with the parsley and remaining cheese.

MACARONI CHEESE

SERVES 4

175 g (6 oz) short-cut macaroni	salt and pepper
40 g (1½ oz) butter	175 g (6 oz) mature Cheddar cheese, grated
60 ml (4 tbsp) plain flour	30 ml (2 tbsp) fresh breadcrumbs
568 ml (1 pint) milk	
pinch of nutmeg, or 2.5 ml (½ tsp) prepared mustard	

1 Cook the macaroni in boiling salted water for 10 minutes, then drain well.
2 Meanwhile melt the butter in a saucepan, stir in the flour and cook gently for 1 minute. Remove from the heat and gradually stir in the milk. Bring to the boil and continue to cook, stirring, until the sauce thickens, then remove from the heat, add the nutmeg or mustard and season to taste. Stir in 100 g (4 oz) cheese and the macaroni.
3 Pour into an ovenproof dish and sprinkle with the remaining cheese and the breadcrumbs.
4 Place on a baking sheet and bake in a preheated oven at 200°C (400°F) mark 6 for about 20 minutes or until golden and bubbling.

TUNA AND PASTA IN SOURED CREAM

SERVES 4

225 g (8 oz) pasta spirals or shells	30 ml (2 tbsp) malt vinegar
salt and pepper	198 g (7 oz) can tuna, drained and flaked
5 ml (1 tsp) vegetable oil	4 eggs, hard-boiled, shelled and finely chopped
25 g (1 oz) butter	
150 ml (5 fl oz) soured cream	60 ml (4 tbsp) chopped parsley
5 ml (1 tsp) anchovy essence	

1 Cook the pasta in plenty of boiling salted water to which the oil has been added, for about 15 minutes or until *al dente* (tender but firm to the bite). Drain well.
2 Melt the butter in a deep frying pan and toss in the pasta. Stir in the soured cream, anchovy essence and vinegar.
3 Add the tuna and egg to the pan with the parsley. Season well and warm through over a low heat, stirring occasionally. Serve immediately.

PASTA BAKE

SERVES 4

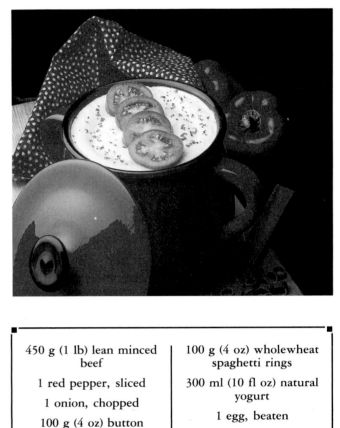

450 g (1 lb) lean minced beef	100 g (4 oz) wholewheat spaghetti rings
1 red pepper, sliced	300 ml (10 fl oz) natural yogurt
1 onion, chopped	1 egg, beaten
100 g (4 oz) button mushrooms, sliced	50 g (2 oz) plain flour
397 g (14 oz) can tomatoes	2 tomatoes, sliced, and chopped fresh parsley, to garnish
5 ml (1 tsp) Tabasco sauce	
salt and pepper	

1 Put the mince in a saucepan and fry gently in its own fat, until turning brown. Drain off any fat. Add the pepper, onion, mushrooms, tomatoes with their juice and Tabasco sauce. Season to taste and simmer gently for 10 minutes.
2 Meanwhile, cook the pasta in boiling salted water for about 10 minutes or until tender, but not soft. Drain well and place in a 1.4 litre (2½ pint) ovenproof dish. Top with the mince mixture.
3 Beat together the yogurt, egg and flour until smooth and pour over the mince. Bake in a preheated oven at 180°C (350°F) mark 4 for 40 minutes. Serve hot, garnished with tomatoes and chopped parsley.

SESAME CHICKEN PITTAS

SERVES 4

30 ml (2 tbsp) sesame oil	100 g (4 oz) beansprouts
1 onion, sliced	15 ml (1 tbsp) dark soy sauce
100 g (4 oz) broccoli, cut into tiny florets	30 ml (2 tbsp) toasted sesame seeds
1 red pepper, diced	4 large pitta breads
225 g (8 oz) cooked chicken breast, sliced into thin strips	

1 Heat the oil in a large frying pan, add the onion and stir-fry for 2 minutes. Add the broccoli and pepper and cook for 3–4 minutes, stirring frequently.
2 Add the chicken strips to the pan, stir well, then add the beansprouts and soy sauce. Continue to cook for 2–3 minutes. Sprinkle over the sesame seeds and stir to combine. Remove from the heat and keep warm.
3 Cut through a long side of each pitta bread and open the cavity to form a pocket. Place the pitta breads on a baking sheet. Bake in a preheated oven at 200°C (400°F) mark 6 for 5–10 minutes to heat.
4 Using a slotted spoon, fill each pitta pocket with the chicken mixture. Serve immediately.

—— TO MICROWAVE ——

Put the oil and onion in a medium bowl. Cover and cook on HIGH for 2–2½ minutes. Add the broccoli and pepper, re-cover and cook on HIGH for 2–2½ minutes. Add the chicken, beansprouts and soy sauce, stir and cook on HIGH for 2–2½ minutes. Stir in the sesame seeds. To warm the pitta breads, place on a double thickness of absorbent kitchen paper and cook on HIGH for 1–1½ minutes or until warm. Complete step 4.

PAN BAGNA WITH AVOCADO

SERVES 6–8

2 ripe avocados	225 g (8 oz) tomatoes, sliced
15 ml (1 tbsp) lemon juice	1 small green pepper, sliced into thin rings
15 ml (1 tbsp) vegetable oil	a few capers and stoned black olives
garlic salt and black pepper	
63 g (2½ oz) can anchovies, drained	
two 35 cm (14 inch) French loaves	

1 Halve the avocados and remove the stones. Mash the flesh with the lemon juice and oil and season to taste with garlic salt and pepper. Cut the anchovies into thin strips.
2 Halve the loaves lengthways. Pull out and discard some of the crumb. Spread the bases with the avocado mixture and top with tomatoes and pepper. Arrange the anchovy strips in a lattice pattern on top and sprinkle with capers and olives. Position the top of the loaf over the filling to make a sandwich, cut the loaf in chunks and serve.

CHICKEN TACOS

SERVES 6

6 Mexican taco shells	salt and pepper
25 g (1 oz) butter or margarine	shredded lettuce
1 medium onion, chopped	100 g (4 oz) Cheddar cheese, grated
450 g (1 lb) cooked chicken meat, diced	Tabasco sauce
4 tomatoes, skinned and chopped	

1 Put the taco shells in the oven to warm according to the instructions on the packet.
2 To make the filling, melt the butter or margarine in a frying pan, add the onion and fry for about 5 minutes or until soft but not coloured. Stir in the chicken and half the tomatoes, season to taste and heat through.
3 Spoon 15–30 ml (1–2 tbsp) filling into each shell. Add a little lettuce, the remaining tomatoes and the cheese with a few drops of Tabasco sauce. Serve immediately.

CRISPY STUFFED POTATO SKINS

SERVES 4–6

4 medium baking potatoes, scrubbed and pricked	25 g (1 oz) fresh breadcrumbs
175 g (6 oz) mature Cheddar cheese, grated	FOR THE DIPPING SAUCE
45 ml (3 tbsp) snipped chives or 15 ml (1 tbsp) dried	30 ml (2 tbsp) snipped chives or 10 ml (2 tsp) dried
salt and pepper	300 ml (10 fl oz) soured cream
vegetable oil, for deep frying	

1 Place the potatoes on a baking sheet and bake in a preheated oven at 220°C (425°F) mark 7 for 1–1½ hours.
2 Cut each potato in half and scoop out the flesh. Chop the flesh into chunks and place in a medium bowl. Add 100 g (4 oz) of the cheese and 30 ml (2 tbsp) of the snipped fresh chives or 10 ml (2 tsp) dried. Season to taste and cover with foil to keep warm.
3 Heat the oil in a deep fat fryer to 190°C (375°F) and deep-fry the potato skins in batches for 3–4 minutes or until crisp. Drain well and arrange, hollow side up, on a baking sheet.
4 Spoon the potato mixture into the skins. Mix the remaining cheese, chives and breadcrumbs together and sprinkle over each stuffed potato skin. Put under a pre-heated grill until golden. For the dipping sauce, stir the chives into the soured cream and serve with the stuffed potato skins.

TO MICROWAVE
Place the potatoes on a double thickness of absorbent kitchen paper. Cook on HIGH for 10–15 minutes, rearranging. Stand for 5 minutes. Complete steps 2–4.

SALADS

Needing little or no accompaniment, these salads are complete meals on their own, combining cooked meats, fish, eggs or cheese with dried beans, grains and vegetables as well as more usual salad ingredients. They are the perfect choice for a summer lunch or buffet for family or friends.

CRAB SALAD

SERVES 2

CHEF'S SALAD

SERVES 4

CRAB SALAD

15 ml (1 tbsp) lemon juice	2 tomatoes, skinned and cubed
15 ml (1 tbsp) mayonnaise	50 g (2 oz) pasta shells, cooked
15 ml (1 tbsp) natural yogurt	pepper
225 g (8 oz) cooked crab meat, thawed if frozen	lettuce, shredded
½ cucumber, diced	cucumber and lemon slices, to garnish

1 Mix together the lemon juice, mayonnaise and yogurt.
2 Combine the dressing with the remaining ingredients, except the lettuce. Serve the crab salad on a bed of shredded lettuce, garnished with cucumber and lemon slices.

CHEF'S SALAD

225 g (8 oz) cooked ham	6 small tomatoes, halved, or 2 large tomatoes, quartered
225 g (8 oz) cold cooked chicken	3 spring onions, finely chopped
225 g (8 oz) Emmenthal cheese	French or blue cheese dressing, to serve
1 Iceberg or Webb's lettuce	
2 eggs, hard-boiled, shelled and quartered	

1 Using a sharp knife, cut the ham and chicken into fine strips and set aside. Remove any rind from the cheese. Carefully cut the cheese into small dice. Wash the lettuce under cold running water and pat it dry.
2 Finely shred the lettuce leaves, or leave them whole, and use to line an oval serving dish.
3 To serve, arrange the meat and cheese alternately around the edge of a large dish. Add the egg and tomatoes and sprinkle over the finely chopped spring onions. Serve the dressing separately.

PORK AND MUSHROOM SALAD

SERVES 6

DEVILLED DUCKLING SALAD

SERVES 6

two 350 g (12 oz) pork fillets (tenderloins)	10 green olives, stoned and chopped
vegetable oil	150 ml (5 fl oz) soured cream
knob of butter	1.25 ml (¼ tsp) mustard powder
225 g (8 oz) small button mushrooms	salt and pepper
juice of ½ lemon	5 ml (1 tsp) chopped marjoram or mint
1 small onion, finely sliced	
1 small green pepper, finely shredded	lemon wedges, to garnish

1 Cut the pork into 1 cm (½ inch) slices on the diagonal, then cut each slice into neat strips.

2 Heat a little oil and the butter in a large frying pan, add half the pork and fry quickly to brown and seal the meal. Repeat with the remaining meat, then return all to the pan. Lower the heat and cook slowly for 10–15 minutes or until very tender. Using a slotted spoon, lift the meat out of the pan and leave to cool.

3 Add the mushrooms to the pan with 50 ml (2 fl oz) water and the lemon juice. Cook, stirring, for 1–2 minutes. Using a slotted spoon, remove from the pan and cool.

4 Put the onion and green pepper in a pan of cold water, bring to the boil and simmer for 1–2 minutes. Drain and cool under cold running water. Stir into the pork with the cooled mushrooms and the olives.

5 Mix the soured cream with the mustard, season to taste and stir into the pork. Cover and chill for at least 3 hours.

6 Stir the salad well before serving sprinkled with marjoram or mint and garnished with lemon wedges.

two 1.4 kg (3 lb) oven-ready ducklings	15 ml (1 tbsp) mild curry paste
salt	salt and pepper
150 ml (5 fl oz) soured cream	50 g (2 oz) cashew nuts
90 ml (6 tbsp) mayonnaise	350 g (12 oz) fresh apricots, stoned and thickly sliced
15 ml (1 tbsp) clear honey	endive leaves, to serve

1 Cut away any surplus fat from the ducklings, then wipe them with a damp cloth. Pat dry.

2 Prick the birds all over with a sharp fork or skewer and sprinkle generously with salt. Place the ducklings, breast-side down, side by side, on a wire rack or trivet in a large roasting tin.

3 Roast in a preheated oven at 180°C (350°F) mark 4 for about 1¾ hours or until the birds are really tender, basting occasionally. Half-way through the cooking time, turn the birds over so they are standing breast-side up.

4 Meanwhile, prepare the dressing. In a large bowl, mix together the soured cream, mayonnaise, honey and curry paste. Season and stir in the cashew nuts and apricots.

5 While the ducklings are still warm, strip off the crisp breast skin and reserve. Remove the meat from the bones.

6 Coarsely shred the meat, discarding all the remaining skin, fat and bones. Fold the shredded duckling meat into the dressing, cover and chill for 2–3 hours.

7 Using a pair of kitchen scissors, cut the reserved duckling skin into strips and quickly crisp it further under a hot grill.

8 To serve, spoon the duckling salad down the centre of a large flat platter, then arrange the crisp duck skin over the top. Serve on a bed of endive leaves.

CHICKEN AND GRAPE SALAD

SERVES 4–6

1.4 kg (3 lb) roasting chicken	150 ml (5 fl oz) whipping cream
1 onion	225 g (8 oz) green grapes, halved and seeded
1 carrot	50 g (2 oz) seedless raisins
1 bay leaf	salt and pepper
6 peppercorns	lettuce and paprika, to garnish
2 eggs	
90 ml (6 tbsp) lemon juice	
45 ml (3 tbsp) clear honey	

1 Put the chicken in a large saucepan with the onion, carrot, bay leaf and peppercorns, cover with water and poach for about 50 minutes or until tender. Leave to cool in the stock.

2 Remove the chicken from the stock and cut all the meat off the bones, discarding the skin. Cut the meat into bite-sized pieces.

3 Beat the eggs with 60 ml (4 tbsp) lemon juice and the honey. Put in the top of a double saucepan or in a heatproof bowl standing over a saucepan of hot water and heat gently, stirring, until thick. Cover with damp greaseproof paper and leave to cool.

4 Whip the cream until softly stiff and fold into the cold lemon mixture.

5 Add the remaining lemon juice to the grapes, then combine with the chicken, raisins and sauce.

6 Serve garnished with lettuce and paprika.

SMOKED CHICKEN AND AVOCADO SALAD

SERVES 4–6

1 kg (2 lb) smoked chicken	2.5 ml (½ tsp) green peppercorn mustard
135 ml (9 tbsp) olive oil	2 ripe avocados
juice of 1 lemon	salt and pepper
5 ml (1 tsp) bottled grated horseradish	sprigs of fresh coriander and lemon slices, to garnish

1 Remove all the meat from the chicken carcass, taking care to cut thin, even slices which will look attractive in the finished dish.

2 To make the dressing, whisk together the oil, lemon juice, horseradish and mustard. Add the chicken and coat in the dressing. Cover and leave for 30 minutes to 1 hour.

3 Halve the avocados and remove the stones. Peel off the skin, then cut the flesh lengthways into thin, even slices.

4 Arrange the chicken and avocado slices alternately on a flat, round plate, overlapping them in a 'Catherine-wheel' shape.

5 Chop any remaining oddly-shaped pieces of chicken and avocado and toss them together. Pile this mixture into the centre of the plate.

6 Season the dressing remaining in the bowl and brush over the avocado slices to prevent discoloration.

7 Garnish the centre of the salad with fresh coriander and lemon slices, and serve immediately with the dressing.

CHICKEN WITH CURRIED LEMON MAYONNAISE

SERVES 4

1.4 kg (3 lb) chicken	2 celery sticks, finely chopped
150 ml (¼ pint) dry white wine	175 ml (6 fl oz) thick mayonnaise
1 strip of lemon rind	30 ml (2 tbsp) apricot jam
bouquet garni	finely grated rind and juice of 1 lemon
6 black peppercorns	
salt and pepper	1 red or green pepper, diced
15 g (½ oz) butter	2 red-skinned eating apples
1 small onion, chopped	150 ml (5 fl oz) double or whipping cream
15 ml (1 tbsp) curry powder	lettuce, to serve

1 Put the chicken in a deep saucepan with the wine, enough water just to cover, the strip of lemon rind, bouquet garni, peppercorns and a good pinch of salt. Cover and simmer for 1–1¼ hours or until the chicken is tender, then leave to cool in the liquid for about 2 hours.

2 Remove the chicken from the liquid. Strain the liquid into a saucepan, then boil until reduced to a few tablespoons. Cool for 5 minutes. Meanwhile, remove the chicken from the bones and dice the meat, discarding all skin.

3 Melt the butter, add the onion and curry powder and fry for 5 minutes or until soft. Add the celery and fry for 2 minutes, stirring. Cool for 10 minutes.

4 Add the onion and celery to the mayonnaise with the apricot jam, grated lemon rind and juice and the diced pepper. Thin with the reduced cooking liquid. Season.

5 Core and dice or slice the apples. Whip the cream until thick, then fold into the mayonnaise with the apples and chicken. Chill for 30 minutes. Serve on a bed of lettuce.

BEEF AND OLIVE SALAD

SERVES 4

450 g (1 lb) rolled lean brisket	12 black olives
1 bay leaf	450 g (1 lb) French beans
6 peppercorns	salt and pepper
	45 ml (3 tbsp) soy sauce
1 large bunch of spring onions	20 ml (4 tsp) lemon juice

1 Put the beef, bay leaf and peppercorns in a small saucepan and add enough water to cover. Bring to the boil, cover and simmer gently for about 1 hour or until the meat is tender. Leave to cool in the cooking liquid for about 2 hours.

2 Slice the spring onions diagonally into thick pieces. Quarter and stone the olives. Trim and halve the French beans. Cook the beans in boiling salted water for 5–10 minutes or until just tender. Drain well, rinse under cold running water and drain again thoroughly.

3 Drain the beef and trim off the fat. Slice thinly and cut into 4 cm (1½ inch) long shreds.

4 Put the beef in a bowl, add the spring onions, olives, beans, soy sauce and lemon juice. Toss well together, then season with pepper. (The soy sauce should provide sufficent salt.) Cover and chill in the refrigerator for about 30 minutes before serving.

AVOCADO AND LEMON SALAD WITH OMELETTE RINGS

SERVES 4–6

4 eggs	5 ml (1 tsp) coriander seeds
50 g (2 oz) Cheddar cheese, grated	90 ml (6 tbsp) olive or vegetable oil
salt and pepper	45 ml (3 tbsp) lemon juice
25 g (1 oz) butter or margarine	2 ripe avocados
5 ml (1 tsp) black peppercorns	parsley sprigs, to garnish (optional)

1 Put the eggs in a bowl with the cheese and 15 ml (1 tbsp) water. Season to taste and whisk together.
2 Melt a quarter of the butter or margarine in an omelette pan or small non-stick frying pan. When foaming, pour in a quarter of the egg mixture. After a few seconds, push the set egg mixture into the centre of the pan and tilt the pan to allow the egg to run to the edges. Cook until just set.
3 Brown the omelette under a preheated hot grill. Turn out on to a plate. Repeat with the remaining egg mixture to make another three omelettes.
4 While the omelettes are still warm, roll them up loosely. Wrap in greaseproof paper and leave to cool.
5 Meanwhile, crush the peppercorns and coriander seeds coarsely with a pestle and mortar, or with the end of a rolling pin in a strong bowl.
6 Whisk together the oil, lemon juice and crushed spices and season to taste. Halve, stone and peel the avocados, then slice thickly into the dressing. Toss gently to coat.
7 Slice the rolled omelettes thinly. Arrange the omelette rings and avocado slices in individual serving plates. Spoon over the dressing and garnish with sprigs of parsley, if liked. Serve immediately.

CHEESE AND CHICORY SALAD

SERVES 4

2 large heads of chicory, trimmed	45 ml (3 tbsp) white wine vinegar
100 g (4 oz) Cotswold or Cheddar cheese, cubed	5–10 ml (1–2 tsp) soft brown sugar
1 green pepper, chopped	1 small garlic clove, crushed
2 celery sticks, chopped	
100 g (4 oz) radishes, sliced	salt and pepper
30 ml (2 tbsp) beef stock	100 g (4 oz) walnut halves
90 ml (6 tbsp) vegetable oil	

1 Chop the chicory coarsely. Place the cheese cubes in a salad bowl with the chicory. Add the pepper, celery and radishes and mix together.
2 Place the stock, oil, vinegar, sugar and garlic in a screw-topped jar, season to taste, and shake well to combine. Pour over the salad and stir in the walnuts.

─── **COOK'S TIP** ───
Cotswold cheese is a variety of Double Gloucester flavoured with chopped chives and onion.

CHEDDAR CHEESE AND APPLE SALAD

SERVES 4

½ round lettuce	2 eating apples, peeled, cored and diced
150 ml (5 fl oz) soured cream	225 g (8 oz) Cheddar cheese, diced
45 ml (3 tbsp) milk	2 canned pineapple rings, coarsely chopped
5 ml (1 tsp) lemon juice	4 orange slices and 8 black olives, to garnish
5 ml (1 tsp) icing or caster sugar	
1.25 ml (¼ tsp) salt	

I Tear the lettuce leaves into bite-sized pieces and use to cover the base of a serving dish.
2 Combine the soured cream with the milk, lemon juice, sugar and salt.
3 Add the apples, cheese and pineapple to the soured cream mixture and toss lightly together. Pile on to the lettuce and garnish with orange slices and olives.

GOAT'S CHEESE WITH PEAR AND WALNUT SALAD

SERVES 2

a few lettuce leaves, such as Webb's and radicchio, torn into pieces	50 g (2 oz) walnuts, chopped
100 g (4 oz) goat's cheese, halved into 2 discs	½ bunch of watercress
2 ripe pears, cored and cut into chunks	30 ml (2 tbsp) lemon juice
	45 ml (3 tbsp) vegetable oil

I Arrange the lettuce on two serving plates and top with the goat's cheese. Mix together the pears, walnuts and watercress.
2 Blend the lemon juice and oil together, add to the pear mixture and toss to coat. Spoon on to the cheese to serve.

—— VARIATION ——

Caerphilly with Pear and Walnut Salad

If you prefer not to use goat's cheese, Caerphilly makes a delicious substitute, as do other white cheeses, such as Lancashire, Wensleydale or white Stilton.

WHOLE WHEAT BRAZIL NUT SALAD

SERVES 4–6

75 g (3 oz) dried black-eyed beans, soaked in cold water overnight	45 ml (3 tbsp) chopped mint
	salt and pepper
100 g (4 oz) whole wheat grain, soaked in cold water overnight	½ cucumber, diced
	225 g (8 oz) tomatoes, skinned and roughly chopped
90 ml (6 tbsp) natural yogurt	
30 ml (2 tbsp) olive oil	100 g (4 oz) cheese, grated
45 ml (3 tbsp) lemon juice	100 g (4 oz) Brazil nuts, chopped

1 Drain the beans and place in a saucepan of water. Bring to the boil and simmer gently for 1½ hours or until tender.
2 Meanwhile, drain the whole wheat and place in a saucepan of water. Bring to the boil and simmer gently for 20–25 minutes or until tender. Drain, rinse well with cold water and cool for 30 minutes. When the beans are cooked, drain and cool for 30 minutes.
3 Whisk the yogurt and olive oil together with the lemon juice and mint. Season to taste.
4 Put the whole wheat, beans, cucumber, tomatoes, cheese and Brazil nuts in a bowl. Pour over the dressing and mix well.
5 Garnish and chill before serving.

WINTER SALAD

SERVES 4–6

1 eating apple, cored and chopped	2.5 ml (½ tsp) sugar
	60 ml (4 tbsp) single cream
1 head of celery, sliced	10 ml (2 tsp) white wine vinegar
1 cooked beetroot, peeled and sliced	
	salt and pepper
2 heads of chicory, trimmed and sliced	3 eggs, hard-boiled, shelled and cut into wedges
1 punnet of salad cress	
2.5 ml (½ tsp) prepared English mustard	

1 Lightly mix the apple, celery, beetroot and chicory together with the cress in a large salad bowl.
2 To make the dressing, whisk the mustard, sugar, cream and vinegar together. Season to taste. Pour over the salad and toss together so that everything is coated in the dressing. Add the eggs, then serve at once.

BEAN, CHEESE AND AVOCADO SALAD

SERVES 4

![Bean, cheese and avocado salad]

225 g (8 oz) dried red kidney beans, soaked in cold water overnight	1 small onion, finely chopped
90 ml (6 tbsp) olive oil	2 celery sticks, finely chopped
juice and finely grated rind of 1 lemon	2 tomatoes, skinned and chopped
1.25 ml (¼ tsp) Tabasco sauce	1 ripe avocado
salt and pepper	celery leaves, to garnish
175 g (6 oz) Edam cheese, diced	

1 Drain the kidney beans and rinse under cold running water. Put in a saucepan, cover with fresh cold water and bring to the boil. Boil rapidly for 10 minutes, then simmer for 1–1½ hours or until tender.

2 Drain the beans and put in a bowl. Add the oil, lemon juice and rind and Tabasco. Season to taste. Toss well, then leave until cold.

3 Add the cheese, onion, celery and tomatoes to the beans and toss again to mix the ingredients together. Cover and chill.

4 When ready to serve, cut the avocado in half and remove the stone. Peel and chop the flesh into chunky pieces. Fold the avocado pieces gently into the bean salad and taste and adjust the seasoning. Garnish and serve.

MIXED BEAN SALAD

SERVES 4

450 g (1 lb) broad beans	15 ml (1 tbsp) lemon juice
salt and pepper	397 g (14 oz) can red kidney beans, drained and rinsed
225 g (8 oz) French beans	
15 ml (1 tbsp) vegetable oil	225 g (8 oz) Charnwood or Applewood cheese, cubed
150 ml (5 fl oz) natural yogurt	
15 ml (1 tbsp) mild whole grain mustard	chopped parsley, to garnish

1 Shell the broad beans and cook in boiling salted water for 10 minutes. Add the French beans and continue to cook for 5–10 minutes or until both are tender.

2 Meanwhile, mix together the oil, yogurt, mustard and lemon juice. Season to taste and beat until well blended.

3 Drain the cooked beans and, while still hot, combine with the kidney beans and dressing. Leave to cool.

4 Toss in the cubes of cheese and garnish with chopped fresh parsley just before serving.

─── **TO MICROWAVE** ───

Put the broad beans in a small bowl with 30 ml (2 tbsp) water. Cover and cook on HIGH for 10–12 minutes or until tender. Put the French beans and 15 ml (1 tbsp) water in a small bowl, cover and cook on HIGH for 4–5 minutes or until tender, stirring once. Complete steps 2, 3 and 4.

─── **COOK'S TIP** ───

Charnwood or Applewood cheeses are varieties of mature Cheddar, smoked and coated with paprika.

INDEX